# THE GUYS' GUIDE TO GUYS' VIDEOS

Enjoy!
Happy Birthday
and Happy Viewing
Deb, Ralph
Eric

# THE GUYS' GUIDE TO GUYS' VIDEOS

## Scott Meyer

another idea from
becker&mayer!

AVON BOOKS · NEW YORK

AVON BOOKS
A division of
The Hearst Corporation
1350 Avenue of the Americas
New York, New York 10019

Copyright © 1997 by Scott Meyer
Interior design by Stanley S. Drate/Folio Graphics Company, Inc.
Published by arrangement with becker&mayer!, Ltd.
Visit our website at http://www.AvonBooks.com
ISBN: 0-380-78705-9

Library of Congress Cataloging in Publication Data:

Meyer, Scott.
    The guys' guide to guys' videos / Scott Meyer.
       p.   cm.
     1. Motion pictures for men—Catalogs.   2. Video recordings—
Catalogs.   I. Title.
   PN1995.9.M46M49   1997                                        97-16675
   016.79143′75′081—dc21                                              CIP

First Avon Books Trade Printing: October 1997

AVON TRADEMARK REG. U.S. PAT. OFF. AND IN OTHER COUNTRIES, MARCH REGISTRADA,
HECHO EN U.S.A.

Printed in the U.S.A.

OPM      10  9  8  7  6  5  4  3  2  1

# CONTENTS

**W**hy do we guys like to watch certain movies over and over again? The guys on the "Get in Touch with Your Inner Warrior while Playing Drums in Your Undies" circuit might say that these movies reflect our most enduring myths, that watching them compensates for the loss of adventure and danger in our lives, or that the heroes and antiheroes we identify with delineate the parameters of contemporary manhood. Psychoanalysts would probably theorize that we're searching for father figures in these movies. Sociologists have been known to argue that we're the victims of a bereft culture, which has conditioned us to expect nothing more or less than visceral thrills and to have an insatiable appetite for them. Our wives and girlfriends could accuse us of being lazy slobs with the remote stuck in a perpetual loop of "play, rewind, play, rewind . . ." Our mothers will insist that we're nothing more than little boys who still haven't outgrown our boyhood fantasies.

I believe we keep coming back to these movies because they're about the kind of fun we love. When I watch two cars rip through city streets, scattering pedestrians and leaving other cars skidding into each other in their wake, I think, "What a blast it must be to drive like that." Watch a cop mow down a row of deserving thugs, or better still, watch a nasty murderer dream up cruel executions for undeserving innocents, and I say to myself, "What a ball they must be having acting out our most primal urges without worrying about consequences." See guys behaving like mindless idiots willing to do anything for a cheap laugh, and we must acknowledge how much we enjoy doing the same. The way I figure it, that's why movies were invented: so you can watch other people doing stuff you can't do in real life.

*The Guys' Guide to Guys' Videos* is my attempt to list and describe movies I believe are worth watching anytime they're on TV, and renting repeatedly when one or the other claims your imagination. Is it a comprehensive list of every guy movie ever made? No, though I will argue that I've included all of the essential ones. And I've tried to add some representative nonessential ones, but I have no doubt that many of you have others you'd rather see on the list.

In each entry I've tried to capture the tone of the movie itself, to point you to the scenes you'll always identify the movie with, and to accurately get down the lines you'll want to repeat when you're reenacting them with other guys. The ratings that accompany the reviews are based on the quantity and quality of violence, profanity, hot babes, chase scenes, and sharp vehicles (I've used the same car symbol for all of them, whether they be motorcycles, airplanes, tanks, cars, or horses) and hero worship—a category that designates how cool the main man, men, or even woman is. Just keep in mind that I rated the movies in each chapter in relation to each other, not to all the movies in the book. So, for example, a topless woman in a T&A movie may be worth no more than a 2, but in a war movie, she'd get the film a 5-babe rating. This, I hope, will make the book handy for you again and again.

Now, before we get to the movies, allow me a few brief acknowledgments. My own initiation into the kinds of movies guys like began while watching lots of late-night TV with my oldest pal Kevin; many of the concepts about what makes for great guy movies crystallized for me while carpooling and movie mauling with my brainy buddy Matt; my compadre Rob scanned his memory for a bunch of suitable selections, listened to my daily reviews, and shot my jacket photo for nothing but my gratitude. And don't let me forget the Friday diner gang. The idea for this book received a warm welcome from my enchanting friend Barbara (and the other great folks at becker&mayer!, Ltd), and was developed with generous encouragement and valuable ideas from her and Stephen S. Power, my editor at Avon Books. Each of these people is hereby awarded a Guys' Guide Medal of Honor, my highest esteem, and undying gratitude. Finally, this book was forged with the most precious alloy I know of: The patience, indulgence, and love of my wife, Dawn.

# BAD DAY AT BLACK ROCK (1954)

## RATINGS

| | |
|---|---|
| VIOLENCE | 🔫 🔫 |
| PROFANITY | |
| BABES | 👄 |
| COOL CARS | 🚗 🚗 🚗 |
| HERO WORSHIP | 🚬 🚬 🚬 |

**WHAT HAPPENS** ■ You can tell just by the name of the town that Black Rock, Arizona, isn't the friendliest place in the West. When a one-armed stranger gets off the train there, the residents of Black Rock do what they can to convince him to leave immediately. But McCready (the right-hand man), just back from the fighting in World War II, has a purpose for stopping in Black Rock and he's determined to see it through. His questions about a local Japanese-American farmer are brushed off, and he gets the feeling the locals are hiding something. That only strengthens his resolve to find out what's going on in the town. Which he does before the day is done.

**THE CAST** ▰ Spencer Tracy is no fresh-faced plowboy back from the adventure of war overseas—he's a little worn and gray to be passed off as fresh in any way. But as Mc-Cready, Tracy carries himself with enough self-assurance to convince us that he wouldn't be scared away by smug thugs like Lee Marvin and Ernest Borgnine. That witless duo take their orders from Robert Ryan, who veers eerily from charming and accommodating to terse and tough. Behind him, Dean Jagger quivers as the sheriff with no authority. Only the ever-happy Walter Brennan sees no harm in the stranger. Anne Francis is one tough chick, but she can't stand up to her conscience.

**WHY GUYS LOVE IT** ▰ A good man with one bad arm is a fair match for four bad guys with eight good arms. Got it?

**HONEY, YOU'LL LIKE THIS MOVIE . . .** ▰ Because only the woman does the right thing for the wrong reason.

**DON'T MISS**
- Tracy playing matador to Ernest Borgnine's raging bull.
- The daredevil driving in the desert.

**MEMORABLE LINES**
"Hey, stranger, you look like you need a hand," the always gracious Lee Marvin offers.

**BEWARE**

Don't mistake this movie for a boring business book about something that happened at CBS, whose headquarters in New York is known as Black Rock.

# THE DESPERATE HOURS (1955)

**RATINGS**

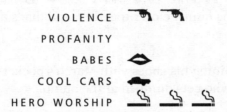

VIOLENCE

PROFANITY

BABES

COOL CARS

HERO WORSHIP

**WHAT HAPPENS** ☛ Killer Glenn Griffin, his brother Hal, and another guy bust out of prison, then surprise a housewife at her home in suburban Indiana. These painfully polite criminals hold the weepy wife and her wimpy banker-husband, their feisty babe daughter, and defiant young son hostage in their house for three days while they wait for money to be delivered by Griffin's girlfriend. As the Griffins' plans (and their alliance) unravel, the father works subtly to exploit their troubles and ultimately proves he's as cunning as any con—and certainly craftier than the cops.

**THE CAST** ☛ A grizzly Humphrey Bogart starts out grinning and guffawing as Glenn Griffin, the killer in control of the situation and reveling in the power he has. But as his plans are disrupted, Bogie begins to brood and bully, terrorizing the family and blowing through enough cigarettes to kill them all with secondhand smoke. Fredric March is the father, and his transformation is the mirror image of Bogie's deterioration: March is at first indignant yet restrained, fearful and submissive. But with each passing minute, he grows more confident and clever. Gig Young is the boyfriend who finally gets the hint.

**WHY GUYS LOVE IT** ▰ If your family was ever held hostage, you know you'd stand at least as tall as March and his family.

**HONEY, YOU'LL LIKE THIS MOVIE . . .** ▰ Because this crisis brings the family closer together, and that's nice, isn't it?

**DON'T MISS**
- Bogart shining his shoes with March's pocket hankie.
- The guy who gets dumped at the dump.

**MEMORABLE LINES**
"Clickety-click, clickety-click. I can see your mind working overtime, Pop," Bogart says to March every time he realizes March has been scheming.

A Classic Remade
# DESPERATE HOURS (1990)

**RATINGS**

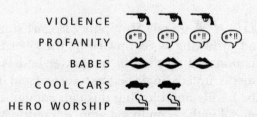

| | | | |
|---|---|---|---|
| VIOLENCE | 🔫 | 🔫 | 🔫 |
| PROFANITY | @*!! | @*!! | @*!! @*!! |
| BABES | 👄 | 👄 | 👄 |
| COOL CARS | 🚗 | 🚗 | |
| HERO WORSHIP | 🚬 | 🚬 | |

**WHAT HAPPENS** ▰ The story is almost exactly the same as the original. A disturbingly polite psychopath, his brother, and a big dumb guy break out of jail, then hold a family hostage while they wait for money to be delivered. The father tries to outwit the psycho, though he's much more confrontational than the father in the original, and the ending roughly follows the first movie's finish. But this version is much more violent, and the actors go ballistic at the first opportunity.

**THE CAST** ☛ Mickey Rourke is the slick killer Michael Bosworth, whose manners seem a put-on from the first. Anthony Hopkins is at his best when he's holding something back, which he does as the father in this movie. His wife is played by Mimi Rogers (the first Mrs. Tom Cruise), who tries hard to look like the dowdy housewife, but we see what Bosworth sees—and she's fair and fine. If Bosworth's lawyer and accomplice, Kelly Lynch (from *Drugstore Cowboy*), would stop crying in every scene, we might enjoy checking out her long legs and big breasts. Lindsay Crouse plays the cop with a grudge against Bosworth—for laughs.

**DON'T MISS**
- A peep at Lynch's handy holster.
- Rogers's bathtub scene in the beginning of the movie.

**MEMORABLE LINES**
"Listen closely while I pull rank on you," says Crouse to a subordinate who disagrees with her plan to catch the cons.

**CHECK OUT**

For an even better look at what director Michael Cimino and Mickey Rourke can do together, see *Year of the Dragon* (on page 133).

# LAWRENCE OF ARABIA (1962)

## RATINGS

VIOLENCE

PROFANITY

BABES

COOL CARS

HERO WORSHIP

**WHAT HAPPENS** ◄ It's an epic (four hours of movie) based on the somewhat true story of T. E. Lawrence, an arrogant young British Army officer in World War I. Lawrence's superiors send him to persuade the leader of a Bedouin tribe to fight the Turks, who had sided with the Germans against the English. Lawrence teaches them modern warfare, leads the tribesmen into battle himself, and recruits other Arab tribes to join in his crusade. He begins to believe the Arabs that call him their savior, which doesn't make him Officer of the Month back at headquarters. There's plenty of interesting history stuff to consume at the end of the movie, but if all you want to see are some of the greatest battle scenes ever filmed, stop watching when the Arabs capture Damascus.

**THE CAST** ◄ Peter O'Toole (surely the most phallic stage name any serious actor has ever had the nerve to take) plays his first starring role with a confidence that Lawrence himself would have admired. With a rigid posture and an upraised chin, O'Toole stares down superior officers, rivals, even the desert. Alec Guinness gives "Lord" Faisel, leader of the Bedouin, the same soft-spoken authority that was so indelible when he was Obi-Wan Kenobe—the old guy who teaches Luke Skywalker about the Force in *Star Wars*. Swarthy Omar Sharif and his very bushy mustache contrast O'Toole's fair, smooth-cheeked looks, which tells you right away that Sharif's Ali (a warrior in Faisel's tribe) will clash with Lawrence. Grizzly Anthony Quinn is clearly living large in the desert as the leader of another Arab tribe. Claude Rains (the greasy French captain in *Casablanca*) oozes onto the screen as the intelligence officer. And look for lots of other familiar faces—this is an epic, after all.

## WHY GUYS LOVE IT ◆ Call him cocky, call him foolish, but this guy feared nothing.

## HONEY, YOU'LL LOVE THIS MOVIE ... ◆ Because it's made by the same director as *Doctor Zhivago*, which you make me watch during the PBS fund-raiser every year.

## DON'T MISS
• The cast-of-thousands attack on the supply train.
• The World War I–style air raid.
• Quinn's rhythmically gifted daughters.

## MEMORABLE LINES
"Nothing is written until we write it," Lawrence declares in response to Ali's statement that they cannot cross the Nefud Desert, known to the Arabs as "The Sun's Anvil."

## AWARDS

*Lawrence of Arabia* won seven Oscars, including Best Director and Best Picture.

# LITTLE CAESAR (1930)

## RATINGS

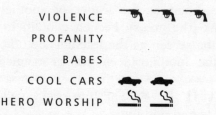

VIOLENCE

PROFANITY

BABES

COOL CARS

HERO WORSHIP

**WHAT HAPPENS** ▰ This is a classic American tale, often told but never better than here. Two small-town boys want to make something of themselves, so they move to an unnamed big city in the East. One, Joey Massara, gets a job dancing at a nightclub and takes up with a beautiful fellow dancer named Olga. The other, Rico, falls in with the mob and works his way up with his willingness to play hard with anybody—including the boss who first hired him. The bad guys hit the nightclub where Joey works, and Rico (now Little Caesar) uses Joey's loyalty to pressure him into helping them pull off the heist. But the job goes bad, and one of the customers gets shot. That customer is a member of the city's Crime Commission, and Joey is pressed to tell what he knows. Little Caesar looks to take the fall, but he never backs down.

**THE CAST** ▰ Edward G. Robinson is pure pit bull as Rico: short, stocky, and mean, calling everybody "Mug" in his characteristic tight-lipped manner that came to be a classic criminal's style. Douglas Fairbanks Jr. is his opposite: lithe, smooth-featured, and genuinely troubled by the conflict between his sense of loyalty and his conscience.

**WHY GUYS LOVE IT** ■ This guy's a gangster not for money or even power, but just because he likes it.

**HONEY, YOU'LL LIKE THIS MOVIE ...** ■ Because Douglas Fairbanks Jr. was the Patrick Swayze of his day.

**DON'T MISS**
- The gang posing for photographers after a shoot-out.
- Little Caesar's agitated phone call to the Crime Commission after they bad-mouth him in the press.

**MEMORABLE LINES**
"If he's looking for trouble," Little Caesar says as an invitation, "that's what we got the most of."

# THE PUBLIC ENEMY (1931)

**RATINGS**

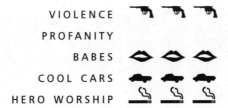

| | | | |
|---|---|---|---|
| VIOLENCE | 🔫 | 🔫 | 🔫 |
| PROFANITY | | | |
| BABES | 👄 | 👄 | 👄 |
| COOL CARS | 🚗 | 🚗 | 🚗 |
| HERO WORSHIP | 🚬 | 🚬 | 🚬 |

**WHAT HAPPENS** ■ The movie opens with the disclaimer, "It is the ambition of the authors of *The Public Enemy* to honestly depict an environment that exists today at a certain strata of American life rather than to glorify the hoodlum or the criminal." But, of course, that's exactly what they do. The story follows a boy, Tom Powers, and his buddy during Prohibition, who start out running beer from a saloon, progress to picking pockets, and finally graduate to full-scale gangsterhood—complete with lots of cash, great suits, and babes. They steal booze from a government warehouse in a gas truck, bully bar owners and even kill a cop. Tom clashes with his self-righteous older brother and then with a rival gang—who kills his boyhood friend and partner. That makes Tom very angry and more than a little foolish. He ends up a special delivery to his mother's house.

## THE CAST ▪ James Cagney's tough, bitter, and mean portrayal of Tom Powers does everything to glorify the hoodlum. The look in his eye is a constant "Please, I beg you, give me a reason to kick your ass." The original blond bombshell, Jean Harlow, takes a turn as Tom's babe of the week, but it is Mae Clarke who is partnered with Cagney in the movie's most famous scene: He grinds a grapefruit in her face because she's nagging him.

## WHY GUYS LOVE IT ▪ Cagney backs down from no one, but no one—not even his ma.

## HONEY, YOU'LL LIKE THIS MOVIE ... ▪ Because Cagney was a great dancer and is liable to break out into a soft-shoe at any moment. He's almost as good as Fred and Gene.

## DON'T MISS
- Cagney's visit to the local gun shop, a scene remade in *The Terminator*.
- Cagney spitting beer in the face of a bartender who dares to use another supplier's brew.

## MEMORABLE LINES
"I wish you was a wishing well, so I could tie a bucket to you and sink it," Cagney says to the nagging broad.

# THE RACKET (1951)

## RATINGS

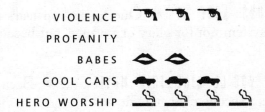

| | |
|---|---|
| VIOLENCE | 🔫 🔫 🔫 |
| PROFANITY | |
| BABES | 👄 👄 |
| COOL CARS | 🚗 🚗 🚗 |
| HERO WORSHIP | 🚬 🚬 🚬 🚬 |

**WHAT HAPPENS** ◾ Long before *Internal Affairs, Prince of the City,* or even *Serpico,* there were cops gone bad and good cops who nailed them and their cronies. Captain McQuigg is one of those good cops and he's assigned to the precinct where the criminals run the show. McQuigg knows that Nick Scanlon, a guy from the old neighborhood who's living a bit too well, is at the root of the problem. So McQuigg turns the heat up by pinching Scanlon's kid brother and his sleazy lounge-singer girlfriend on a trumped-up charge. Nick Scanlon uses every weapon he can—intimidation, influence, etc.—but McQuigg doesn't back down. And that's when Scanlon loses his cool and walks himself and the corrupt Crime Commission out onto a ledge from which there is no escape.

**THE CAST** ◾ Robert Mitchum never flinched in the face of anyone, and as Captain McQuigg he shows not a flicker of fear. Not even when his house gets bombed. He just lowers his sleepy eyelids another notch, drops his deep voice another note, and orders his men to hang tough. Robert Ryan is the dapper and smug Nick Scanlon, a man too impressed by himself to see what's coming—hard. William "Cannon" Conrad is the crime commissioner on the take who tries to walk a line between the cops and the crooks, but he's a heavy who keeps tipping in the wrong direction. Lizabeth Scott is the trashy singer who discovers that straight-arrow cops are as lovable as the crooks.

## WHY GUYS LOVE IT ▰ One tough cop tears down the whole system not for glory or revenge, but because it's his job.

## HONEY, YOU'LL LIKE THIS MOVIE ... ▰ Because a bad girl gets a second chance to do good.

## DON'T MISS
- Scanlon giving his brother relationship advice with the back of his hand.
- McQuigg may be by the book, but when he's finished grappling with one of Scanlon's boys on the rooftop, Mc-Quigg tosses him to the ground.
- The cars they drive may not have been any cooler in those days than a Plymouth Fury squad car is today, but those old machines sure look sharp now.

## MEMORABLE LINES
"He won't stop at anything now," one of the cops says after Scanlon kills a fellow officer right in the station house.

"What makes you think I will?" McQuigg responds.

# SPARTACUS (1960)

RATINGS

| | |
|---|---|
| VIOLENCE | 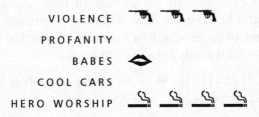 |
| PROFANITY | |
| BABES | |
| COOL CARS | |
| HERO WORSHIP | |

**WHAT HAPPENS** ● They didn't have action movies during the glory days of the Roman Empire, so the Romans satisfied their bloodlust by watching slaves trained as gladiators fight to the death with nasty weapons like the trident and Thracian sword. But one slave, Spartacus, doesn't want to kill other slaves. Instead, he leads a slave revolt against the greatest fighting force yet known—the Roman legions. After Spartacus and his horde humiliate the Garrison of Rome, a new commander is assigned by the Senate to hunt down and crush the rebels, and this commander has a truly "take no prisoners" attitude—he's not content until Spartacus is hung out to dry.

**THE CAST** ● Everything you need to know about Spartacus you can see in the eyes of Kirk Douglas, who produced the movie and took the starring role. Those eyes burn with insolence and contempt from the first to the last moment of the movie. Of course, his Roman tormentors can see it, too. Laurence Olivier, the English actor renowned for his performances in movies based on Shakespeare's plays, is thoroughly political in the most underhanded sense of the word, giving his portrayal of Crassus—the commander assigned to crush the slave revolt—the undercurrent of menace that makes us almost root for him. Less admirable is the head of the gladiator school, played by Peter Ustinov, who seems as much in the business of sucking up to the rich and powerful as he is involved in the buying and selling of slaves. A young Tony Curtis is a manservant to Crassus, who appears resigned to waiting on the nobleman until the slave revolt erupts and he learns to be a man. Jean Simmons is reserved and demure as Spartacus's woman—except for her jutting breasts,which really stand out in a toga.

### WHY GUYS LOVE IT ◄ This gladiator stuff is better than WWF Saturday Night.

### HONEY, YOU'LL LIKE THIS MOVIE . . . ◄ Because the men's outfits are as skimpy—if not skimpier—than the women's.

### DON'T MISS
- The wives perusing and selecting the gladiators they want to watch.
- Jean Simmons's bath—Spartacus doesn't miss it.

### MEMORABLE LINES
- "Those who are about to die salute you," says the trainer before the gladiators fight.
- "I am Spartacus," proclaim all the slaves one by one when Crassus asks them to identify their leader or be executed.

### AWARDS
*Spartacus* won four Oscars, including Ustinov for Best Supporting Actor.

### CHECK OUT

When this classic was restored during the early 1990s, the sound track in a few of the scenes with Laurence Olivier had to be redubbed. But Olivier was dead, so Anthony Hopkins got the job of doing his voice.

# THUNDER ROAD (1958)

## RATINGS

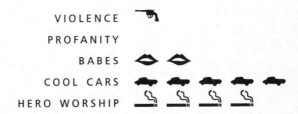

VIOLENCE

PROFANITY

BABES

COOL CARS

HERO WORSHIP

**WHAT HAPPENS ▰** Long before *The Dukes of Hazzard* made running moonshine a popular entertainment, this movie showed how much fun you can have rippin' around country roads, leaving the Feds behind in a cloud of dust, and bringing tax-free booze to the people. A mobster tries to muscle in on a respectable family's illegal business, but older son Luke—a Korean War vet—smokes all comers in his jacked late-model Mercury. And, just to keep things interesting, Luke has a nice girl back home in the holler and a nightclub singer in town.

**THE CAST ▰** Robert Mitchum practically invented the dead-eye squint—which he deploys here as Luke with great effectiveness, whether he's whipping through S-turns or blowing off the kingpin's emissary. No one, save Humphrey Bogart, ever smoked a cigarette with more attitude than Mitchum. His son, Jim Mitchum, plays Luke's younger brother. Gene Barry, best known as TV's Bat Masterson, shows up as Luke's rival for the country girl's affections.

**WHY GUYS LOVE IT ▰** Ninety-two minutes of hot-rod action!

**HONEY, YOU'LL LIKE THIS MOVIE . . .** ◗ Because it illuminates the nuances of Appalachian culture.

**DON'T MISS**
• Luke's handy trunk modification—talk about your party mobiles.

**MEMORABLE LINES**
• "Hey pretty girl," Luke says whenever he sees the girl back home.
• "She's trying to make a living," Luke tells a fat guy who laughs loudly during the nightclub singer's performance. "If you want to bray, find a barnyard."

**TRIVIA**

If you think of Robert Mitchum as simply a tough-guy actor, you'll be surprised to know that he wrote this movie's screenplay and the theme song "Whippoorwill," which became a hit when he sang it.

# THE TREASURE OF THE SIERRA MADRE (1948)

**RATINGS**

| | |
|---|---|
| VIOLENCE | 🔫 🔫 |
| PROFANITY | |
| BABES | |
| COOL CARS | |
| HERO WORSHIP | 🚬 🚬 🚬 |

SHOOTING STAR

Bogie has his eyes set on *The Treasure of the Sierra Madre.*

**WHAT HAPPENS** ⬝ Gold is the magnet that draws together three down-and-out Americans into the hills of Mexico and, sure enough, gold is the explosive that blows them apart. An old gold prospector with a hunch signs on two young partners, and they find a rich vein. They divide the work and the proceeds fair and square—until one of them develops the twin diseases of paranoia and greed. Before long, he turns rabid and snaps at the others. But you'll have to watch until the end to find out where the gold goes.

**THE CAST** ⬝ Humphrey Bogart is as grimy and grizzly as he ever was—both in his physical appearance and his portrayal of Fred C. Dobbs. Dobbs is seen first begging and he never ceases looking at everyone for what they can give him. Tim Holt is the earnest partner, Curtin, who hopes to get just a little money together to buy an orchard. Walter Huston is the old prospector, Howard, who knows all too well the perils of gold fever. His calm and wise manner aggravates Bogart more than pacifies him. John Huston, Walter's son and this movie's director, strolls past Bogart on the streets of the Mexican town during the opening sequence. Robert "Baretta" Blake, Hollywood's official child of the 1940s, is the too-helpful Mexican boy.

## WHY GUYS LOVE IT ☛ We all know that greed isn't good, but it is fun to watch other guys go at it for the love of gold.

## HONEY, YOU'LL LIKE THIS MOVIE . . . ☛ Because the old prospector gives up his gold to save an Indian child. It's all about charity.

## DON'T MISS
- The surprise that greets Dobbs when he goes looking for Curtin after their confrontation.
- Dobbs' carefully considered plan to return his money to the local economy in Tampico, the Mexican town where they met.

## MEMORABLE LINES
"We are the Federales," proclaim a band of Mexicans the three miners encounter. "You know, the mounted police."

"If you are the police, where are your badges," Dobbs asks.

"Badges," the Mexican answers. "We ain't go no badges. We don't need no badges. I don't have to show you no stinkin' badges."

## AWARDS

 Father and son Walter Huston and John Huston won Academy Awards for this movie: Best Supporting Actor for Walter, Best Direction and Best Screenplay for John.

# APOCALYPSE NOW (1979)

## RATINGS

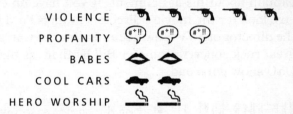

| | |
|---|---|
| VIOLENCE | 🔫 🔫 🔫 🔫 🔫 |
| PROFANITY | @*!! @*!! @*!! |
| BABES | 👄 👄 |
| COOL CARS | 🚗 🚗 |
| HERO WORSHIP | 🚬 🚬 |

**WHAT HAPPENS ▪** During the Vietnam War, Special Forces assassin (and burnout) Captain Willard is ordered to make contact with a renegade officer, Colonel Kurtz, who has established his own outpost deep in the heart of the Cambodian jungle, and "terminate his command." The captain hitches a ride up the Mekong River with a U.S. Navy patrol boat that takes him deeper and deeper into the nightmare of the war. He finds Colonel Kurtz living in a village among the natives and other dropout Americans, indulging in bizarre blood rituals and surfing the edge of sanity. The captain begins to fall under the spell of Kurtz and the place even before he arrives, and when he finally confronts Kurtz, the captain must come to grips with his own moral conflicts about his conduct.

**THE CAST** ▰ As Captain Willard, Martin Sheen looks haggard and drained as he sets off on his mission. His focus on his assignment becomes clearer as he travels up the river, while his questions about how Colonel Kurtz, an unusual but outstanding officer, came unglued plague the captain the closer he gets to him. Marlon Brando has just a few brief scenes as Colonel Kurtz, but his shaved head, dark, brooding eyes, and rumbling, mumbling whisper will haunt you as they did the captain. Robert Duvall plays his part of Lieutenant Colonel Kilgore, a cavalry officer with an unwavering interest in surfing, for laughs—even if they're just nervous laughs. Dennis Hopper is a manic American news photographer caught in Colonel Kurtz's spell. A very young-looking Harrison Ford is one of the officers who briefs the captain about his assignment. If you have an eye for cameos, look for the movie's director, Francis Ford Coppola, as the director of a TV crew documenting the war, and the late, great rock concert promoter Bill Graham as the emcee of a USO show gone bad.

**WHY GUYS LOVE IT** ▰ For the same reason we like roller coasters—the queasy feeling in the pit of your stomach that says nothing is stable here.

**HONEY, YOU'LL LIKE THIS MOVIE . . .** ▰ Because this is a remarkably faithful update of *Heart of Darkness*, a novella by twentieth-century writer Joseph Conrad.

**DON'T MISS**
- Captain Kilgore's thoughtful gesture of sharing his favorite music, Richard Wagner's *Ride of the Valkyries*, with the enemy.
- The boat being attacked by natives with bows and arrows.
- The calling card Colonel Kurtz drops outside the captain's cell to serve notice of where his head is at.

## MEMORABLE LINES

- "I love the smell of napalm in the morning. . . . It smells like victory," says Captain Kilgore.
- "You have no right to judge me," Colonel Kurtz tells the captain. "You have the right to kill me."
- "You're just an errand boy for grocery clerks come to collect the bill," Kurtz says to Willard about his assignment.

**CHECK OUT**

*HEARTS OF DARKNESS: A Filmmaker's Apocalypse* is an equally fascinating study of insanity and excess in the jungle—it's a documentary on the making of *Apocalypse Now*, with footage filmed on location by Eleanor Coppola, the director's wife.

# THE DIRTY DOZEN (1967)

## RATINGS:

| | |
|---|---|
| VIOLENCE | 🔫 🔫 🔫 |
| PROFANITY | #*!! #*!! #*!! |
| BABES | 👄 👄 |
| COOL CARS | 🚗 |
| HERO WORSHIP | 🚬 🚬 🚬 🚬 |

**WHAT HAPPENS** ◼ A tough but unorthodox U.S. Army major is assigned to recruit and train twelve imprisoned soldiers—all of whom have been sentenced to death or life without parole—for a suicide mission into Germany during World War II. Of course, the major whips them into a tight fighting unit, but not before he has broken a few rules and

S.S./SHOOTING STAR

Locked, loaded, and ready to kick ass in *The Dirty Dozen*.

kicked a few asses. They are opposed along the way by a couple of regulation Army officers, who must be humiliated in a war games exercise to prove the worthiness of the Dirty Dozen. And then the twelve are dropped behind enemy lines, where they execute a boldly clever plan to assault a chateau used for high-level drinking and whoring by German officers. Everything goes according to plan, which means fewer than a dozen remain when the smoke clears.

**THE CAST** ◆ Lee Marvin gritted his teeth and uttered dire threats throughout a whole career of tough-guy characters like Major Reisman in this movie. Before Major Reisman earns the respect of the prisoners, he has to go to the mat with Victor Franko, the streetwise prisoner played with pure insolence by John Cassavetes. Charles *"Death Wish"* Bronson, believe it or not, is the smart prisoner, while Donald Sutherland is the one with a permanent "Vacancy" sign on his forehead. Telly "Kojak" Savalas misses out on some big fun because he's a Bible-quotin' Southerner who sees the devil in all good times. Former running back Jim Brown gets to show his moves in the movie's climactic scene. Ernest Borgnine and George Kennedy are the staff officers who support the Dirty Dozen; a pinched Robert Ryan and stiff Robert Webber are the officers who want to see them crack.

**WHY GUYS LOVE IT** ◄ Twelve outcasts get a second chance—which we all wish for sometimes.

**HONEY, YOU'LL LIKE THIS MOVIE ...** ◄ Because it celebrates forgiveness and the potential for good in all men, no matter what their service records show.

## DON'T MISS
- The major's reward to the men for successfully completing their training.
- Sutherland's impersonation of a general and inspection of Ryan's troops.

## MEMORABLE LINES
- "He slipped on a bar of soap" is the response whenever officers catch the men brawling.
- One of the soldiers asks Major Reisman what to do about the captured service staff at the chateau. "Feed the French and kill the Germans," he answers.

## TRIVIA

Three made-for-TV sequels were broadcast in the 1980s: *The Dirty Dozen: The Next Mission, The Deadly Mission,* and *The Fatal Mission.* Lee Marvin appeared in one, Ernest Borgnine was in all three, and, though he was killed in the original, Telly Savalas came back to lead *The Fatal Mission.* The last, and the worst, included boxer Ray "Boom Boom" Mancini.

# FULL METAL JACKET (1987)

RATINGS:

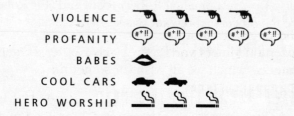

| | |
|---|---|
| VIOLENCE | 🔫 🔫 🔫 🔫 |
| PROFANITY | 💬 💬 💬 💬 💬 |
| BABES | 👄 |
| COOL CARS | 🚗 🚗 |
| HERO WORSHIP | 🚬 🚬 🚬 |

**WHAT HAPPENS** ▰ This movie is divided into two distinct sections that follow U.S. Marines in training on Parris Island and in combat in Vietnam. During the first part, a high-intensity drill sergeant berates, badgers, and bullies a platoon of Marine recruits, with special attention on a lumbering private the sergeant has dubbed "Gomer Pyle." When Pyle short-circuits on graduation day (in a scene that will haunt you for days), the movie shifts its focus to one of Pyle's platoon-mates—dubbed Private Joker—who's assigned to be a reporter in Vietnam for the military newspaper. He and the troops he's covering find themselves "in a world of shit," as the drill sergeant warned them, during the Tet Offensive of 1968, and discover what kind of killing machines they have been trained to be.

**THE CAST** ▰ Vincent D'Onofrio earns our pity as the blubbery and slow-witted Pyle, but our respect goes to Lee Ermey as the lean and mean drill sergeant. Ermey is an ex-soldier who also appeared in *Apocalypse Now* and *The Boys in Company C*. Matthew Modine is Private Joker, the thoughtful Marine who fights to hold on to his irreverence on the ground. Adam Baldwin, younger brother of Alec Baldwin, has a small part as a squad leader fighting off sniper attack.

**WHY GUYS LOVE IT** ■ It's about Marines and their appetite for impersonal sex and impersonal death.

**HONEY, YOU'LL LIKE THIS MOVIE . . .** ■ Because, well, because you made me sit through *Beaches* last week.

**DON'T MISS**
The sergeant's first meeting with the recruits; he reels off a dozen one-liners you can repeat to other guys almost anytime.

**MEMORABLE LINES**
- "Pyle, your ass looks like 150 pounds of chewed bubble gum," says the sergeant. (I find this line especially handy for taunting opponents on the basketball court.)
- "You think we waste gooks for Freedom?" one soldier says to a roving film crew. "If I'm going to get my balls blown off for a word, that word is gonna be Poontang."

**TRIVIA**

Remember the outlawed rap group 2 Live Crew? They sampled the line "Me so horny" from this movie.

# THE GUNS OF NAVARONE (1961)

**RATINGS:**

VIOLENCE
PROFANITY
BABES
COOL CARS
HERO WORSHIP

**WHAT HAPPENS** ✒ During World War II, the British command organizes a crew of experienced soldiers for a secret mission to sabotage a pair of mammoth Nazi cannons housed inside an impregnable fortress overlooking the Aegean Sea. After the ranking British officer is injured at the outset, the team is led by Captain Mallory, a New Zealander who is an expert mountain climber, and his right-hand man, the stealthy and lethal Andreas. Mallory's judgment is continually questioned by Corporal Miller, a by-the-book Englishman who ultimately develops a grudging respect for Mallory and a well-founded fear of Andreas. The team is aided along the way by several natives of the island, particularly a dark-haired beauty named Maria who loathes the Germans and comes to love Mallory. This is a very suspenseful movie, but not because the eventual outcome is in doubt—it's more about *how* they get there than *if* they will.

**THE CAST** ✒ Gregory Peck always seems too serious to be someone you'd like to hang out with, but he's just the kind of guy you'd want as your leader on a dangerous mission: His Captain Mallory is steady, focused, and entirely free of emotions. Even the exotic beauty Irene Papas (who also appeared, no surprise, in *Zorba the Greek*) as Maria can't get his attention. Anthony Quinn (Zorba himself) is equally cool as Andreas, who barely utters a line but whose reactions are swift and decisive. David Niven's Corporal Miller, on the other hand, does little without talking—he'll annoy you nearly as much as he does Captain Mallory. Irish actor Richard "*A Man Called Horse*" Harris is on the crew, too. James Darren, fresh from a date with Gidget, tries (vainly) to be taken seriously in this movie.

**WHY GUYS LOVE IT** ✒ This is war as it was meant to be won: by men performing nearly impossible jobs in the worst possible conditions, with life and death hanging in the balance all the way to the end.

**HONEY, YOU'LL LIKE THIS MOVIE . . .** ☛ Because it's about trying to stop the killing of thousands of men.

**DON'T MISS**
- One minute of the two hours and thirty-seven minutes because none of it is filler.
- The very effective interrogation technique Andreas employs on the eavesdroppers.

# HAMBURGER HILL (1987)

**RATINGS**

| | |
|---|---|
| VIOLENCE | 🔫 🔫 🔫 🔫 |
| PROFANITY | #*!! #*!! #*!! #*!! |
| BABES | |
| COOL CARS | 🚗 |
| HERO WORSHIP | 🚬 🚬 🚬 |

**WHAT HAPPENS** ☛ An infantry unit is sent to take a hill from the North Vietnamese Army—a hill notorious for reducing the toughest soldiers to ground meat. The fighting is close, the scenes very realistic, and the action very intense. Whether they capture the hill or not seems far less important than who will survive. The answer is, as you would expect, not many.

**THE CAST** ☛ All of the players in this movie are very convincing "dogfaces" who are neither too pretty nor too fearless—always a dead giveaway of "Hollywood" soldiers. The only faces you're likely to recognize in this movie are those of Steven Weber, the brother without a conscience on TV's

*Wings*, and Dylan McDermott, Clint Eastwood's doomed partner in *In the Line of Fire*.

## WHY GUYS LOVE IT ▰ This movie, along with *Pork Chop Hill*, are staples in the Guys' High Cholesterol War Diet. Notice they didn't call either of them "Sushi Hill" or "Chef Salad with Dressing on the Side Hill."

## HONEY, YOU'LL LIKE THIS MOVIE ... ▰ Because the guys are man enough to admit they're scared.

## DON'T MISS
- The sergeants' premission bath with a few local pros.
- The medical officer's difficult time identifying one of the new guys, who's lost his head.

## MEMORABLE LINES
- Whenever any of the soldiers screws up or considers violating regulations, everybody says, "What can they do to you, send you to Vietnam?"
- "Drop your weapon," the Vietnamese radio broadcaster offers to the American soldiers, "and Uncle Ho will give you a water buffalo and a rice paddy to shit in."

# MIDWAY (1976)

## RATINGS

| | |
|---|---|
| VIOLENCE | 🔫 🔫 |
| PROFANITY | (#*!!) |
| BABES | 👄 |
| COOL CARS | 🚗 🚗 🚗 |
| HERO WORSHIP | 🚬 🚬 🚬 🚬 |

**WHAT HAPPENS** ✒ The biggest naval battle in history and a major turning point in the war against the Japanese is recounted from both sides, with an emphasis on command-level strategizing rather than extensive combat scenes (though, once the battle begins, about three-quarters of the way through the movie, you do see lots of actual footage from the war). The battle was focused on a Pacific island called Midway, from which American bombers had flown to strike Tokyo. Japanese admiral Yamamoto believed that a massive surprise strike at Midway would crush the American Navy and effectively win the war; U.S. admiral Nimitz placed his faith in some sketchy intelligence and his hunch to trump the Japanese surprise with one of his own.

**THE CAST** ✒ This is an all-star line-up: Henry Fonda is the cool and in-command Admiral Nimitz; Toshiro Mifune is stiff and stern as Admiral Yamamoto; Hal Holbrook is the code cracker who's not sailing on an even keel; Glenn Ford commands the fleet at sea; Charlton Heston delivers the final blow; Robert Mitchum takes a brief spot as Admiral Halsey; and Cliff Robertson, James Coburn, Robert Wagner, Eddie Albert, Dabney Coleman, Pat "Arnold" Morita, Erik Estrada, Kevin Dobson (Kojak's partner, Crocker), a mustacheless Tom Selleck, and Christopher George (who got his combat experience on *Rat Patrol*) all have their moments.

**WHY GUYS LOVE IT** ✒ Two hundred ships, thousands of planes, and some of the coolest guys ever to snap off a salute.

**HONEY, YOU'LL LIKE THIS MOVIE . . .** ✒ Because there's a whole illicit love thing going on between Charlton Heston's son and a Japanese-American girl.

## DON'T MISS
- The clever trick Holbrook devises to confirm his suspicions about the Japanese's plans.
- Watching those Japanese carriers blow up. More than fifty years later, you still want to jump up and shout when they go boom.

## MEMORABLE LINES
- "You're guessing," Heston says to Holbrook.
  "We like to think of it as analysis," Holbrook answers.
- "You go to sea, you find Yamamoto, you chew his ass off. That's all there is to it," Mitchum explains to Ford, who has doubts about his ability to command in combat.

# PATTON (1970)

## RATINGS

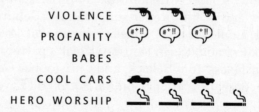

| | | |
|---|---|---|
| VIOLENCE | | |
| PROFANITY | | |
| BABES | | |
| COOL CARS | | |
| HERO WORSHIP | | |

**WHAT HAPPENS** ▰ This is the true story of the toughest, most arrogant, most uncontrollable, most dangerous (and thus most interesting) son of a bitch ever to pin a star on his collar. General George S. Patton commanded tank divisions that smashed the brigades of the wily German General Rommel in North Africa, and then chased the Huns through Italy and France. He did not lead from a command post, but from the battlefield itself and he would hear of no strategy but attack, always attack. Problem was, he had to take orders from the Supreme Allied Commander in Chief, General Eisenhower, and though Patton was a believer in military discipline, he didn't take orders very well—particularly those that directed him to be politic. That left Patton on the sidelines during some of the war's biggest battles, where he slowly lost his grip.

THE CAST ◆ There are hundreds of actors in this movie, but only one ever occupies your attention. From the moment George C. Scott swaggers onto the screen and begins his crude, but inspiring speech backed by a huge American flag, you can see how full of himself and zeal for war Patton is. But the way that Scott makes Patton seem so real and vivid is in his sly smile—as if Patton is letting us see that it's all an act he puts on for the men. The delusion is so complete because he has deluded himself. Oh yeah, Karl Malden is General Omar Bradley—at first Patton's second-in-command, but later promoted past Patton and put in the unfortunate job of reining him in.

WHY GUYS LOVE IT ◆ He may be insane, but he's crazy like a fox—just the sort of guy you'd charge a tank for.

HONEY, YOU'LL LIKE THIS MOVIE . . . ◆ Because some critics have called this an important antiwar movie.

DON'T MISS
- Patton standing in the middle of the street during an air raid firing his pistol at the German planes bombing all around him.
- Patton slapping the combat-fatigued soldier and chasing him out of the hospital with taunts of "coward."
- Patton without irony asking the chaplain to write a "better-weather prayer."

## MEMORABLE LINES

"No dumb bastard ever won a war by dying for his country," Patton tells the men in his opening speech. "You win by making the other poor bastard die for his country." Simple enough?

**TRIVIA**

Believe it or not, Francis Ford Coppola (director of *Apocalypse Now*) wrote this movie's screenplay, for which he won an Academy Award.

# PLATOON (1986)

## RATINGS

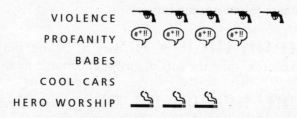

| VIOLENCE | 🔫 🔫 🔫 🔫 🔫 |
| PROFANITY | 💬 💬 💬 💬 |
| BABES | |
| COOL CARS | |
| HERO WORSHIP | 🚬 🚬 🚬 |

**WHAT HAPPENS** ▪ This is a grunt's-eye view of the Vietnam War. And what the grunt who narrates this movie sees are two different kinds of soldiers: those who just do their duty and try to stay alive, and those who are a bit more enthusiastic about doing their duty. The two types of soldiers are definitively represented by Sergeant Elias, brave, tough, and compassionate toward the "fresh meat"; and Sergeant Barnes, mean, scornful, and coldly lethal. When the platoon comes upon a village that has hidden food and weapons for the North Vietnamese Army, the sergeants clash over Barnes's methods of extracting information from the villagers. That clash polarizes the platoon and leaves our grunt with a blurry sense of right and wrong. All of this goes down amidst some of the most realistic combat action ever fabricated for the movies.

THE CAST ► Why does the narrator's voice sound strangely familiar? Because Charlie Sheen's voice-over has the same rasp as that of his father, Martin Sheen, who narrates *Apocalypse Now*. But that's where their similarities end. In this movie, Charlie is an innocent (in *Apocalypse Now*, Martin's character is anything but an innocent) who enlisted because he didn't want to stay in college. Even after a few months in the jungle, he's still surprised and indignant about how some of the others behave. His most telling moment comes when he confronts a cripple in the village and is as frightened and unsure about how to behave as the unarmed one-legged guy. Willem Dafoe's intensity burns in his eyes, but his portrayal of Sergeant Elias is softened by a loopy grin. Tom Berenger's face is crosshatched with so many scars that you can tell Sergeant Barnes has looked into the eyes of men he's killed. Forest Whitaker's character is troubled by their actions, Kevin Dillon's wishes he'd see more action. Also in the platoon are Johnny Depp and Corey Glover (singer for the defunct rock band Living Colour). Don't blink during the climactic firefight and you'll spot director Oliver Stone, who wrote this movie based on his own experiences in Vietnam.

WHY GUYS LOVE IT ► This is war at its most grim— fought on the ground, at close range.

HONEY, YOU'LL LIKE THIS MOVIE ... ► Because it's filled with eighteen- and nineteen-year-old boys, dressed in khakis you'd pay a fortune for at The Gap.

## DON'T MISS

- Sergeant Elias's idea of a shotgun hit of dope—down the barrel of an M16.
- How Bunny (Kevin Dillon) busts the language barrier with the crippled villager.

## MEMORABLE LINES

- "Hey, O'Neill, take a break, you don't have to be an asshole every day of your life," Elias says to one of the other sergeants.
- "You talkin' about death? You all experts?" Barnes challenges the dopers one night. "I'd like to hear about it, potheads. You smoke this shit to escape from reality. I don't need this shit. I am reality."

## AWARDS

*Platoon* won Oscars for Best Picture and Best Director.

Can someone please tell me why the videotape of this movie opens with Lee Iacocca doing a Jeep commercial? Am I supposed to go buy a Grand Cherokee after watching these guys march through the jungle, blasting away at the natives and each other?

# PORK CHOP HILL (1959)

## RATINGS

VIOLENCE    🔫 🔫

PROFANITY

BABES

COOL CARS

HERO WORSHIP    🚬 🚬 🚬 🚬

**WHAT HAPPENS** ▰ Based on a true story and shot in gritty black and white, this movie is unlike most other war films you've seen—and not just because it takes place during the Korean War. World War II movies typically have casts of thousands, shift focus from one battle line to another, and celebrate uncommon (often unbelievable) acts of heroism; too many of the Vietnam War movies rely on the shocking brutality of war to keep your attention. This riveting movie follows one company of soldiers as they work in carefully coordinated maneuvers to capture the eponymous hill from the Chinese Communists; the tension that builds as they climb the hill finds its way into the pit of *your* stomach. The company's leader, Lieutenant Clemons, is tough and demanding, but not entirely without compassion—and he has a strangely insatiable hunger for raisins, which he munches at every pause in the action. He prods his company on in their all-night assault in the face of heavy casualties and without the support they are promised. They triumph because he insists that they rely on each other to do their jobs and that no one take an unnecessary risk.

**THE CAST** ▰ What is it about Gregory Peck that makes him the most reliable guy in every war movie he ever appeared in? It could be his deep, authoritative voice or his clear, watchful eyes. Or maybe it's his never-faltering seriousness—can you remember him ever smiling in a war movie? Whatever it is, when he (as Lieutenant Clemons) commands his men to climb a mountain in the face of enemy fire, they race to do it. He has plenty of star power at his side in this movie—like George *"A-Team"* Peppard, Martin Landau, and Rip Torn—as well as lower caliber talents like Robert "Barretta" Blake, Norman "Mr. Roper" Fell, and Harry Guardino. Keep your eyes and ears open and you'll spot a young Harry Dean Stanton and an already balding Gavin MacLeod (*The Love Boat*'s Captain Stubing).

## WHY GUYS LOVE IT ▰ War doesn't get any more real than this.

## HONEY, YOU'LL LIKE THIS MOVIE ... ▰ Because for once the men work together, not against each other.

## DON'T MISS
The general at the peace talks explaining the crucial significance of the hill at the end.

## MEMORABLE LINES
"Welcome to the meat grinder," announces the Chinese broadcaster as the American soldiers begin their assault.

# RUN SILENT, RUN DEEP (1958)

## RATINGS

| | |
|---|---|
| VIOLENCE | 🔫 🔫 |
| PROFANITY | |
| BABES | |
| COOL CARS | 🚗 🚗 🚗 |
| HERO WORSHIP | 🚬 🚬 🚬 |

**WHAT HAPPENS ▪** During World War II, a submarine commander loses a ship and most of his crew to the Japanese in a battle in the Bungo Straits—where three other American subs had been sunk. When he is assigned to a new ship, he defies orders and returns to the same place to defeat the Japanese commander who sunk his first sub. The second-in-command and the crew question his decisions, then sign on to his crusade. When the commander is wounded during a skirmish, the exec takes up the fight. Though the plot isn't all that novel and the special effects are primitive, the combat strategies are very authentic and engrossing.

**THE CAST ▪** Clark "Rhett Butler" Gable is the headstrong commander, P. J. Richardson, who sets a collision course with both his men and the enemy. (I know that Gable's pencil-thin mustache is a trademark, but please tell me how he got to be the only man in the Navy with facial hair.) Burt Lancaster is steady as she goes as the executive officer waiting for his opportunity to lead. Jack Warden's gunnery officer remains ready to punch out anyone disloyal to the commander. Seaman Don Rickles—already bald—has not a single punch line.

**WHY GUYS LOVE IT** ▰ In a sub, everybody must be the strong, silent type.

**HONEY, YOU'LL LIKE THIS MOVIE ...** ▰ Because before there were oddly attractive guys like Harrison Ford, women watched movies with Clark Gable.

**DON'T MISS**
The commander's wily ploy to fool the Japanese into thinking they had sunk the sub.

**MEMORABLE LINES**
"You're going back because you've been there; you have to go back," says the commander to the exec.

# BAT*21 (1988)

## RATINGS

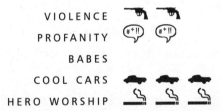

| | |
|---|---|
| VIOLENCE | |
| PROFANITY | |
| BABES | |
| COOL CARS | |
| HERO WORSHIP | |

**WHAT HAPPENS** ▬ About the only action Air Force officer Iceal Hambleton sees in Vietnam is on the golf course. But just before a big American offensive, his commanding officer suggests he go along on a surveillance flight to use his expertise to identify North Vietnamese antiaircraft defenses. Those defenses, it turns out, are good enough to take down Hambleton's plane, killing everybody but him. Once on the ground, he finds himself right in the middle of enemy territory and the planned site of an American carpet-bombing attack. After he goes down, Hambleton is contacted by a spotter plane flown by a guy calling himself Birddog. For the next three days, Hambleton gets a view of the war from the ground and works his way to a safe pickup site, following a route he relates to Birddog by matching his movements to holes on Air Force base golf courses.

**THE CAST** ■ Gene Hackman is Hambleton, so you know the officer will be a real guy with relaxed confidence and a practical, commonsense view of his situation. Yet Hackman also lets us see through the cracks as Hambleton becomes anxious about being captured, and the workings of his conscience as he gets closer to the ground action. Danny Glover's Birddog is his only contact—he's a very real guy, too, with his own anxieties, buzzing around in his prop plane. He is pulled into personal involvement with the men on the ground. Country singer Jerry Reed is Birddog's superior and he has to work to reel Birddog in.

**WHY GUYS LOVE IT** ■ Airplanes and golf. Now that's how to wage a war.

**HONEY, YOU'LL LIKE THIS MOVIE ...** ■ Because a man learns up close about the consequences of his actions.

**DON'T MISS**
- How Hambleton's life is saved from a deadly trap by a little Vietnamese kid.
- How the North Vietnamese use prisoners to sweep minefields.

**MEMORABLE LINES**
"I've been in the service most of my adult life," Hambleton tells Birddog. "This is the first time I ever saw any war."

**TRIVIA**

 This is a true story based on the experiences of Lieutenant Colonel Iceal Hambleton, who served as the movie's technical advisor.

# BLUE THUNDER (1983)

**WHAT HAPPENS** ☛ At the start of the movie we are told that "The hardware, weaponry, and surveillance systems depicted in this film are real and in use in the United States today." So close your curtains and talk softly. Okay, you ready? Murphy flies a Los Angeles police force helicopter for surveillance and support, and even though he's not a regulation kind of guy, he's chosen to test a brand-new armed and armored chopper the federal government has developed because he's a combat (Vietnam) experienced veteran and the force's best pilot. Along with its state-of-the-art weapons, the helicopter (called the Blue Thunder) also has high-tech listening devices that allow the pilots to eavesdrop on conversations inside buildings. When Murphy and his partner accidentally overhear a plot by the helicopter's developers to stir up trouble in the city, they become targets and Murphy must use the Blue Thunder itself to thwart them. He does this with some dry-palmed flying around L.A., evading jets and another Blue Thunder.

**THE CAST** ☛ Murphy has the occasional flashback to Vietnam, but Roy Scheider doesn't overdo the dramatics of that or lay the insolence on too thick. Rather, he seems like a guy who wants to be left alone to do his job. Murphy's rookie partner, Daniel Stern, thinks he's having a good time, right up until his last scene. Their captain, Warren Oates, is too busy thinking up funny insults to be having a good time. Murphy's rival, Malcolm McDowell, wants to have a good time with Murphy, but he's a government-trained killing machine, and fun isn't in his program.

## WHY GUYS LOVE IT ▰ A dogfight between two attack helicopters over Los Angeles is almost as deadly as a traffic jam on the Santa Ana Freeway.

## HONEY, YOU'LL LIKE THIS MOVIE... ▰ Because Murphy protects his girlfriend and her Vega with the Blue Thunder.

## DON'T MISS
- The woman doing nude yoga in the privacy of her own home while Murphy and his partner do their surveillance duty outside her window.
- When chicken rains down on the streets of L.A. after heat-seeking missiles fired from F16s miss the Blue Thunder and hit a barbecue shack. Even in L.A., drumsticks, thighs, and wings dropping from the sky are strange.

## MEMORABLE LINES
"You're a rookie, you're supposed to be stupid," the captain tells Murphy's partner. "Don't abuse the privilege."

# FIREBIRDS (1990)

## RATINGS

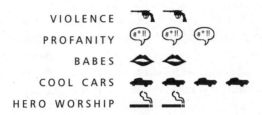

VIOLENCE

PROFANITY

BABES

COOL CARS

HERO WORSHIP

**WHAT HAPPENS** ➤ No one fires on American pilots and then just flies away into the wild blue yonder. When American Cobra and Blackhawk helicopters on a search-and-destroy mission against South American drug lords are flamed by the cartel's Scorpion helicopter and its hotshot pilot, the Army gets mad. The best chopper pilots we've got are brought together with the best teacher and are trained for a retaliation mission with Apache attack helicopters. While the salty old teacher peppers his trainees with down-home sayings and drills them with a rigorous program designed to get them ready for combat, the group's hottest pilot, Preston, tries to revive an old romance with a tough and wary woman pilot. Preston does prove himself on all fronts, but not without dodging a lot of flak first.

**THE CAST** ➤ The best compliment I believe you can give an actor in a movie so similar to *Top Gun* is to say he's no Tom Cruise. And Nicolas Cage as Preston is no Tom Cruise. Sure, he's an arrogant hotdog unwilling to discipline himself. But where Cruise wants to score with the babe to affirm what a desirable guy he is, you're sure that Preston wants her because she turns him on as much as flying in under enemy radar does. Or almost as much. You know, you could say many of the same things about Sean Young, saucy as always in her role as the target of Preston's fire. Tommy Lee Jones pulls out his Texas accent to deliver all the adages as the middle-aged teacher who still would like a bit of action.

### WHY GUYS LOVE IT ▰ Attack helicopters are the coolest innovation in warfare since the air-to-air missile.

### HONEY, YOU'LL LIKE THIS MOVIE . . . ▰ Because this is the new military, and not all the pilots are guys.

### DON'T MISS
- How the teacher uses a pair of red panties to help Preston overcome his problem flying with a scope.
- The 360-degree showdown between Preston and the Scorpion.

### MEMORABLE LINES
"You're going to be busier than a three-peckered goat," the teacher tells Preston.

# FIREFOX (1982)

### RATINGS

| | |
|---|---|
| VIOLENCE | 🔫 🔫 🔫 |
| PROFANITY | 💬 💬 |
| BABES | |
| COOL CARS | 🚗 🚗 🚗 🚗 🚗 |
| HERO WORSHIP | 🚬 🚬 🚬 |

### WHAT HAPPENS ▰ The Russians develop an amazing airplane (actually two of them) that flies at Mach V, can't be

detected by radar, and fires its weapons on commands that are thought by the pilot. This bird is so hot that the United States has to try to steal it, and to do that the government must press into service the best pilot we've got, Mitchell Gant, who turns out to be a reclusive Vietnam vet with a nagging flashback problem. But never mind, he accepts the challenge and drops into Moscow in the guise of a Western drug dealer being watched by the KGB—pretty clever, these CIA guys, dressing up this new guy as someone already known by the KGB, so the Russkies won't think to put extra surveillance on him until it's too late. Anyway, with the help of dissident scientists, Gant gets the Firefox out of its hangar and on its way to the U.S., but before he's in the clear he has to fight a high-tech air battle against the only conceivable opponent worthy of this plane: its twin, piloted by the best the Russians have to fly it.

**THE CAST** ✒ Clint Eastwood plays Mitchell Gant (and produced and directed this movie) and he handles the plane and the flashbacks with a minimum of comment. As always, Clint does the job without overdoing it. If you have a sharp eye, you may spot John "Cliff Clavin" Ratzenberger as a sailor aboard the refueling submarine.

**WHY GUYS LOVE IT** ✒ Boost a car for a joyride and you're daring; steal an experimental airplane and you've got balls of steel.

**HONEY, YOU'LL LIKE THIS MOVIE . . .** ✒ Because Clint Eastwood looks as clean and well-groomed as he did in *The Bridges of Madison County.*

**DON'T MISS**
- What Gant's Russian contacts do to the real drug dealer.
- Gant's men's room standoff with a KGB agent.

## MEMORABLE LINES

"Can you use this?" one of the Russians says to Gant about a gun he gives him.

"Yeah, I can use it," Gant answers with slight indignation.

"Don't," the Russian tells him, "except when absolutely necessary."

# FLIGHT OF THE
# INTRUDER (1990)

## RATINGS

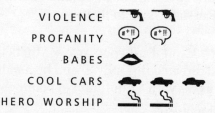

| VIOLENCE | 🔫 🔫 |
| PROFANITY | 💬 💬 |
| BABES | 👄 |
| COOL CARS | 🚗 🚗 🚗 |
| HERO WORSHIP | 🚬 🚬 |

## WHAT HAPPENS ▬ While so many Vietnam movies focus on guys whining about the meaninglessness of the war, this one has guys who do something about it. An experienced navigator with a steely nerve is paired with a bomber pilot who has just lost his buddy on a bombing raid of a strategically worthless target. The navigator teaches the pilot how to dodge missiles and MIGs, and together they develop a plan to hit a "big target" that is not in their orders. After completing an assigned mission, they head on to Hanoi and destroy a major antiaircraft missile depot. Their tough superior officer wants them court-martialed, but the charges are dropped for political reasons. This turns out to be good news for the officer, because his plane goes down behind enemy lines and these two must rescue him—but not with-

out some casualties on both sides. There's also a subplot about the officer's search for the "Phantom Shitter," a member of the squadron who sends a none-too-subtle message to the aircraft carrier's unpopular executive officer.

THE CAST ■ Tom Sizemore (who often appeared in TV's Vietnam-based soap opera *China Beach*) has the all-American looks to be convincing as the pilot who's angry and disappointed at his friend's death. Likewise, you'll have no trouble believing Willem Dafoe is a cynical navigator on his third tour of duty who teaches Sizemore's character how to be cool in the face of the enemy. Danny Glover as their commanding officer conveys genuine concern about his pilots behind his tough talk. Rosanna Arquette shows up briefly to give Sizemore solace, which her bathing suit clearly does. The crew also includes Ving Rhames—who played Marsellus the kingpin in *Pulp Fiction*—and a brief appearance by David Schwimmer, whose haircut you'll recognize as belonging to Ross from *Friends*.

WHY GUYS LOVE IT ■ Combat flight scenes more realistic than anything you'll see on Microsoft's *Flight Simulator*.

HONEY, YOU'LL LIKE THIS MOVIE . . . ■ Because it has that guy from *China Beach*, which you watch in reruns on Lifetime when I'm not around . . . and don't think I don't know it.

DON'T MISS
The warm reception the pilots give to new guys in their squadron—especially the process of choosing nicknames.

MEMORABLE LINES
Young pilot asks the squadron commander, "Are you ever afraid of dying?"
The commander sets him straight: "You gotta have permission to die. I'll tell you when that is."

# HELL'S ANGELS (1930)

## RATINGS

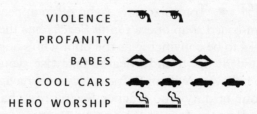

VIOLENCE
PROFANITY
BABES
COOL CARS
HERO WORSHIP

**WHAT HAPPENS** ▬ This movie has nothing to do with the infamous motorcycle gang of the 1960s that went by the name Hell's Angels. Rather, it's about two English brothers, Roy and Monte Rutledge; Roy's too-hot-to-handle girlfriend, Helen; and their service as pilots in World War I. Roy is the uptight, proper brother; Monte parties harder. When the war breaks out, they both enlist in the Royal Flying Service, but before they ship out to France to get into the fighting, Helen makes a move on her boyfriend's brother, Monte. Then she follows them to France (she's a bartender at their officers' club), where she takes up with yet another officer—which Roy discovers on the night before their perilous mission to destroy a German ammo dump. That dose of reality pales before the hard decision Roy has to make when they are captured by the Germans.

**THE CAST** ▬ Jean Harlow became the first blond bombshell of the movies with her appearance in a sheer and skimpy gown at the dance thrown for all the fighting men. The lusty way she draws on a cigarette, her lips pursed and her chest expanding with the smoke, is every bit as alluring as watching contemporary actresses like Sharon Stone do the same thing—then, as now, sensible women don't smoke.

James Hall plays Roy as the ever-chipper innocent, happy that his brother and girlfriend have hit it off so well. As Monte, Ben Lyon lays on the cynicism that is at the heart of a guy who lives, as they say, for wine, women, and song.

## WHY GUYS LOVE IT ▬ Dogfights with biplanes is air combat at its purest.

## HONEY, YOU'LL LIKE THIS MOVIE . . . ▬ Because Jean Harlow is a truly modern woman who will not be bullied by what's right—she does what she wants.

## DON'T MISS
- The British pilot dive-bombing the German zeppelin that's come to attack London.
- The final dogfight, which involves 170 planes and includes Baron von Richthofen—better known as the Red Baron.

## MEMORABLE LINES
- With these words, Jean Harlow laid out her place in movie history: "Would you be shocked if I put on something more comfortable?"
- When the German zeppelin is being overtaken by British planes, some of the crew volunteer to lighten the zeppelin's load. As one of them steps up, he salutes and says, "Fur Gott, Kaiser und Reich" ("For God, King, and Country"), then plummets to his death.

## TRIVIA

Billionaire Howard Hughes directed some of this movie and had a few scenes colorized.

# IRON EAGLE (1986)

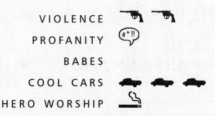

## RATINGS

| | |
|---|---|
| VIOLENCE | |
| PROFANITY | |
| BABES | |
| COOL CARS | |
| HERO WORSHIP | |

**WHAT HAPPENS** ◆ Sixteen-year-old Doug Masters is all fired up when his father, an Air Force colonel, is shot down on a reconnaissance mission over a hostile Middle Eastern country and captured. The U.S. government decides to negotiate rather than invade, so Doug takes matters in his own hands—with help from his friends, the Junior Eagles (or is it the Little Rascals?), and a tough retired officer who must teach Doug about discipline before he agrees to go on this unauthorized mission in a pair of stolen F16s. This is a movie that fears no clichés, but the flight and combat scenes are cool enough to overcome the corny dialogue, obvious characterizations, and cheesy eighties schlock rock that Doug must listen to while he flies. (Fortunately, the colonel listens to Al Green, or the sound track would be a complete goner.)

**THE CAST** ◆ You can't expect Jason Gedrick to play Doug any differently than he does: As the hotshot son of a top-notch pilot who doesn't take anything seriously, he's no heavyweight. Still, just watching him in the flight simulator is enough to convince you that he'd at least win a free game. You've seen Lou Gossett Jr.'s act before: He may have been tougher on Richard Gere (in the chick and gay guy extravaganza, *An Officer and a Gentleman*), but it's the same stern manner and clipped speech that turned Gere into a man.

## WHY GUYS LOVE IT ▰ Dad loves son, son loves dad. Dad shot down, son shoot back.

## HONEY, YOU'LL LIKE THIS MOVIE ... ▰ Because it's a healthy, noncompetitive, father-son thing.

## DON'T MISS
- Doug's drag race against a motorcycle.
- How Doug outclasses the whole Libyan/Iraqi/Whatever air force.

## MEMORABLE LINES
"I must say, I admire the way you handle pain," says the father's interrogator. "I'm looking forward to seeing you handle death."

## BEWARE

The two sequels to this movie are so bad that even decent flight sequences don't compensate.

# THE RIGHT STUFF (1983)

## RATINGS

| | | | | | |
|---|---|---|---|---|---|
| VIOLENCE | | | | | |
| PROFANITY | (#*!!) | (#*!!) | | | |
| BABES | ◆ | ◆ | | | |
| COOL CARS | 🚗 | 🚗 | 🚗 | 🚗 | 🚗 |
| HERO WORSHIP | 🚬 | 🚬 | 🚬 | 🚬 | |

**WHAT HAPPENS** ▬ **A** true story of the bravest guys ever to hold a stick between their legs: They are the airplane pilots who broke the sound barrier in the nineteen fifties and sixties, then joined the space program and became the first guys to boldly go where no guy had gone before them. The pace is set by World War II ace Chuck Yeager, who survived

Dennis Quaid has always had *The Right Stuff.*

flying at Mach I, the speed of sound, when many thought it couldn't be done. The others were recruited to participate in the Mercury manned space program and go into orbit. They begin as competitors, but end up a well-knit team whose wives spend their time talking about them.

## THE CAST ▰ A real gathering of real guys: Cowboy playwright and professional brooder Sam Shepard is Chuck Yeager, while the real Chuck Yeager drops in for a cameo as the bartender in the pilots' hangout. Dennis Quaid grins and struts as the cocky Gordon Cooper. Fred Ward is Cooper's pal Gus Grissom, who later died on the launchpad on *Apollo 11*. Ed Harris is the straightest arrow, John Glenn, first man to orbit the earth and a future senator. Scott Glenn is Alan Shepard, who was the commander of the ill-fated *Apollo 13*. Barbara Hershey gets her afterburners fired as Yeager's (Sam Shephard's) wife. Watch for Jeff Goldblum and Harry Shearer as NASA bureaucrats with problems running a projector. And fans of The Band will recognize drummer Levon Helm as one of the other NASA guys.

## WHY GUYS LOVE IT ▰ It's a true story with lots of accurate details of guys proving who has the biggest balls in planes and spaceships.

## HONEY, YOU'LL LIKE THIS MOVIE ... ▰ Because you love guys in uniforms.

## DON'T MISS
John Glenn and Gordon Cooper humming the Marine and Air Force hymns (respectively) in adjacent stalls as they whip up the sperm sample required for their NASA physicals.

## MEMORABLE LINES
A ladies' choice: While the guys are competing for who can withstand the most physical abuse, one of the wives says

to the others: "Sometimes they're just assholes—but they're handy assholes."

# TWELVE O'CLOCH HIGH (1949)

## RATINGS

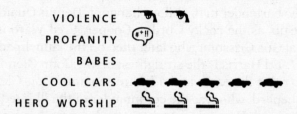

VIOLENCE
PROFANITY
BABES
COOL CARS
HERO WORSHIP

**WHAT HAPPENS** ▬ Squadron 918 was a bomber group based in England flying daylight precision missions over Germany during World War II. After the squadron takes a few hits and morale falls, they get a new commander, Brigadier General Frank Savage, who's the prototypical tough but fair leader. He enforces discipline and preps them for their hardest mission: a nighttime attack on a munitions factory. The pilots and crew grow into men, and General Savage then passes on command to a new leader.

**THE CAST** ▬ Stern, no-nonsense Gregory Peck is Frank Savage, who isn't colorful or complex or even interesting in any way—except that he's a very realistic depiction of the kind of tough military officer for whom we'd fly into hell itself. Dean Jagger won an Oscar for his role as the major who tries to hold the squadron together.

**WHY GUYS LOVE IT** ▬ If you have to die, you might as well die flying.

## HONEY, YOU'LL LIKE THIS MOVIE ...  ◗ Because it's a
war movie with very little blood and not a single whore.

## DON'T MISS
Any of the combat footage, because it was all filmed by
American and Luftwaffe pilots during real battles.

## MEMORABLE LINES
- "I don't have a lot of patience for this 'What are we fighting for?' stuff," Savage says to his pilots. "We're in a
  shooting war, we've got to fight. And some of us have got
  to die."
- "They're not boys, they're men," Savage tells another officer. "It's a pity they have to find that out so young."

### TRIVIA

Alfred Newman, the uncle of singer–songwriter
Randy Newman, composed this movie's score.

# BUTCH CASSIDY AND THE SUNDANCE KID (1969)

## RATINGS

| | |
|---|---|
| VIOLENCE | 🔫 🔫 |
| PROFANITY | #*!! #*!! |
| BABES | 👄 👄 |
| COOL CARS | 🚗 🚗 |
| HERO WORSHIP | 🚬 🚬 🚬 🚬 |

**WHAT HAPPENS** ▪ It's nothing but fun when two legendary outlaws plunder banks and trains alone and with the Hole in the Wall Gang. They even have a good time evading a posse comprising the best lawmen and trackers in the West. And when the posse pushes them over the edge, they pack up their boots, hats, snappy one-liners, and the woman they share and go to South America to start all over again. There they rob banks—overcoming the language barrier with dynamite—hire on to protect a company's payroll, and shoot it out with some of the native-bred banditos. Like all worthy legends, they go out in a blaze of glory and ammunition.

S.S./SHOOTING STAR

*Butch Cassidy and the Sundance Kid* go out in a blaze of glory.

**THE CAST** ☛ Paul Newman is the smart one, Butch. Robert Redford and his mustache are the Kid, who draws faster than you can blink. These guys may be the superhunks of yesteryear—you can tell a lot about any woman over forty by asking her which of these two she favored—but they don't act like they know it. The very unschoolmarmish Katharine Ross is the teacher Etta, who can't pick one or the other. Ted Cassidy (remember the Addams's butler, Lurch?) tries to take over the gang from Butch, but he's brought up short by Butch's rules—and his foot. Strother Martin (Newman's nemesis from *Cool Hand Luke*) puts the boys to work. Cloris Leachman just misses a roll with Butch when the posse pulls into town.

**WHY GUYS LOVE IT** ☛ Picture you and your best buddy pulling jobs and nailing broads, with nary a care in the world—even that price on your heads.

**HONEY, YOU'LL LIKE THIS MOVIE . . .** ▰ Because you, like Etta, can have them both.

**DON'T MISS**
- Sundance's cold-as-steel foreplay with Etta.
- The clever bit of ventriloquism Butch uses to trick the foolishly dedicated railroad employee into opening the freight car door.
- Butch and Sundance discussing the merits of fighting their way out of a corner or jumping from the cliff.

**MEMORABLE LINES**
- "Sundance, when it's over and he's dead, you're welcome to stay," Butch's challenger offers the Kid.

  "I don't mean to be a sore loser," Butch tells Sundance, "but when it's over, if I'm dead, kill him."

  "My pleasure," Sundance says.
- "Just how good are you, Kid?" a gambler makes the mistake of asking Sundance.

**TRIVIA**

Don't bother watching *Butch and Sundance: The Early Days,* a prequel starring Tom Berenger and William *"Greatest American Hero"* Katt as the boys.

# HIGH NOON (1952)

## RATINGS

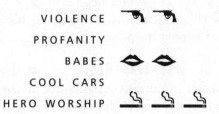

VIOLENCE

PROFANITY

BABES

COOL CARS

HERO WORSHIP

**WHAT HAPPENS** ▰ Marshal Will Kane gets married at 10:40 one morning and prepares to leave town with his pretty and pious new wife, a pacifistic Quaker who has convinced the marshal to quit his job. Problem is: Frank Miller, a gunman the marshal had sent to prison years before, is due to arrive on the 12 P.M. train to give the marshal some monogrammed lead as a wedding present. As the minutes tick away (the running time of this movie corresponds to the time elapsing in the story), the marshal finds himself abandoned by the cowardly townspeople in his plan to take on Miller and three of his henchmen. Still, the marshal stands tall and, with a bit of help from his wife, he turns that present into a homecoming gift for Miller.

**THE CAST** ▰ Gary Cooper's perfect posture and sharp jawline prove that his Marshal Kane is a man of conscience and commitment. You know he's going to stay and fight before he even thinks about it. You'd think that Grace Kelly's classic and classy beauty would seem wasted beneath her Quaker bonnet, but she's so willful and righteous that you forget the bonnet and see only her shining eyes. Lee Van Cleef (the "Bad" in *The Good, the Bad and the Ugly*), Lon Chaney Jr., and Sheb Wooley are Miller's men, lazing around at the train station waiting for the noon train to arrive. Harry "Colonel Potter" Morgan and Lloyd Bridges (who must have used his entire pomade budget for just a couple of scenes) are both spineless townspeople.

**WHY GUYS LOVE IT** ☛ Honeymoon or not, no self-respecting guy slips out of town when the big challenge is pulling in on the next train.

**HONEY, YOU'LL LIKE THIS MOVIE . . .** ☛ Because these newlyweds learn important lessons about conflict resolution on their first day married.

## DON'T MISS
- The marshal and Lloyd Bridges in a prelim bout outside the livery stable a few short minutes before the Main Event.
- Helen Ramirez, a local business magnate who seems to know more about Marshal Kane than he'd like her to share with the new Mrs. Marshal Kane.

## MEMORABLE LINES
"If you're smart, you'll get out," Helen Ramirez says to the marshal.
"I can't," the marshal insists.
"I know," she answers.

**AWARDS**

Cooper won the Oscar for Best Actor.

# THE INDIAN FIGHTER (1955)

## RATINGS

VIOLENCE
PROFANITY
BABES
COOL CARS
HERO WORSHIP

**WHAT HAPPENS** ▪ Johnny Hawks is hired to lead a wagon train through the Dakotas—Sioux territory. So he pays a visit to Chief Red Cloud to ask for safe passage. As Hawks is leaving with the chief's promise of no harrassment if the settlers just pass through without bothering the Indians, Hawks catches a glimpse (or even more) of the chief's daughter bathing in the river and sets his sights on her. All goes well for Hawks and the wagon train until two greedy white men try to bribe some of the members of the tribe with liquor to tell them where a secret Indian gold mine is. When one of them kills Red Cloud's brother, the Indians attack—which ticks off Hawks because he's got something going with Onahti, the sexy squaw.

**THE CAST** ▪ Kirk Douglas has a great time as Johnny Hawks: He smirks through the whole movie—even when the wagon train is in peril—maybe because he is going to score with a prime Indian maiden. She's played by Elsa Martinelli with a fire in her eye—a fire that starts as revulsion but changes to passion. Lon Chaney Jr. and Walter Matthau are having a good time, too, as the gold-hungry white men who prey on the Indians' taste for whiskey. Alan Hale Jr. (the Skipper from *Gilligan's Island*) shows up as part of the wagon train crew.

**WHY GUYS LOVE IT** ▪ Sex and violence in the ol' West is pure fun.

**HONEY, YOU'LL LIKE THIS MOVIE . . .** ▪ Because it's one of those intercultural love stories; you know, like *West Side Story*.

**DON'T MISS**

- Johnny Hawks's policy of smooch first, ask permission later.
- Onahti preventing Hawks from pulling a "Wham, bam, thank you, ma'am" on her with postcoital bondage.

# THE MAGNIFICENT SEVEN (1960)

**RATINGS**

| | |
|---|---|
| VIOLENCE | 🔫 🔫 🔫 |
| PROFANITY | 💢 |
| BABES | 💋 |
| COOL CARS | 🚗 |
| HERO WORSHIP | 🚬 🚬 🚬 🚬 |

**WHAT HAPPENS** ▪ A little Mexican farming village is repeatedly raided by a cruel bandito and his men. The farmers decide to fight back by hiring a gunfighter and paying him to find six others who will defend their town for cash. The gunfighter, Chris, has no trouble finding the other mercenaries he wants: a sharpshooter, a muscle man, a head case with a lightnin' fast draw, a knife expert, a tough guy, and an eager kid. Together they confront Calvera, the bandito, on his next ride through town. But Calvera will not be scared off—first he offers Chris and his bunch a bribe, then

*The Magnificent Seven* mounted up.

S.S./SHOOTING STAR

returns with more men when the seven turn him down. The townspeople get scared along the way, but even they cannot derail the inevitable final shoot-out that reduces the seven to three.

THE CAST ✏ Yul Brynner in a Western? The Pharaoh a gunfighter? Believe it, it's true. Sure, he keeps his black hat on throughout the movie so you don't really see his cue-ball head. But he is cool and curt enough to be convincing as Chris, the gunfighter in charge. He's well-matched against Eli Wallach's Calvera, who is gleefully cruel. Steve McQueen is the sharpshooter and he enjoys the action, too. Charles Bronson is as earnest as he is strong, but don't hold that against him—he kills as well as the others, even if he does it for good reasons instead of for money. On the other hand, Robert Vaughn has several freak-outs that don't keep him from proving he's quicker than the average bandito.

James Coburn is the calm and collected knife thrower, in contrast to Horst Buchholz, who plays the kid foolishly determined to match his mettle to these men.

## WHY GUYS LOVE IT ▬ There is honor among killers.

## HONEY, YOU'LL LIKE THIS MOVIE . . . ▬ Because these guys are really good guys at heart, trust me.

## DON'T MISS

- How the young guy earns his stripes by walking right into the bandito's camp.
- The little boys who reassure Bronson by promising they'll care for his grave.

## MEMORABLE LINES

"If God didn't want them to be sheared," Wallach says to Brynner about the villagers, "why did he make them sheep?"

## CHECK OUT

Check out an excellent Japanese movie called *The Seven Samurai,* on which this movie is based. It has even more graphic violence because the seven use swords instead of guns.

Want to see more of Yul in a cowboy hat? Look for *Westworld,* a movie about an incredible resort where men can live out their fantasies. Yul is a gun-slinging machine on the fritz in this movie written and directed by the master of science gone beserk, Michael Crichton.

# A MAN CALLED HORSE (1970)

## RATINGS

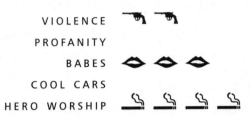

VIOLENCE

PROFANITY

BABES

COOL CARS

HERO WORSHIP

**WHAT HAPPENS** ✒ This is most definitely not *Dances with Wolves*. In this movie, Lord John Morgan is a rich English-man hunting big game on the American Plains. A band of Sioux warriors attacks Morgan's camp and kills everyone but him. They take him back to their village, where he's scorned like an outcast rather than guarded as a prisoner. To survive, he learns their ways with the help of a few native outcasts. When Morgan figures he's mastered enough to be a real part of the tribe, he decides he'd like one of the squaws—specifically, the chief's sister. The chief is will-ing—if Morgan will undergo the tribe's Vow to the Sun, which doesn't involve saying a little prayer. Rather, it re-quires him to hang in the broiling sun by straps attached to sharp sticks driven into his chest and back muscles. Sure it sounds horrible, but if you've been without a squaw for a long time . . .

**THE CAST** ✒ Richard Harris is Morgan, and he keeps his growing respect and appreciation for the beauty of native cultures to himself (unlike other actor/director/producers we can name). Instead, Harris just gives Morgan the dignity to fight for his life and to hang in there (ouch) while he's trying to prove himself worthy. The other actors don't speak much, but they all seem very credible; they include Corinna Tsopei, Iron Eyes Cody, Richard Fools Bull, Lloyd One Star, and James Never Miss a Shot.

**WHY GUYS LOVE IT** ▬ You thought frat hazing was hard.

**HONEY, YOU'LL LIKE THIS MOVIE...** ▬ Because this Englishman endures excrutiating pain for the love of a woman.

**DON'T MISS**
- The Indian brave looking for a scalp on the bald white guy.
- The widow hacking off her finger when the war party brings back the body of her husband.
- The topless squaws.

**MEMORABLE LINES**
"I am not a horse, I am not an animal, I am a man," Morgan shrieks at them after they try to corral him. But he's wasting his time—you know how nicknames stick.

**CHECK OUT**

In *The Return of a Man Called Horse* (1976), Morgan comes back from England to help the tribe in its fight against white society and to watch a dozen braves take the Vow to the Sun. Don't bother with *Triumphs of a Man Called Horse* (1983) because no one new takes the Sun Vow.

# THE MAN FROM COLORADO (1948)

## RATINGS

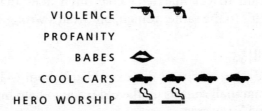

| | |
|---|---|
| VIOLENCE | 🔫 🔫 |
| PROFANITY | |
| BABES | 👄 |
| COOL CARS | 🚗 🚗 🚗 🚗 |
| HERO WORSHIP | 🚬 🚬 |

**WHAT HAPPENS** ☞ At the end of the Civil War, a Union colonel with a bloodthirsty streak and his second-in-command, a captain with a conscience, return home to a hero's welcome by their hometown and their mutual sweetheart. The colonel is appointed federal judge for the territory and he taps the captain to be his U.S. marshal, who reluctantly agrees. But the judge seems to have left his sense of right and wrong on the battlefield. Soon they clash over proper law enforcement and, eventually, over the woman. Their inevitable showdown is fiery.

**THE CAST** ☞ From your first look at Glenn Ford's eyes—through the binoculars he uses to see a white flag waved by Confederates he orders shelled—you can see they're open too wide and they don't blink enough for the colonel to be in complete command of his faculties. As the movie progresses and his sanity egresses, those eyes get wilder. In contrast, William Holden, as the captain, becomes more sure that the colonel has lost it and we don't need close-ups to see it; the set of Holden's jaw tells us a confrontation is coming. You have good eyes if you can spot a young Denver "Uncle Duke" Pyle among the troop.

**WHY GUYS LOVE IT** ◾ If your boss goes wacko, you have a right, nay, an obligation, to take him on.

**HONEY, YOU'LL LIKE THIS MOVIE . . .** ◾ Because two men want to get married—how often does that happen? (Okay, it's to the same women, but what's wrong with that?)

**DON'T MISS**
- The daring rescue of five ex-soldiers about to be hanged; the marshall rounds up the old troop to help him stop the colonel's revenge.
- The great horse chase after two deserters who go on a crime spree.

# THE SEARCHERS (1956)

**RATINGS**

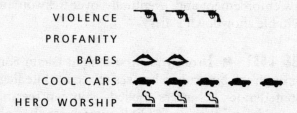

| | |
|---|---|
| VIOLENCE | 🔫 🔫 🔫 |
| PROFANITY | |
| BABES | 👄 👄 |
| COOL CARS | 🚗 🚗 🚗 🚗 🚗 |
| HERO WORSHIP | 🚬 🚬 🚬 |

**WHAT HAPPENS** ◾ Three years after the end of the Civil War, a Confederate soldier comes home to his brother's house in Texas, where he's received warmly by the brother's family, especially his wife. But the happy reunion is spoiled when a band of murderous Comanches (was there any other kind?) kill the brother and his children, except for the two daughters, whom they kidnap. The soldier, Ethan Edwards, and a half-breed who lives with the family, Martin Pawley, find the brutalized body of the older daughter and devote five years to tracking down the Comanches and retrieving the younger one. Meanwhile, Pawley's betrothed back home tires of waiting for him to return and plans to marry another suitor. When the searchers find the girl and discover that she has adopted Indian ways, they clash about what to do about her.

THE CAST ◾ John Wayne plays Ethan Edwards in the standard Duke style: levelheaded, coldhearted, sharp-tongued, and eager to kick ass. Jeffrey Hunter (who also was in *The Longest Day* with Wayne) is the foster son and is the Duke's opposite in many ways, but equally stubborn about finding the girl, who is played in the beginning of the movie by Lana Wood but as a young woman at the end of the movie by Natalie Wood. Vera Miles (the sister in *Psycho*) is the girl pining for Hunter back home. A young Patrick Wayne, the Duke's oldest son, also got a part—he's a soldier in a regiment that comes looking for John Wayne.

WHY GUYS LOVE IT ◾ John Wayne forgives no one, and he'd devote half a decade to proving it.

HONEY, YOU'LL LIKE THIS MOVIE ... ◾ Because they're searching for an innocent young girl.

DON'T MISS
• The Duke shooting out the eyes of a dead Comanche so he can't see his way in the Happy Hunting Grounds.
• The bargain the half-breed gets from an Indian trader.

MEMORABLE LINES
Whenever anyone threatens the Duke, he responds in his oft-imitated style, "That'll be the day."

## CHECK OUT

Director John Ford made many of the best-known movies from the Golden Age of Westerns—including *Stagecoach, My Darling Clementine,* and *She Wore a Yellow Ribbon*—and you won't go wrong with any of them.

# SHANE (1953)

## RATINGS

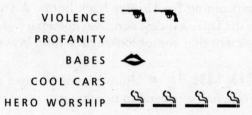

VIOLENCE

PROFANITY

BABES

COOL CARS

HERO WORSHIP

**WHAT HAPPENS** ▰ This is a very familiar Western plot, but this movie is an original and all the others are ripped off from it. Shane, a retired gunfighter turned drifter, takes a job laboring for a homesteader in the Old West, and just in time, because a local rancher is trying to bully the homesteaders off their land so that he can use it. Shane gives the homesteaders the courage to stand up to the rancher—maybe because he beats a couple of the rancher's hired thugs in the nearby town's saloon—but in the end he has to take on the toughest of the thugs himself.

**THE CAST** ✒ Alan Ladd tries to make Shane look like a guy who wants nothing more than steady work and a warm bed, but you can see the gunfighter still alive in him. He's poised for action all the time. Jack Palance (credited as Walter Jack Palance) is the lead thug; then, as now, Palance's face looks weathered and mean, and that's enough to make him credible. Van Heflin is the homesteader who wants to stand up as strong as Shane and impress his wife and son, too, but he shrinks whenever he's confronted by the thugs. Listen for the distinctive voice of Nancy Kulp (you remember, she was Miss Hathaway, the banker's secretary, on *The Beverly Hillbillies*) and you'll spot her among the homesteaders.

**WHY GUYS LOVE IT** ✒ Gunfighters are good guys—they like kids, they don't jump on other guy's wives, and they help people in need.

**HONEY, YOU'LL LIKE THIS MOVIE . . .** ✒ Because there's a real cute kid in it who idolizes Shane.

**DON'T MISS**
- Shane stomping a thug in the saloon.
- The homesteader who gets drunk and makes the mistake of confronting Palance.

**MEMORABLE LINES**
- "A gun is a tool, no better or worse than the man using it," Shane tells the homesteader's wife.
- "A man's got to be what he is, there's no breaking the mold," Shane explains to the homesteader's son. "I tried it and it didn't work for me. There's no living with a killing."

## AWARDS

Ultimate tough-guy Jack Palance was nominated for an Academy Award for Best Supporting Actor for his part in this movie, but he didn't actually win an Oscar until 1991 for his much sillier role in *City Slickers.*

# THE WILD BUNCH (1969)

## RATINGS

| | | | | |
|---|---|---|---|---|
| VIOLENCE | | | | |
| PROFANITY | | | | |
| BABES | | | | |
| COOL CARS | | | | |
| HERO WORSHIP | | | | |

**WHAT HAPPENS** ▰ In 1913, a band of aging but crisply professional outlaws loyal to nothing save each other—and even that is questionable—are tracked by a scruffy, undisciplined posse and a former partner of the outlaws, who have been hired by the railroads to stop the criminals from robbing trains. The outlaws get in some hard drinking and whoring before they make plans for one final job. When the final showdown arrives, the outlaws are caught between the posse and the Mexican Army.

**THE CAST** ▰ William Holden is the band's leader, Pike Bishop, and his weariness with their life and crimes seeps into each of the other criminals. His most doggedly loyal partner is Dutch Engstrom, a part that proves Ernest Borgnine could be genuinely gritty without losing Commander McHale's affability. Warren Oates and Ben Johnson (who was a real cowboy and rodeo star before becoming an actor) add menace to the outlaw band in their parts as Lyle and Tector Gorch. The posse on their trail is led by Deke Thornton, a man Pike once betrayed. Robert Ryan portrays him as reluctant but businesslike; he works hard just to keep his unruly deputies, especially Strother Martin, focused on their duties.

**WHY GUYS LOVE IT** ▬ This is unquestionably the bloodiest Western ever filmed.

**HONEY, YOU'LL LIKE THIS MOVIE . . .** ▬ Because some high culture critic said that the violence in this film is balletic, and you love the ballet.

**DON'T MISS**
- The Brothers Gorch cavorting in the bath with balloon-breasted Mexican whores.
- One of the outlaws tonguing the ear of a woman from the Temperance Society while he makes her sing.

**MEMORABLE LINES**
"They'll be waiting for us," Engstrom says to Pike as they plot their next heist.

"I wouldn't have it any other way," Pike replies.

**CHECK OUT**

Two versions of this controversial movie are available on video: Be sure to rent the uncut 144-minute version so you can see a few key scenes (including one with the babes) that had been dropped without director Sam Peckinpah's permission after the film was originally released.

## Clint's Best Westerns

The gunfighters Clint Eastwood has played in the dozen Westerns he has appeared in embody virtues that all guys can admire: He speaks little but says a lot, is quick to defend the weak and bash the bully, and he's invariably the last to draw but the first to kill. Most of all, he hides behind no pretenses; he's strictly honest about his self-serving intentions. You won't go wrong with almost any Clint Western (though beware of *Paint Your Wagon*—it's a musical). Here two that are often overlooked but have all the elements that a guy will love. And if your woman needs to be convinced to watch any of these Westerns with you, just tell her that the French think Clint Eastwood is a great American film auteur.

# HIGH PLAINS DRIFTER (1973)

**RATINGS**

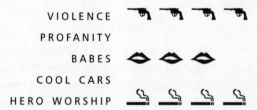

VIOLENCE

PROFANITY

BABES

COOL CARS

HERO WORSHIP

**WHAT HAPPENS** ▬ A stranger rides into a small mining town and stops for a drink. A few tough guys persist in harassing him, and he's forced to aerate them in short order. A local broad berates him, so he knows what she wants— and he gives it to her, with relish (and a dash of mustard). After a warm welcome like that, how could this dangerous stranger leave town? He takes himself a room at the town's hotel and gets a much-needed bath. Then the town's businessmen hire him to help them ambush three bad guys with a grudge against the town who are soon to be released from prison. The stranger drills the townsfolk in preparation for the arrival of the bad guys, while he avails himself of the free liquor and women they've provided for him. And he mocks them by naming a midget as their new mayor and sheriff. When the bad guys finally arrive, the town's defenses crumble, and the stranger does the job himself— including horsewhipping one guy to death. When it's over, the stranger reveals his identity to the midget.

**THE CAST** ✒ Clint Eastwood, who also directed the movie, puts on a virtuoso performance of minimalist acting, relying on his squint and the slightest hint of a smile to convey the mysterious aura of the title character. You've seen the dermatology problems of head bad guy Geoffrey Lewis in lots of Westerns—he doesn't feel out of place because the whole town is filled with unattractive people Clint has shot or beaten in other movies. John Hillerman, who was the uptight Englishman Higgins on TV's *Magnum P.I.*, is one of the shopkeepers in town.

**WHY GUYS LOVE IT** ✒ Anyone who has ever crossed Clint—and that's just about everyone—gets paid back.

**DON'T MISS**
Clint's smooth technique with the ladies, but don't try it yourself unless you, too, are heavily armed.

## MEMORABLE LINES

The midget says to Clint about killing the bad guys, "What do we do after we do it?"

Clint replies, "You live with it."

**TRIVIA**

Geoffrey Lewis, who plays the bad guy number one, is the father of Juliette Lewis, who appeared in *Cape Fear*, *Kalifornia*, and a Melissa Etheridge music video.

# TWO MULES FOR SISTER SARA (1970)

## RATINGS

| | |
|---|---|
| VIOLENCE | 🔫 🔫 🔫 🔫 |
| PROFANITY | @*!! |
| BABES | 👄 👄 |
| COOL CARS | 🚗 🚗 🚗 |
| HERO WORSHIP | 🚬 🚬 🚬 🚬 |

**WHAT HAPPENS** ▬ Hogan, a solitary gunslinger traveling through Texas, helps a naked woman escape the clutches of a band of leering Mexicans. When the woman gets her clothes on, Hogan is surprised to see that she's a nun. But she's a nun being tracked by the French army garrison that occupies Mexico, and she needs Hogan's help to escape. Once they do, she convinces him to join her in infiltrating the garrison's barracks to liberate gold she's promised him is there for the taking. He goes along—at least as much because the nun is a babe as because he wants the loot. After Hogan shoots or blows up a mess of Frog soldiers, he discovers that she's not what she appears to be. Or, rather, she is just what she appears to be.

**THE CAST** ▰ Clint plays this part as he does all of his Western characters—terse, wary, and abrupt—but you can also sense his ardor for the babe nun. A young Shirley MacLaine as the nun is as tough and determined as Clint is, and she looks great, too. All of the other actors come straight from stock Hollywood casting: the fat French officer, the banditos, the pious peasant who sells Sister Sara the burro.

**WHY GUYS LOVE IT** ▰ Hot nun fantasy finishes a close second to hot nurse fantasy.

**DON'T MISS**
- Clint's crude but effective surgical technique for removing an arrow from his shoulder.
- The bath.

**MEMORABLE LINES**
"It ain't natural for a woman who looks like you to be a nun."

Other Surefire Clint Eastwood Westerns
# A FISTFUL OF DOLLARS (1964)

## RATINGS

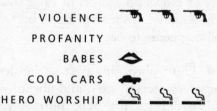

| | |
|---|---|
| VIOLENCE | 🔫 🔫 🔫 |
| PROFANITY | |
| BABES | 👄 |
| COOL CARS | 🚗 |
| HERO WORSHIP | 🚬 🚬 🚬 |

**WHAT HAPPENS** ▰ A stranger who's handy with guns rides into a Mexican town where a gang of weapons smugglers is battling a gang of liquor smugglers for control. After the stranger survives a couple of attacks by both parties, he ingratiates himself with the two gangs, taking money from each side to sabotage the other. He finally leads the gangs into a full-scale confrontation that has them destroying each other, leaving himself out and the town free of them.

**THE CAST** ▰ Clint Eastwood is fresh from the TV series *Rawhide* in this, his first feature film. But already he knows that to show he's a no-bullshit guy ready to face down any and all comers he needs to keep the acting to a minimum. The props that would become Clint's signature—the poncho, the little cigars, the grimy hat—are already there. The other important player in this movie is behind the camera: Italian director Sergio Leone. He shot the movie in Spain and uses the barren hillsides to convey the desolation the people feel in a landscape where natural forces of all kinds make their lives hard.

**WHY GUYS LOVE IT** ▰ If two gangs of bad guys want to mess with each other, why shouldn't another guy have some fun with them?

## DON'T MISS

- The two dead guys who come in handy for Clint's scheme to lead the two gangs to a final battle.
- Clint's homemade body armor—crude but cleverly effective.

## MEMORABLE LINES

As Clint walks toward three guys who have a mind to take a shot at him, he says to the undertaker he passes along the way, "Get three coffins ready." As he walks back past the undertaker after having shot an additional who was concealed, Clint says, "I was wrong—make that four coffins."

**CHECK OUT**

This movie, like *Last Man Standing,* has the same plot as *Yojimbo,* a Japanese samurai movie directed by Akira Kurosawa.

# THE GOOD, THE BAD AND THE UGLY (1966)

## RATINGS

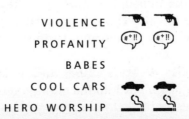

| | |
|---|---|
| VIOLENCE | 🔫 🔫 |
| PROFANITY | 💬 💬 |
| BABES | |
| COOL CARS | 🚗 🚗 |
| HERO WORSHIP | 🚬 🚬 |

**WHAT HAPPENS** ☛ The three guys identified by the title—none of whom is what you could call virtuous or attractive—all chase after $200,000 in gold coins stashed by a Confederate soldier. The Good and the Ugly first raise some cash by fooling with the law: The Ugly has a reward on his head, so the Good turns him in and then sets him loose, only to turn him in again. The Bad wastes no time on anything but searching for the money, and he's even willing to enlist in the Union Army in the hopes of getting closer to the cash. All three eventually must rely on each other to get the money, though only one of them will ride away with it.

**THE CAST** ☛ Clint is the Good (though the other two keep calling him Blondie) and he's good only in the sense that he won't completely double-cross the Ugly, Eli Wallach. You can tell Lee Van Cleef is the Bad because he wears all-black clothes.

**WHY GUYS LOVE IT** ☛ You hear the unforgettable theme music in your head everytime you're confronted by three or four thugs whom you are about to beat, maybe even kill.

**DON'T MISS**
• How the Ugly uses a train to remove his handcuffs when the Good leaves him out in the desert.
• The great Civil War battle for the bridge.

**MEMORABLE LINES**
"There are two kinds of people in this world, my friend," the Ugly informs the Good. "Those with a rope around their neck and those who do the cutting. I run the risks, so next time I want more than half."

The Good smiles, lights a cigar, and answers simply, "You may run the risks, but I do the cutting. If we cut down on my percentage, it's liable to interfere with my aim."

**CHECK OUT**

Rent the letter-box edition of this movie instead of the pan-and-scan version if you can because the battle is so much bigger than your TV screen can do justice to otherwise.

# THE OUTLAW JOSEY WALES (1976)

## RATINGS

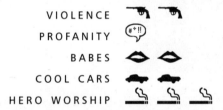

VIOLENCE

PROFANITY

BABES

COOL CARS

HERO WORSHIP

**WHAT HAPPENS** ▰ For some guys the war is over when they say it's over. After Josey Wales sees his family and then a troop of Confederates killed in cold blood by Union soldiers, he goes on a rampage and slaughters a slew of the boys in blue. That puts a price on Josey's head, which many foolish, greedy men try to collect—but, of course, he perforates them with incomparable speed. Josey moves ever West, is joined by an outcast Indian, and then takes a family of homesteaders from Kansas under his wing. Josey faces down a Comanche war party and helps the family set up their new home—either out of the goodness of his heart or because they have a fresh-faced young daughter he'd like to swoop on.

S.S./SHOOTING STAR

*The Outlaw Josey Wales:* The man with a name, but still few words and much action.

**THE CAST** ☛ Josey Wales isn't the mystery man that so many of Clint's Western characters are, but he is every bit the man of few words, and all of those sharp and to the point. Clint's longtime girlfriend, Sondra Locke, makes her first appearance in one of his movies as the shy girl from Kansas. Chief Dan George is his loyal Native sidekick with a sardonic sense of humor. John Vernon is Fletcher, a Confederate officer who is double-crossed by the Union guys.

**WHY GUYS LOVE IT** ☛ This Josey is no pussycat.

**DON'T MISS**
- How the wounded Confederate kid Josey rescued distracts the bandits and saves Josey's tail.
- The chief making nik-nik with the squaw.

## MEMORABLE LINES

- "You a bounty hunter?" Josey asks a guy who comes into the saloon looking for him.

  "A man's got to make a living these days," the guy says, finally.

  "Dying ain't much of a living," Clint tries to warn him.

- "You promised my men would be treated decently," the Confederate officer complains to the senator on the scene. "They were decently fed and decently shot."

# PALE RIDER (1985)

## RATINGS

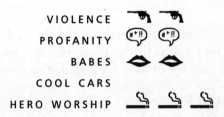

| | |
|---|---|
| VIOLENCE | |
| PROFANITY | |
| BABES | |
| COOL CARS | |
| HERO WORSHIP | |

**WHAT HAPPENS** ■ This is the Shane story (see page 74), Clint Eastwood style. In this movie, a mysterious preacher arrives to help a gold prospector and his compatriots stand up to a mining company bent on driving them off and then ravishing the landscape. The prospector's woman and her daughter fall for the preacher, but, perhaps because he's a man of the cloth, the preacher passes up the dark, sweet daughter and takes on only her mother. This preacher inspires the other tin-panners to stand up for themselves, delivers them to the Valley of the Shadow of Death, and then smites the minions of evil with his blessed six-shooters.

**THE CAST** ✏ Clint directed and starred in this movie from a screenplay he commissioned for a story idea he had. In short, it's Clint's movie and he creates contemporary villains from these bad guys of the Old West, then mows them down most righteously. He appears out of nowhere to aid Hull Barret, a miner being beaten for the crime of being a miner. Michael Moriarty's Hull wants desperately to be a brave man of action like the preacher, but he has the will without the skill. Richard Dyshart is Coy LaHood, the fat cat mining company owner who is used to getting his way, and Chris Penn is his punk son, Josh, who hasn't yet gotten his way. Carrie Snodgrass is Hull's frightened fiancée, who sacrifices herself to keep her daughter, Megan (Sydney Penny), from tempting damnation with the preacher.

**WHY GUYS LOVE IT** ✏ Clint kills in the name of the Lord.

**DON'T MISS**
- Clint demonstrating the versatility of the hickory stick.
- Richard Kiel ("Jaws" in the Bond movies) and Clint discussing all manner of uses for a sledgehammer.

**MEMORABLE LINES**
"And I looked and beheld a pale horse," Megan reads from the Bible, "and his name that sat on him was Death, and Hell followed with him."

# UNFORGIVEN (1992)

RATINGS

| | |
|---|---|
| VIOLENCE | 🔫 🔫 🔫 🔫 |
| PROFANITY | @*!! @*!! @*!! |
| BABES | 👄 👄 👄 |
| COOL CARS | |
| HERO WORSHIP | 🚬 🚬 🚬 |

**WHAT HAPPENS** ▬ The Old West wasn't just a bunch of fun-lovin' cowboys carousing with saloon girls and sleeping under the stars. A cowboy who got mad at a girl might mutilate her, and the cruel sheriff won't do much to punish him, so the girls pool their cash and offer it to any gunfighter who will pay back the cowboy. A legendary gunfighter-turned-pig-farmer, William Munny, could be coaxed out of retirement for the money, and he goes along with his ex-partner and a myopic kid to claim it. The sheriff won't like the looks of these guys any more than he took to the others (least of all the one called English Bob) and he'll do what he must to send them packing. Munny, however, takes his work seriously, dead-seriously.

**THE CAST** ▬ The many lines on Clint's face have settled into creases, and his voice has faded into a whisper. The only sentiment he registers is quiet anger in Munny's eyes when his pal Ned Logan is hurt. In ways both physical and theatrical, Morgan Freeman's Logan is Munny's negative image. The sheriff Gene Hackman depicts is more colorful than either, but even he's pale beside the flamboyant English Bob of Richard Harris.

## WHY GUYS LOVE IT ▪ Clint keeps the Western alive and kicking.

## DON'T MISS
- The touching conversation Clint has with the mutilated girl about freebies.
- The cowboy who gets it while he's going.
- Clint taking slow, careful aim at a man who's got the muzzle of Clint's rifle resting on the bridge of his nose.

## MEMORABLE LINES
"I don't deserve to die like this," the sheriff pleads to Munny.

"Deserve's got nothing to do with it," Munny croaks back.

## AWARDS
This movie won Academy Awards for Best Picture, Director (Clint), and Supporting Actor (Hackman). The last real Western to win Best Picture was *Cimarron* in 1931—*Dances with Wolves* doesn't count, and *Midnight Cowboy* really doesn't, either.

## Criminals Ya Just Love

# AT CLOSE RANGE (1986)

---

**RATINGS**

| | |
|---|---|
| VIOLENCE |  |
| PROFANITY | |
| BABES | |
| COOL CARS | |
| HERO WORSHIP | |

**WHAT HAPPENS** ▪ Brad Whitewood's dad ain't exactly Ward Cleaver: He always has lots of cash to pass around, a fast car to cruise around in, and a young babe in place of Brad's mom. So, of course, Brad Jr. looks up to Brad Sr., even if—or maybe because—the elder Brad runs a gang of professional thieves. Brad Jr. joins in the family business and runs a gang of his own, including his half-brother Tommy and their spaced-out friend Lucas. At the same time, he finds a country girl looking for excitement, which she gets by the trunkload. When the heat is on, Brad Jr. discovers just how low his daddy will go, and he doesn't like the looks of it.

**THE CAST** ✒ Many actors would have chosen to portray Brad with a sneer, but Sean Penn—who can sneer with the best—instead emphasizes his sincerity. And that makes plausible Brad's indignation when he finally explodes in his father's face. Christopher Walken takes Brad Sr. in the opposite direction: He's so oily, you want to watch your footing whenever you're near him or you may slip and fall. Chris Penn, Sean's younger brother, places Tommy squarely in line with his TV-dulled mother and grandmother. You may recognize Crispin Glover as the goony father in *Back to the Future*, but in this role as their spaced-out pal he's closer to the scary speed freak he played in *River's Edge*. Mary Stuart Masterson has country girl freshness to spare, though it is hard to see her character's initial attraction to an apparent lowlife like Brad. David Strathairn shows up in Brad Sr.'s gang; Keifer Sutherland is the most dangerous man in Brad Jr.'s crew.

**WHY GUYS LOVE IT** ✒ We honor any father who spends quality time with his sons—even if the activity is boosting tractors.

**HONEY, YOU'LL LIKE THIS MOVIE . . .** ✒ Because you'll find plenty of material here for a two-hour rant about the violence and greed inherent in our patriachal society.

**DON'T MISS**
- Sean Penn windshield surfing in the movie's opening sequence.
- His low-tech pedicure technique.

**TRIVIA**

Believe it or not, this is based on a true story about a father and son in rural Pennsylvania.

# BONNIE AND CLYDE (1967)

## RATINGS

VIOLENCE    🔫 🔫 🔫

PROFANITY    @*!!

BABES    👄 👄

COOL CARS    🚗 🚗 🚗 🚗

HERO WORSHIP    🚬 🚬 🚬 🚬

## WHAT HAPPENS ▪ A pair of Depression-era outlaws (who are remarkably more attractive than anyone else around

*Bonnie and Clyde:*
Have guns, sex, style,
will travel.

them) rob banks and work out their complicated sexuality against the grim landscape of the black-and-white West. Their exploits and odd generosity make them folk heroes, and they seduce an adoring auto mechanic they meet into riding with them. Later, Clyde loads up his brother and raggin' sister-in-law, and the five of them hit banks and make themselves the targets of all sorts of cops and do-gooders. When they make the mistake of fooling with a Texas Ranger, they fuel his frenzy until he catches them in slow motion.

**THE CAST** ✒ Warren Beatty's cheeky grin and aw-shucks charisma make Clyde Barrow seem more an entertainer than a lover or a killer. Faye Dunaway's Bonnie Parker is hot for action, and for Clyde, too. Come to think of it, you can say the same about the mechanic C. W. Moss, played by the very Radar O'Reilly-like Michael J. Pollard. Buck Barrow doesn't have his brother's charm, but then again Gene Hackman is not Warren Beatty; just a regular guy the folks can relate to. Buck is so durn proud to be a member of the Barrow Gang, while his wife (a shrill Estelle Parsons) wants no part of the whole business except a share of the loot. Denver Pyle (Uncle Duke from *The Dukes of Hazzard*) is the Ranger raging for revenge. Gene Wilder gets scooped up by the gang and then dumped right quick.

**WHY GUYS LOVE IT** ✒ It's an insightful study of the relationship between violence and sex with plenty of both.

**HONEY, YOU'LL LIKE THIS MOVIE . . .** ✒ Because it's an insightful study of the relationship between violence and sex, dressed in classic 1930s styles and colors.

**DON'T MISS**
- A peak at what Bonnie is (not) wearing behind the blinds in the opening scene
- Clyde's crisis when he sticks up a failed bank.

## MEMORABLE LINE

"I'm an undertaker," Gene Wilder tells the Barrow Gang, bringing their merriment to a screeching halt.

## AWARDS

Parsons won an Oscar for Best Supporting Actress.

# BLUE VELVET (1986)

## RATINGS

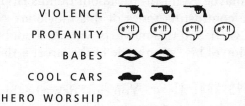

VIOLENCE

PROFANITY

BABES

COOL CARS

HERO WORSHIP

## WHAT HAPPENS ▪ The cozy little Northwest town of Lumberton is a lot more happenin' than you'd think. Oh sure, the firemen wave to the children, little dogs play in the grass, and sunny blond Sandy (the policeman's daughter) dates wholesome Jeffrey, who comes home from college when his father collapses from cardiac arrest while he's watering the lawn. But at the seedy lounge on the edge of town, there's a dark, mysterious singer named Dorothy Vallens and she's wrapped up in a twisted dominant/submissive sexual relationship with a nitrous-sucking psychotic, Frank Booth. And man, does he know some weird people. Jeffrey gets in on the excitement when he finds a human ear in an abandoned lot that leads him to Dorothy and Frank. Jeffrey can't resist peering into Dorothy's world, but he becomes more participant than spectator.

THE CAST ☛ With his smooth-featured, boyish face Kyle MacLachlan is the boy next door, but he shows us Jeffrey lusting for something more than than the predictable pattern of teenage dating he's embarked on with Sandy (Laura Dern). He's encouraged by Sandy's enthusiasm, but the secrets of Dorothy Vallens are what he wants to probe. Dorothy, played without a flinch by Isabella Rossellini (daughter of primal movie beauty Ingrid Bergman and Italian director Roberto Rossellini), is caught in the deviant sexuality of Frank Booth, an outlaw running a gang of kidnappers, drug dealers, and oddballs. It is Frank's unnerving friendliness and his sudden attacks of lucidity as much as his explosive temper and drug-aided depravity that fascinate Jeffrey and us and maybe even Dorothy about Dennis Hopper's character. The contrasting tones of this movie are conducted by David Lynch, and this movie is without a doubt the clearest expression of his "sunny side of the street is dark" vision.

WHY GUYS LOVE IT ☛ You can't describe this movie without using the terms "pervert," "kinky," or "deviant."

HONEY, YOU'LL LIKE THIS MOVIE ... ☛ Because it has the former Lancôme model, who you say looks so much classier than that trashy Christie Brinkley.

DON'T MISS
• Dean Stockwell's creepy rendition of Roy Orbison's "In Dreams"—you'll never hear that song again without thinking of this scene.
• Dorothy's visit to the police detective's house, battered, bruised, and totally nude.

MEMORABLE LINES
• "What kind of beer do you like?" Frank asks Jeffrey on their joyride.

"Heineken," Jeffrey squeaks out.

"Heineken," Frank shrieks. "Fuck that shit. Pabst Blue Ribbon."

- "Baby wants to fuck," Frank wails at Dorothy. (Warning: I advise that you don't use this line on a woman unless you happen to have a hostage.)

# DRUGSTORE COWBOY (1989)

## RATINGS

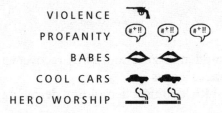

| | |
|---|---|
| VIOLENCE | 🔫 |
| PROFANITY | 💬 💬 💬 |
| BABES | 💋 💋 |
| COOL CARS | 🚗 🚗 |
| HERO WORSHIP | 🚬 🚬 |

**WHAT HAPPENS** ☛ Bob and Dianne, Rick and Nadine rob pharmacies and hospitals. Why? Because that's where the drugs are. They get the drugs and then they take the drugs. They're not picky about the drugs—though they have a special fondness for those in the heroin/morphine family—but they do have some rules: 1) If someone ODs, the other three get to divide up his or her share of the drugs. 2) Never leave a hat on the bed. When the rules are violated, Bob bails. But he can't get completely clear, and the past is likely to follow him home and club him over the head.

**THE CAST** ☛ You'd think that Matt Dillon's Bob gets as high on the action as he does on the drugs. When he's plotting a job, his pupils dilate, his forehead gets sweaty, and he starts yammering at warp speed. Once he's scored, he has no energy left for anything—least of all Dianne. Which, if you've seen long, leggy Kelly Lynch, is a damn shame. She thinks it is, too. Rick (James LeGros) can't decide if he loves Nadine (Heather Graham) more than he loves stealing drugs with Bob. William S. Burroughs, author of *Naked Lunch*, has always been sure about his love for drugs, and he keeps the passion alive as Father Tom, the junky priest.

## WHY GUYS LOVE IT ■ This is good shit, 100 percent pure, pharmaceutical, man.

## HONEY, YOU'LL LIKE THIS MOVIE ... ■ Because it portrays the difficulties facing many alternative family structures.

## DON'T MISS
- Nadine's sudden seizure and swift recovery right before the pharmacist's eyes.
- Dianne and Rick doing a demolition derby for the doctors and nurses.

## MEMORABLE LINES
- "You never fuck me and I always have to drive," Dianne complains to Bob.
- When Bob gives Father Tom a full vial of Dilaudid, the priest blesses him and says, "This should earn you an indulgence."
- "Most people don't know how they're going to feel from one moment to the next," Bob informs us. "But a dope fiend has a pretty good idea. All you have to do is look at the labels on the bottles."

# GOODFELLAS (1990)

**RATINGS**

VIOLENCE
PROFANITY
BABES
COOL CARS
HERO WORSHIP

**WHAT HAPPENS** ■ Henry Hill tries real hard to be a Good-Fella. Henry takes care of the don's business just the way the don likes it done—quiet and cool—and he doesn't kick up trouble like his ballistic buddies, Tommy DeVito and Jimmy Conway, do. Henry marries a nice Jewish girl who gives him healthy children. Most of all, Henry does his time righteous when he gets pinched. But Henry can't stay away from his girlfriends, he falls even harder for cocaine snorting and selling, and he follows Jimmy and Tommy into trouble. And when the Feds bust Henry and his wife, Henry buys a ticket for the Witness Protection Program, and worst of all, tells his story to a paisan journalist, who writes a book about the family that gets made into a movie. So is Henry a GoodFella?

**THE CAST** ■ Henry Hill is only half-Italian, so he can never be "made" a true insider in the family, and that only makes him more eager to please the don. Not that Ray Liotta has Henry toadying up to the don, Paul Sorvino's Paul Cicero. The sensible Pauly sees the fire in Henry's eyes, but he also trusts that Henry will be more subtle than Joe Pesci's explosive Tommy or Robert De Niro's vicious Jimmy. As Karen Hill, Henry's wife, Lorraine Bracco loves the danger of Henry first and the cash of Henry later. Catherine Scorsese (the director's mother) handles the role of Tommy's mother, serving a meal at a ridiculous hour and avoiding bothersome questions. Comedian Henny Youngman and singer Jerry Vale each handle the very demanding roles of Henny Youngman and Jerry Vale.

## WHY GUYS LOVE IT ☛ These hardworking, lunch pail kind of guys don't sit around and give orders, they're out on the streets, running numbers, selling tax-free booze and smokes, taking bets, and making collections. Guys like us, only with better-paying jobs.

## HONEY, YOU'LL LIKE THIS MOVIE ... ☛ Because Henry cares for Karen enough to pistol-whip another guy who looks at her.

## DON'T MISS
- If you think you know some guys who are poor tippers, check out Tommy's tips for the waiter at the club who asks Tommy to square his $7,000 tab.
- Karen's wake-up call for Henry. Try to count how many years off his life he loses when he opens his eyes to see her straddling him with a pistol pointed right at his head.

## MEMORABLE LINES
- "Why don't you get a nice girl?" Tommy's mother asks him.
  "I get a nice girl every night," Tommy answers.
  "I mean, why don't you get a nice girl and settle down?" she says.
  "I settle down every night, and then in the morning, I'm free," he says. Try that out on your mother sometime.
- "In prison, dinner was always a big thing. We had a pasta course and then we had a meat or fish. Pauly did all the prep work—he was doing a year for contempt—and he had a wonderful system for doing the garlic. He used a razor blade and he used to slice it so thin that it used to liquefy in the pan with just a little oil."

## AWARDS

Pesci won an Oscar for Best Supporting Actor.

**TRIVIA**

It's true, Henry Hill did tell his story, this story, to Nicholas Pileggi, who wrote about him in *Wiseguy*, the source for the screenplay Pileggi and Martin Scorcese wrote for this movie.

# THE KRAYS (1990)

## RATINGS

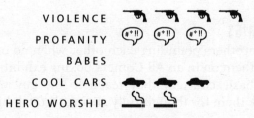

VIOLENCE

PROFANITY

BABES

COOL CARS

HERO WORSHIP

**WHAT HAPPENS** ▬ Two working-class boys in Britian grow up to be violent criminals who manage a club and an extensive crime network, while remaining devoted to their overprotective mother. I have to warn you that one of the brothers (Ron Kray) is gay, not that there is anything wrong with that, especially because he's much more vicious than his brother (Reg Kray), who marries a pretty, innocent girl. The brothers keep themselves busy with extortion and intimidation, and the good clean fun of beating and mutilating rival gang members.

**THE CAST** ▰ The brothers in this movie are played by the real-life brothers Gary and Martin Kemp, founders of the band Spandau Ballet. The one who plays Ron doesn't force the obvious conclusion that he's overcompensating for his homosexuality by being especially nasty. He is cruel to his boyfriend, but Ron doesn't single him out—he spits on everyone, except his mother. Reg, on the other hand, has a charming side he shows to his girl, though he takes his share of glee in their brutality, too. Steven Berkoff (the evil Victor in *Beverly Hills Cop*) is their main rival.

**WHY GUYS LOVE IT** ▰ Brothers should stick together, no matter what their personal problems are.

**HONEY, YOU'LL LIKE THIS MOVIE . . .** ▰ Because, whatever their failings, these boys love their mum.

**DON'T MISS**
- The brothers pounding each other when no one else will take them on in an All-Comers boxing exhibition.
- The basic courtesy they teach to the guy who doesn't thank them for thoughtfully slicing through his hand.

**MEMORABLE LINES**
- "Men are born children and they stay children," the boys' grandmother keeps reciting, as if there were something wrong with that.
- "Do you know the Beatles?" an American mobster asks the Krays.
  "I believe they know us," Ron answers.

# LITTLE ODESSA (1994)

## RATINGS

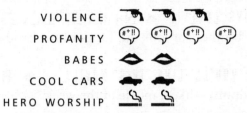

| | |
|---|---|
| VIOLENCE | 🔫 🔫 🔫 |
| PROFANITY | @*!! @*!! @*!! @*!! |
| BABES | 👄 👄 |
| COOL CARS | 🚗 🚗 |
| HERO WORSHIP | 🚬 🚬 |

**WHAT HAPPENS** ▰ When Joshua returns to the Brooklyn neighborhood where his Russian immigrant parents and younger brother still live, many people are surprised to see him. But not everyone is happy to see him. His philandering father sure isn't, but his dying mother and admiring brother are. His former cronies are unnerved that Josh has the guts to come back, and his ex-girlfriend can't decide how she feels about seeing him. And there's one guy who doesn't know it but he certainly won't be glad to see this professional killer execute the assignment that brings him home. Joshua must confront all of these people, and his past, present, and future before we see the movie's last shot.

**THE CAST** ▰ Tim Roth uses all the oil he slathered on his role in *Pulp Fiction* and is even more menacing as Joshua than he was as Ringo, the armed robber. He also allows us to see a flicker of life in his eyes before they go cold when he gets to work. After his conscience, Joshua must grapple with his father, Arkady, played with appropriately hollow self-righteousness by Maximilian Schell. As Reuben, Edward Furlong (who was the kid in *Terminator 2*) is trapped between the brother he looks up to and the father he knows is right—like any normal kid, he can't resist his brother. Just glimpses of Vanessa Redgrave as Joshua's mother in the last throes of cancer are enough to convey that her deterioration parallels that of this immigrant family.

**WHY GUYS LOVE IT** ▰ No matter what, we all look up to our big brothers or look out for our little brothers.

**HONEY, YOU'LL LIKE THIS MOVIE . . .** ▰ Because it's a family drama—like a movie of the week.

**DON'T MISS**
- Joshua's breakthrough with Alla, his ex.
- How Joshua finally lays bare his relationship with his father.

**MEMORABLE LINES**
- "The biggest killer in the world is rumors," Joshua tells Reuben.
- "Do you believe in God?" Joshua asks his target. "We'll wait ten seconds to see if God saves you."

# OCEAN'S ELEVEN (1960)

**RATINGS**

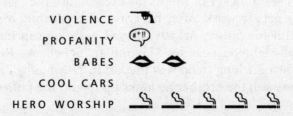

| | |
|---|---|
| VIOLENCE | 🔫 |
| PROFANITY | (#*!!) |
| BABES | 👄 👄 |
| COOL CARS | |
| HERO WORSHIP | 🚬 🚬 🚬 🚬 🚬 |

**WHAT HAPPENS** ▰ **W**hen Danny Ocean gathers the boys from the old 82nd Airborne commando squad for a reunion, you know it's gonna be one for the books—with plenty of booze and broads for everyone. But Danny has more in mind for the boys than reliving the old days: He's planning to pull a whopper of a job that will make them all rich. At a minute after midnight on New Year's Eve, they hit five casinos in Vegas simultaneously. Danny has even come up with a plan to keep the money safe until the heat dies down and they can divvy it up. Only the heat turns out to be a lot hotter than they guessed, and all their careful plotting threatens to go up in smoke.

**THE CAST** ▰ **H**ey, baby, we're talking about the all-star team here, the Rat Pack, in its full glory. Leading off is The Man himself, Frank Sinatra, as the mastermind Danny Ocean—and he's not whistling or even singing, he's just playing it cool and playing it tough. He's got all the backup he needs in Peter Lawford, a cynical rich boy who wants for once to earn (or at least steal) his own money instead of begging for it from his mother, and Dean Martin, who croons and stays totally tuned from start to finish. Sammy (Davis Jr.) is beautiful, and I mean it, babe, stashing the cash after they've grabbed it good. Angie Dickinson's Beatrice Ocean may have divorced The Man, but he still punches her buttons and she resists but doesn't refuse. Shirley MacLaine staggers through long enough to get a wet one from Dino. Cesar Romero is the rich mommy's beau who tries to worm his way in on the deal when he figures it all out—and he lets loose a big Joker cackle at the moment of truth. There's even a walk-on for Red Skelton, because Frank is a generous, bighearted guy.

**WHY GUYS LOVE IT** ▰ **F**rank says so, and nobody, but nobody, contradicts Frank.

**HONEY, YOU'LL LIKE THIS MOVIE . . .** ■ Because these are the coolest guys on the planet trying so hard to look like criminals they can't possibly be criminals.

## DON'T MISS

- How Frank educates a one-night stand who mistakes herself for something more.
- Norman "Mr. Roper" Fell forcing a casino employee to sing "Auld Lang Syne" in the dark.
- Sinatra, Lawford, and Dino discussing what they'll do with their share of the loot. Lawford says he plans to buy an ambassadorship, which was not entirely out of the realm of possibilities since he was married to President John Kennedy's sister.

## MEMORABLE LINES

- "If you're not careful," Sinatra says to Lawford while he's getting a massage from a hot babe, "she'll rub you out."
- "You better stop getting prettier every day," Dino tells Angie Dickinson, "or you'll turn into a monopoly."

# POINT BLANK (1967)

## RATINGS

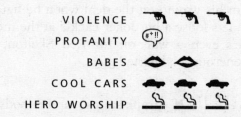

VIOLENCE

PROFANITY

BABES

COOL CARS

HERO WORSHIP

**WHAT HAPPENS** ◆ Reese begs Walker to help him with a heist, but Reese double-crosses Walker, then steals Walker's wife and shoots him, leaving him for dead. But Walker declines all offers to die until he gets his share of the money. Which means taking on not just Reese, but the whole ruthless organization he works for. Walker works his way up the organization's management ladder, politely asks each guy for his cut of the money and, when they refuse, impolitely shoots them. He is aided in his quest by a mysterious benefactor and his very babe-o-rific sister-in-law.

**THE CAST** ◆ Lee Marvin, master of the steeliest stare in the movies, isn't an expert fighter or marksman—but he turns Walker, hardly a hero, into a fearless tough guy we can all admire. Walker's battle begins with Reese, who's played by John "Dean Wormer" Vernon as coldly calculating and essentially gutless. Walker also takes on a phony lawyer (portrayed by veteran TV bad guy Lloyd Bochner) and a glad-handing mobster named Brewster (Carroll "Archie Bunker" O'Connor). Angie Dickinson (at her very ripest) is Walker's very close sister-in-law who has her own reasons for wanting revenge. You'll recognize James B. Sikking as the sharpshooter; he was the SWAT team commander in *Hill Street Blues*.

**WHY GUYS LOVE IT** ◆ Revenge is one of the very best reasons to not die.

**HONEY, YOU'LL LIKE THIS MOVIE ...** ◆ Because director John Boorman used a lot of those weird camera angles and other arty techniques you like to explain to me afterwards.

**DON'T MISS**
- Marvin working over a used car—and a used-car dealer—to get information he wants.

- The many lingering camera shots of Dickinson's body in various stages of undress.

## MEMORABLE LINES

When Walker reappears after he was thought to have been killed, his wife (who took up with Reese) says, "I'm glad you're not dead." Walker, however, is not able to return the sentiment.

# THE POPE OF GREENWICH VILLAGE (1984)

## RATINGS

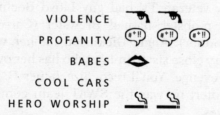

|                |     |     |     |
| -------------- | --- | --- | --- |
| VIOLENCE       | 🔫  | 🔫  |     |
| PROFANITY      | @*!! | @*!! | @*!! |
| BABES          | 👄  |     |     |
| COOL CARS      |     |     |     |
| HERO WORSHIP   | 🚬  | 🚬  |     |

**WHAT HAPPENS** ▬ Charlie has a lot going for him. He's good-looking and suave, he has a long-limbed blond dancer for a girlfriend, and he's the maître d' at a nice Italian restaurant. Charlie's only problem is Paulie, his sticky-fingered, dim-witted cousin who gets them fired from their jobs at the restaurant. Charlie wants to buy a restaurant of his own, Paulie thinks his way out will be a racehorse sired by sperm stolen from a champion. Charlie lets Paulie talk him into teaming up with an experienced safecracker to rip off cash from an office, so they can each pursue their ambitions. The money, however, belongs to the mob and crooked cops. And they intend to make Charlie and Paulie pay it back, with interest.

**THE CAST** ◗ Mickey Rourke is a slick Charlie with a strut in his walk and a half-smile of exasperation for his fast-talking cousin, played by Eric Roberts, who gives dumb a good name. You have no trouble seeing why Charlie feels protective of Paulie, but you can't imagine why Charlie allows himself to be dragged into Paulie's schemes. Burly actor Kenneth McMillan is their anxious safecracking partner with a good reason for doing the job. Charlie's girlfriend, Diane (Daryl Hannah), spends most of her time in her underwear, stretching her legs and trying to convince Charlie to be legit. Burt Young is mob boss Bed Bug Eddie, and Tony "Toma" Musante is his Goon #1, and they give Paulie the big thumbs-down. Geraldine Page gives motherhood a bad name as the bitter alcoholic mom of the cop on the take.

**WHY GUYS LOVE IT** ◗ Everybody talks with their mouths full; it's enough to send Miss Manners into cardiac arrest.

**HONEY, YOU'LL LIKE THIS MOVIE . . .** ◗ Because it's about a family that sticks together.

**DON'T MISS**
- Paulie getting his revenge on the cop who towed his car by spiking his drink—with horse laxative.
- What happens to the crooked cop who takes the elevator DOWN.

**MEMORABLE LINES**
- "Why are you always just an inch away from being a good person?" says Diane to Charlie, demonstrating her poor grasp of weights and measures.
- "You ever hear of artificial inspiration?" Paulie asks Char-

lie as he launches into a hilarious explanation of horse genetics.

# PULP FICTION (1994)

## RATINGS

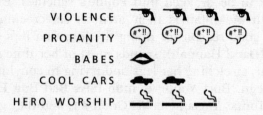

| | |
|---|---|
| VIOLENCE | |
| PROFANITY | |
| BABES | |
| COOL CARS | |
| HERO WORSHIP | |

**WHAT HAPPENS** ✒ A lot of stuff happens, so pay attention. Two chatty hit men, Vinny and Jules, stop by to visit with a group of enterprising college kids, pick up a briefcase, and debate the implications of a foot massage. Vinny does the Twist with his boss's wife, Mia, before she goes on the nod. A professional boxer makes a deal to go down, then breaks the deal and ends up nose to nose with the boss. A couple of lovebirds, Hunny Bunny and Pumpkin, try to stick up the coffee shop. Do you follow any of this? You don't? Watch it twice and then you'll know where it starts and where it ends.

**THE CAST** ✒ Vinny Vega may not be the brightest guy who ever lived, but he's no Vinny Barbarino. John Travolta gives this Vinny a low-key, businesslike approach to his job of shooting people for Marsellus (Ving Rhames), who issues orders in a deep, soft bass that speaks with unquestionable authority. Vinny might be better off turning down Marsellus's request that Vinny entertain his wife, Mia, one night. Uma Thurman's graceful beauty and glancing flirtatiousness are sure to attract Vinny to Mia, but it's Mia's nose that really leads to trouble. He seeks help from his dopey dealer friend, Eric Stoltz, and his wife (Rosanna Arquette), the human pincushion. Samuel L. Jackson's Jules puts the fire and brimstone into his work with Vinny. Boxer Butch (Bruce Willis) refuses to go down—for Marsellus or their new friend Zed. Tim Roth and Amanda Plummer are the love-blinded robbers who can't see whom they're messing with. When director Quentin Tarantino has a few uninvited guests, Harvey Keitel helps with the cleanup chores.

**WHY GUYS LOVE IT** ▰ You've never laughed so much at graphic violence or been so disturbed by bloody comedy . . . you make the call.

*Pulp Fiction,* or Saturday Night Uma.

**HONEY, YOU'LL LIKE THIS MOVIE ...** ▬ Because if you just remember it's nothing but fake blood being spilled for fun.

## DON'T MISS

- Christopher Walken recounting with pure reverence to a young Butch the deep, dark, uncomfortable secret of the family pocket watch.
- Vinny's first home medical procedure and Mia's dramatic recovery in his hands.

## MEMORABLE LINES

- "Your method of foot massage may differ from mine," Jules insists to Vinny, "but you know that touching his wife's feet and sticking your tongue in the holiest of holies ain't in the same ballpark, they ain't in the same league, they ain't even the same sport."
- "I'm gonna get medieval on your ass," Marsellus tells Zed.
- "The path of the righteous is beset on all sides by the inequities of the selfish and the tyranny of evil men. Blessed is he who in the name of charity and goodwill shepherds the weak through the Valley of Darkness for he is truly his brother's keeper and the finder of lost children. And I will strike down upon thee with great vengeance and furious anger those who attempt to poison or destroy my brother and you will know my name is the Lord when I lay my vengeance upon thee." Jules shares these lines with those most in need of spiritual uplift, but his claim that it is from Ezekial 25:17 is wrong—the words don't even come from the Bible at all, though I know a few guys who consider the *Pulp Fiction* script a holy book.

## AWARDS

Tarantino and Roger Avary took the Oscar for Best Original Screenplay.

Some devotees of this movie have argued that the contents of the briefcase—which remain unseen but have a golden glow, and which Marsellus desperately wants back—is Marsellus's soul. Do you buy that?

# RESERVOIR DOGS (1992)

## RATINGS

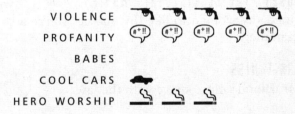

VIOLENCE
PROFANITY
BABES
COOL CARS
HERO WORSHIP

**WHAT HAPPENS** ▰ A weather-beaten old thug, Joe Cabot, convenes a crew of six hoodlums who don't know each other to steal diamonds. For secrecy's sake, each of the crew is given a color-coded name. But they're so busy jawing about nothing that they bungle the plan. When they regroup after the failed heist, they determine that a cop among them has sabotaged their plan, but they disagree about which of them is the cop. Meanwhile, Mr. Blond has brought back a uniformed cop, whom he tortures brutally. So much blood splatters everywhere before the movie is over that you'll want to change your own shirt.

**THE CAST** ▬ They've been given code names by Cabot, played by gravelly voiced Lawrence Tierney, who has been intimidating lawmen and outlaws since he first appeared as John Dillinger in the 1940s. Harvey Keitel is the thoughtful Mr. White; Michael Madsen is the sadistic Mr. Blond. Mr. Orange, played by Tim Roth, lays jabbering and bleeding throughout most of the movie. Steve Buscemi's Mr. Pink has no loyalty to any of his colleagues. And the director, Quentin Tarantino, gives himself a few choice lines as Mr. Brown. Chris Penn is Cabot's son, who talks the talk but doesn't walk the walk that his father does.

**WHY GUYS LOVE IT** ▬ It's a new standard in screen violence.

**HONEY, YOU'LL LIKE THIS MOVIE . . .** ▬ (If you can convince any woman to like this movie, you're a smarter man than me.)

**DON'T MISS**
Mr. Blond's close shave with the law.

**MEMORABLE LINES**
"Be glad I didn't name you Mr. Yellow," says Cabot in answer to Mr. Pink's complaint about his handle.

# RUTHLESS PEOPLE (1986)

## RATINGS

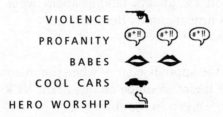

VIOLENCE
PROFANITY
BABES
COOL CARS
HERO WORSHIP

**WHAT HAPPENS** ☛ Miniskirt magnate Sam Stone plots to kill his pampered wife, Barbara, but he lucks out when she is kidnapped first—so he can decline to pay the ransom and devote his full attention to killing her poodle. The kidnappers, a middle-class couple seeking revenge for Stone's unscrupulous business tactics, don't luck out, because the wife is an unholy bitch. Meanwhile, Stone's mistress plots to blackmail him by videotaping the dirty deed—only her dimwitted other boyfriend films the wrong dirty deed. When all of these plotlines collide, the guilty wind up innocent and the innocent guilty.

**THE CAST** ☛ Danny DeVito's Sam Stone sniggers and licks his chops as events fall in his favor, then nearly swallows his tongue when they change course. As Barbara Stone, Bette Midler shrieks, bellows, and throws an elbow or two at her kidnappers, played almost childlike by Helen "Supergirl" Slater and Judge Reinhold. Though Anita Morris isn't fresh from the pages of *Playboy,* her lascivious manner and her silky underwear (or is that her silky manner and lascivious underwear?) occupy Sam Stone's attention, but all she wants is to take Stone's money and run off with the airheaded mimbo played by Bill Pullman.

**WHY GUYS LOVE IT** ■ It proves that morals and inhibitions are for the squeamish.

**HONEY, YOU'LL LIKE THIS MOVIE ...** ■ Because it has Bette, and you are always talking about what a multitalented entertainment genuis Bette is.

### DON'T MISS
The scene at the appliance store when the mistress and her boyfriend put their videotape on one of the VCRs and it appears on every screen in the store.

### MEMORABLE LINES
When Sam Stone gets a wrong-number call for a "Debbie," he says to the caller, "I'm sorry, Debbie can't come to the phone right now—she's got my dick in her mouth," then hangs up and adds with a grin to the cop sitting in his office, "I just love getting wrong numbers, don't you?"

**TRIVIA**

Mick Jagger found time in his busy schedule to sing the cheesy title song.

# SCARFACE (1983)

## RATINGS

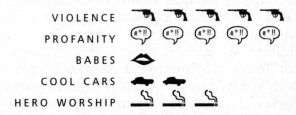

| | |
|---|---|
| VIOLENCE | 🔫 🔫 🔫 🔫 🔫 |
| PROFANITY | @*!! @*!! @*!! @*!! @*!! |
| BABES | 👄 |
| COOL CARS | 🚗 🚗 |
| HERO WORSHIP | 🚬 🚬 🚬 |

**WHAT HAPPENS** ✒ The American immigrant experience has lots of faces, and one of them is the scarred and sneering mug of Tony Montana, a refugee who comes from Cuba during the brief mass migration in the late 1970s when Fidel Castro emptied his country's jails on our shores. Tony ("a political prisoner" in Cuba) wastes no time in meeting up with some of Miami's most prosperous importers of South American products and ingratiating himself with his hard-nosed negotiating tactics and loyalty. Fueled by the immigrant's boundless ambition, Tony climbs the ladder in his organization, stepping right over everyone who would impede his road to success. Ultimately, Tony achieves the American Dream: a lavish mansion with a mammoth sunken bathtub and six TVs; a beautiful blond wife who loves his wealth and disdains him; a devoted cadre of heavily armed bodyguards; and a mountain of cocaine he can stick his face into whenever he needs a lift.

**THE CAST** ✒ You'll see lots of the qualities Al Pacino has brought to other movie roles in his portrayal of Tony Montana: Michael Corleone's calm under fire; the explosive temper of bank robber Sonny from *Dog Day Afternoon;* Serpico's relentless drive; but since this is a movie about excess, he piled all of those attributes on top of each other and used them as a launching pad to jump over the top, way over the top. By the time he welcomes the Colombian army into his house at the end, he's got us believing he may be as unstoppable as he thinks he is. His frosty and snow-blind wife is not the Michelle Pfeiffer we usually see—she dresses in spare, slinky evening gowns, but she's so distant that she invites nothing but looks. By contrast, Tony's sister (Mary Elizabeth Mastrantonio) wants closer contact, especially with Tony's one true friend, Manolo (Stephen Bauer)—which sends Tony into a blind rage. Ever-steady Robert Loggia and a cautious F. Murray Abraham have the misfortune of standing in Tony's way.

## WHY GUYS LOVE IT ▰ It proves one of our favorite maxims: Too much of everything is just enough.

## HONEY, YOU'LL LIKE THIS MOVIE . . . ▰ Because when one of Tony's targets is joined in his car by a woman and two children, Tony refuses to execute the assignment.

## DON'T MISS
- The chain saw–dismembering Tony is forced to watch and the revenge shots Tony fires in the middle of the street right after.
- A staggeringly stoned Tony lecturing the upper crust at a posh restaurant about the sociological role of the "bad guy" in American culture.
- Manolo's subtle approach with the bikinis.

## MEMORABLE LINES
The Gospel according to Tony Montana:
- "I've only got two things in this world, my word and my balls, and I don't break neither for nobody."
- "First you get the money. Then you get the power. Then you get the beautiful woman."
- "Fuck you, meng."

TRIVIA

You won't be surprised to know that the Emperor of Excess, Oliver Stone, wrote the screenplay for this movie.

# THE USUAL SUSPECTS (1995)

## RATINGS

VIOLENCE

PROFANITY

BABES

COOL CARS

HERO WORSHIP

**WHAT HAPPENS** ■ Five guys who are hauled in for a police lineup hatch a plan for another job. And what do you know, each of them has a different specialty: There's a sharp-shooter, an explosives expert, a vicious punk, a smart guy, and a slow, gimpy con artist, who narrates the movie and their tale to a Fed. They execute a clever heist involving the New York City police, then head west where they ambush an L.A. drug dealer. A mysterious lawyer meets them and puts them up to disrupting a huge deal on a ship. When they do, nothing is what it seems. Then buckle your seat belt, because you'll hit several sharp turns before the end.

**THE CAST** ■ Irish actor Gabriel Byrne (*Miller's Crossing; Siesta*) broods from start to finish as the smart guy. Stephen

Baldwin, youngest of the overacting Baldwins, is the hot-shot sharpshooter long on attitude and short on hair. Kevin Pollak plays the fearless explosives expert. Benicio Del Toro is the manic mumbling punk. And Kevin Spacey is the gimp who tells the tale and knows it all too well. Pete Postel-thwaite's portrayal of the lawyer is quietly disquieting. The cops on the case include Chazz Palminteri as the Fed who interrogates Spacey; Dan Hedya as the local cop; and Gian-carlo Esposito as the FBI agent with the critical detail.

## WHY GUYS LOVE IT ▰ We all wish we could lie so well.

## HONEY, YOU'LL LIKE THIS MOVIE . . . ▰ Because if you like a brunette, we've got Gabriel Byrne. Prefer a blond? How about Stephen Baldwin? Rather an intellectual? Kevin Spacey. A funny guy? Comic Kevin Pollak. Have an eye for the exotic? Benicio Del Toro. You want a girl? Willowy Suzi Amis gets several minutes of screen time.

## DON'T MISS
One minute or you'll be lost.

## MEMORABLE LINES
- Cop says to Pollak, "You know what happens if you do another turn in the joint."
   He answers, "I fuck your father in the shower and then have a snack."
- Baldwin, sighting his rifle's scope at a group of men, says to himself, "Oswald was a faggot."

# BAD LIEUTENANT (1992)

## RATINGS

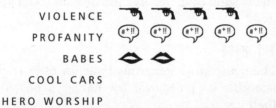

| | |
|---|---|
| VIOLENCE | 🔫 🔫 🔫 🔫 |
| PROFANITY | @*!! @*!! @*!! @*!! @*!! |
| BABES | 👄 👄 |
| COOL CARS | |
| HERO WORSHIP | |

**WHAT HAPPENS ▪** Even cops like to have fun, only this New York City detective has taken it to new depths. He snorts coke for breakfast, shakes down dealers for freebies, drinks and parties with whores, and blows a lot of cash betting on the N.Y. Mets (which proves he's really gone). He's definitely headed for a sudden crash at the bottom when he's assigned to investigate the rape of a young, good-looking nun. She forgives the young men who did it and refuses to cooperate, which sends the lieutenant into a tailspin that brings him into direct confrontation with his own soul. But don't worry about that—the movie may have serious themes, yet they don't get in the way of the fun of watching this cop self-destruct.

**THE CAST** ▪ Harvey Keitel lets us see every wrinkle and flaw of the lieutenant without remorse. He bares himself in every way (be prepared to cover your eyes), and never shies away from the grossest details. Almost everyone else in the cast is unfamiliar to people who don't see Off-Broadway plays, except for Paul Hipp, who starred in *The Buddy Holly Story* On Broadway and who went to my high school (in case anyone cares). Stella Keitel plays the part of the lieutenant's daughter, which must not be too hard since she is Harvey Keitel's daughter.

**WHY GUYS LOVE IT** ▪ This cop is baaaaaad.

**HONEY, YOU'LL LIKE THIS MOVIE . . .** ▪ Because it's a very human portrait of a man in a difficult job grappling with his soul. And, just like in *The Piano,* you get to see Harv naked.

**DON'T MISS**
- The lieutenant's generous leniency offer to the two teen-age girls he pulls over for having a busted taillight on their car.
- His reaction when he hears of another Mets loss on his car radio. He satisfies an urge we've all felt when our team lets us down with money riding on the game.

**MEMORABLE LINES**
"Vampires are lucky, they can feed on others; we only get to eat away at ourselves," says a junkie chick to the lieutenant.

# BULLITT (1968)

## RATINGS

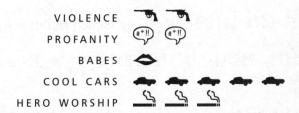

| | |
|---|---|
| VIOLENCE | 🔫 🔫 |
| PROFANITY | #*!! #*!! |
| BABES | 👄 |
| COOL CARS | 🚗 🚗 🚗 🚗 🚗 |
| HERO WORSHIP | 🚬 🚬 🚬 |

**WHAT HAPPENS** ▬ A witness in a high-visibility mob trial in San Francisco needs police protection, so the city's district attorney (who's running for mayor) asks that the best detective on the police force be assigned to guard the witness. That detective is Bullitt, a cool-as-a-cucumber cop with a distinct distaste for politicians. Bullitt gets hot under the collar when he figures out that he's been guarding a decoy, and that the D.A. and a police captain have more at stake than their dedication to upholding the law. In direct defiance of his orders, Bullitt takes over the case himself and brings it to a shattering conclusion.

**THE CAST** ▬ You don't have to be told that Steve McQueen's Bullitt is not a by-the-book cop: Watch how painful it is for him to be polite to D.A. Chalmers and you can see he holds little but contempt for the politician's posturing. Robert Vaughn pours on the posturing as Chalmers, dripping with gooey charm one moment and then hardening into the tough power broker full of hollow threats the next. On his side is the flunky police captain played by Norman "Mr. Roper" Fell, who has his own less potent arsenal of threat aimed at Bullitt. Our hero is supported by his immediate supervisor, truly tough Simon Oakland, his partner

Robert Duvall, and more warmly by his artist girlfriend, the luscious Jacqueline Bisset. You'll also recognize Georg Sanford Brown, one of the cops from *The Rookies* on TV, as the doc.

## WHY GUYS LOVE IT ▬ A cop named Bullitt is no flatfoot.

## HONEY, YOU'LL LIKE THIS MOVIE ... ▬ Because it's not Dirty Harry.

## DON'T MISS
- The seven-minute car chase through the up-and-down streets of San Francisco with Bullitt gunning his Mustang GT in pursuit of hit men in a Dodge Challenger. They stay just ahead of the 'Stang until their very sudden stop at the gas pump.
- Bullitt taking just a few brief minutes to remind his girlfriend that he's loaded and aimed at her target.

## MEMORABLE LINES
"You work your side of the street and I'll work mine," Bullitt warns the D.A. when they first meet.

# THE FRENCH CONNECTION (1971)

## RATINGS

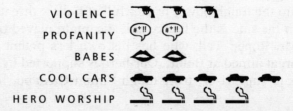

| | | | | | |
|---|---|---|---|---|---|
| VIOLENCE | 🔫 | 🔫 | 🔫 | | |
| PROFANITY | @*!! | @*!! | | | |
| BABES | 👄 | 👄 | | | |
| COOL CARS | 🚗 | 🚗 | 🚗 | 🚗 | 🚗 |
| HERO WORSHIP | 🚬 | 🚬 | 🚬 | 🚬 | |

In *The French Connection,* Popeye Doyle administers his own brand of Miranda Rights.

**WHAT HAPPENS** ▰ Based on a true story—though obvious liberties have been taken with the truth. A very urbane French businessman comes to New York to arrange a major heroin deal. The activities of the French guy come to the attention of a slovenly cop named Popeye Doyle, who has never heard of probable cause or rights of any kind. Doyle and his partner, Buddy Russo, tail the French guy and his associates, bust up bars in Harlem, irritate their supervisors, and bicker with the Feds. They finally show up to bust the drug deal, and Doyle chases the Frenchman into an abandoned warehouse—where he makes a lethal mistake that leads to the sequel.

**THE CAST** ▰ You can almost smell the liquor and B.O. on Gene Hackman's portrayal of Popeye Doyle. Only his partner, played by Roy Scheider, seems to tolerate him. They stand in sharp contrast to the French businessman Fernando Rey, whose stylish, upright manner immediately makes him suspect. The Three Degrees are The Three Degrees.

## WHY GUYS LOVE IT ⬛ This cop thinks that Miranda Rights is some hooker he busted last week.

## HONEY, YOU'LL WANT TO WATCH THIS MOVIE . . . ⬛ Because it has subtitled French dialogue, like those foreign films you love so much.

## DON'T MISS
- Doyle chasing the elevated train through the streets of New York—for eight minutes of screen time, Doyle violates every traffic law on the books and leaves people dying and wounded all around him just to catch one bad guy.
- Doyle's demonstration of the use of handcuffs for more pleasurable restraint.

## MEMORABLE LINES
Roy Scheider makes contact with the babe wife of a mobster by saying, "I like your blouse. I'd like to get one just like it for my girlfriend. But I want you to model it."

She says, "How much?"

"Fifty dollars an hour," Scheider replies.

"I'll do it for two hundred dollars," she says.

## AWARDS

*The French Connection* is one of the few movies to win the five top Oscars.

# MIDNIGHT RIDE (1992)

## RATINGS

VIOLENCE
PROFANITY
BABES
COOL CARS
HERO WORSHIP

**WHAT HAPPENS** ▬ A cop's wife decides to leave her husband one night and go stay with a friend, but he chases her. She picks up a sweet-faced guy hitchhiking—a bad idea because he terrorizes her and takes time to perform quick eye surgery on a surly motel owner (who must belong to one of those cheap, small-business HMOs) and to help another young woman get home safely from a date with an abusive guy. At each opportunity, the cop's wife tries to escape the psychotic hitchhiker and the husband who continues to chase them. Eventually, all three of them end up at a psychiatric hospital, where the hitchhiker hopes to shock the woman's troubles right out of her head. The ride is never over, you should remember, until the elevator doors open on your floor.

**THE CAST** ▬ Mark "Luke Skywalker" Hamill must be still traumatized after discovering that Darth Vader is his father, or maybe he's just pissed that Harrison Ford gets the princess and a career, and he got stuck with the two robots and *Corvette Summer*. Either way, Hamill's wide-eyed innocence has been transformed into beady-eyed mania in this role as the hitchhiker. Robert Mitchum shows up briefly to play the hitchhiker's psychiatrist and to collect his paycheck.

**WHY GUYS LOVE IT** ■ One look at this movie and your woman will think twice about running out on you.

**HONEY, YOU'LL LIKE THIS MOVIE . . .** ■ Because it focuses on a woman who sets out on her own to make a new life for herself, but discovers how much she loved the security of her husband.

**DON'T MISS**
Hamill dragging the cop . . . literally

# RICOCHET (1991)

**RATINGS:**

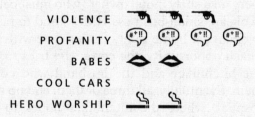

| | |
|---|---|
| VIOLENCE | 🔫 🔫 🔫 |
| PROFANITY | @*!! @*!! @*!! @*!! |
| BABES | 👄 👄 |
| COOL CARS | |
| HERO WORSHIP | 🚬 🚬 |

**WHAT HAPPENS** ■ Boy from the hood makes good as a cop who daringly confronts a psychotic killer and rescues a young girl. The hero catches the wave of media acclaim and rides it to a promising political future as a prosecutor and mayoral candidate, while the psycho makes no friends in prison. Inevitably, the psycho and his grudge bust out and he gets busy exacting his revenge on the hero. There's a subplot about the hero and the drug-dealing gang from the hood, but it's just a sideshow. That's because when the psycho and the hero meet for their final showdown, the hero from the hood turns to his homeboys for backup rather than the cops. The ending gives new meaning to the phrase "Stuck for an answer."

**THE CAST** ⬛ Denzel Washington has the smooth features, nice teeth, and boundless charm that every hero needs to turn an act of bravery in the line of duty into a career. Your first look at John Lithgow's eyes tell you that he was the kid who ate the fly while the merely cruel ones just pulled its wings off. Rapper/actor Ice-T is the only choice for the gang leader who dislikes but has respect for the cop. Kevin Pollak is the cop's partner and the last person to lose his faith in him. Watch for Lindsay "Bionic Woman" Wagner.

**WHY GUYS LOVE IT** ⬛ A good psycho is hard to find; a case-hardened one even better.

**HONEY, YOU'LL LIKE THIS MOVIE . . .** ⬛ Because Denzel is Denzel in all his charm and good looks.

**DON'T MISS**
- The cruel and barbarous but strangely satisfying torture Lithgow subjects Denzel to and videotapes for his enjoyment later.
- A prison-style joust between Lithgow and the second meanest guy in the joint.

**MEMORABLE LINES**
When the psycho is asked by a parole board member what would be the first thing he'd do upon his release, the psycho answers, "Come over to your house to fuck your wife. And your daughter. And your dog." (Prison life must be even lonelier than you'd think, isn't it?)

# UNDER COVER (1987)

**RATINGS:**

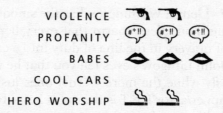

| VIOLENCE | 🔫 🔫 |
| PROFANITY | @*!! @*!! @*!! |
| BABES | 👄 👄 👄 |
| COOL CARS | |
| HERO WORSHIP | 🚬 🚬 |

**WHAT HAPPENS** ▰ When a narc in a high school undercover operation gets killed, his best friend goes under to find out what happened. He joins the baseball team, befriends a couple students, gets stoned with them, and asks a lot of questions. Eventually, he finds a few adults lurking in the shadows of the mystery—who are ready to play hardball with him, too. He is helped by a saucy fellow narc who wears her badges prominently.

**THE CAST** ▰ David Neidorf (whom you may, or may not, recognize as one of the basketball players in *Hoosiers*) successfully convinces most of the kids he's one of the guys, even if you might have a hard time figuring how he got away with a receding hairline and razor stubble. Jennifer Jason Leigh as Tanille Lareaux, the other narc in the school, extracts lots of secrets from the boys that help put together the case, and she certainly gets results because of the subtlety of her investigative techniques. Barry Corbin (the astronaut Maurice Minnifield from TV's *Northern Exposure*) lays on the good ol' boy charm with a butter knife in portraying shifty Irwin Lee, the cop in charge of the narc program. Kathleen Wilhoite is Corinne, a ditzy receptionist in the police department who provides information and interest to the main narc. The kids came right out of the class of 1985 yearbook.

**WHY GUYS LOVE IT** ■ How cool to go back to high school with a gun and lord it over all the punks.

**HONEY, YOU'LL LIKE THIS MOVIE . . .** ■ Because without the woman narc, he'd be dead.

**DON'T MISS**
The topless interrogation in the whorehouse.

**CHECK OUT**

Jennifer Jason Leigh went undercover again—well, she does in every movie . . . let's rephrase that: She played a narc again in *Rush*.

# WALKING TALL (1973)

**RATINGS**

| | | | | |
|---|---|---|---|---|
| VIOLENCE | 🔫 | 🔫 | 🔫 | 🔫 |
| PROFANITY | @#*!! | @#*!! | | |
| BABES | 👄 | 👄 | | |
| COOL CARS | 🚗 | 🚗 | 🚗 | 🚗 |
| HERO WORSHIP | 🚬 | 🚬 | 🚬 | 🚬 |

**WHAT HAPPENS** ■ If your name is Buford Pusser, what kinds of careers are open to you? Would you trust Buford Pusser, C.P.A., to do your taxes? Care to discuss your health with Dr. Buford Pusser, urologist? Not a chance. With that name, B. P. had to be either a professional wrestler or the sheriff of a small, violent Southern town. Or both. After a successful stint putting lesser men in headlocks, "Wild Bull" Buford decides to settle down with his family in his quaint little hometown in Tennessee. Only the town's charm has been marred by two "social clubs" run by organized crime and staffed by vicious goons. An indignant Buford Pusser becomes the sheriff and sets about to break the stranglehold the gangsters have on the town—mostly with the aid of a big stick. Of course, every confrontation Buford has with the thugs just raises the ante until nobody and nothing involved is left standing.

**THE CAST** ◾ Joe Don Baker (whose two first names instantly identify him as a proper Southerner) doesn't have the physique of today's superjacked pro wrestlers, but he has the heft and the menace of a real "rassler." Those qualities come in handy in his portrayal of Buford Pusser, who takes the worst that the hoodlums visit upon him and keeps on coming. Elizabeth Hartman is his pacifist wife; you can see her cringe each time the stakes go up. Noah Beery is in the familiar role of Buford's father; you'll recognize Beery as Jim Rockford's father from the very guys' guy TV series *The Rockford Files*.

**WHY GUYS LOVE IT** ◾ Walk softly and carry a big stick? Bullshit. Walk anyway you want and carry a *really* big stick.

**HONEY, YOU'LL LIKE THIS MOVIE . . .** ◾ Because it's about small-town values.

**DON'T MISS**
- The generous treatment Sheriff Buford has for the pro who helps him.
- The nasty treatment the goons have for that same pro and the sheriff's treatment of them when he catches them.

## MEMORABLE LINES

"Looking don't cost a thing," says the pro to Buford the first time they meet.

This movie is based, very loosely, on the real-life story of Sheriff Buford Pusser.

# YEAR OF THE DRAGON (1985)

## RATINGS

| | |
|---|---|
| VIOLENCE | 🔫 🔫 🔫 🔫 |
| PROFANITY | (#*!!) (#*!!) (#*!!) (#*!!) |
| BABES | 👄 👄 |
| COOL CARS | |
| HERO WORSHIP | 🚬 🚬 🚬 |

**WHAT HAPPENS** ◄ When mob rule turns bloody in New York City's Chinatown, the new captain in charge of the precinct (a Vietnam vet) ignores orders from his superiors and launches an all-out offensive against the syndicate, enlisting the help of a brash and beautiful Asian-American TV news reporter. Meanwhile, the young leader of the Chinese mob is busy defying his elders and increasing his share of the city's drug traffic. The clash between the captain and the kid turns personal and ends in a brutal face-to-face that you'll hear coming down the tracks.

S.S./SHOOTING STAR

In *Year of the Dragon,* Rourke doesn't let Ariane's screaming disrupt his aim.

**THE CAST** ▪ Mickey Rourke as Captain Stanley White has his usual impudent look on his face, but he's otherwise as sloppy as he is normally slick. His hair is even a bit gray around the edges. It is the young boss on the block, Joey Tai, played by John Lone, who's as slick as an oil spill in this movie—that is, until he's had enough of White. As Tracy Tzu—determined TV reporter, Ariane veers sharply from being enchanted and exasperated by White.

**WHY GUYS LOVE IT** ▪ There's something about hot-tempered young guys running over levelheaded older guys to get to their own destruction that gets us everytime.

**HONEY, YOU'LL LIKE THIS MOVIE . . .** ▪ Because an hour after watching it, you'll want to watch it again.

## DON'T MISS

- Tracy's very warm bath.
- Captain White continuing to beat the guy who killed his wife after the guy is already dead.

## MEMORABLE LINES

"Let no motherless fuck raise his head between us again," says Joey Tai to his trading partners as he pulls the severed head of a rival out of a sack and places it on the table.

Asia-obsessed director Oliver Stone co-wrote the screenplay for this movie, which Michael *"The Deerhunter"* Cimino directed.

# *Dirty Harry*

Inspector Harry Callahan is more than just an enduring character (who appeared in five movies in seventeen years) and a major influence on lots of other movie cops. He's a national icon who was quoted by President Reagan. Harry stands for our frustration at the way politics and corruption have given criminals the upper hand in our society. He plays by the same rules as the killers—disregarding the police handbook, orders from his superiors, even the U.S. Constitution when necessary. And he wages his one-man war on crime armed with his famed Magnum and his highly sensitive bullshit detector. In any of these five movies, you'll find a cop who believes that every action deserves an equal and opposite reaction.

# DIRTY HARRY (1971)

## RATINGS

VIOLENCE

PROFANITY

BABES

COOL CARS

HERO WORSHIP

S.S./SHOOTING STAR

*Dirty Harry* counting his shots.

**WHAT HAPPENS** ✒ A serial killer with really bad skin who calls himself "Scorpio" (hey, Psycho, what's your sign?) demands money from the city of San Francisco to cease his kidnapping-and-murder spree. The mayor and police chief agree to the killer's demands—which include having Harry deliver the money. When Harry collars the creep, he questions the guy a little too vigorously—and the killer gets released and then gets pissed. The psycho kidnaps a school bus full of kids, Harry climbs aboard, and eventually gets to pop the big question to the psycho.

**THE CAST** ✒ To play Harry Callahan, Clint Eastwood took off his poncho and boots, and brushed his hair up into a pomp that Jack Lord would envy, but he's still the same man of few words as he was in the Westerns he starred in. And when Clint does utter a line or two, they pack a punch that'd knock over dialogue ten times their size. Andy Robinson gives Scorpio some balance: One moment he's a wild-eyed madman gleefully terrorizing his victims, and the next he's a beady-eyed whiner feeling terrorized by the relentless cop. You won't feel the slightest twinge of sympathy when he gets his. The mayor (John "Dean Wormer" Vernon) is a model for many other weaselly politicians; Harry Guardino plays Callahan's superior, caught between his respect for Callahan and his job.

**HONEY, YOU'LL LIKE THIS MOVIE . . .** ✒ Because Clint's main concern is the safety of women and children.

**DON'T MISS**
- Harry calmly eating his lunch before he busts up a bank robbery; he chews up the last few bites as he guns down three crooks.
- His carefully calibrated interrogation of Scorpio on the fifty-yard line of a football stadium.

## MEMORABLE LINES

Both the opening and closing sequences of the movie end with Harry pointing his Magnum at a criminal whose gun is within reach. "I know what you're thinking," Harry says each time. "Did he fire six shots, or only five? To tell you the truth, in all this excitement, I kind of lost track myself. But being as this is a .44 Magnum, the most powerful handgun in the world, and would blow your head clean off, you have to ask yourself one question: 'Do I feel lucky?' Well, do you, punk?"

## TRIVIA

 Believe it or not, Andy Robinson, the unforgettable psycho killer in this movie, played the title part in *Liberace*, a made-for-TV movie.

# MAGNUM FORCE (1973)

## RATINGS

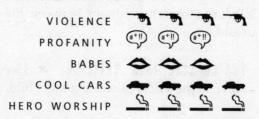

| | | | | |
|---|---|---|---|---|
| VIOLENCE | 🔫 | 🔫 | 🔫 | 🔫 |
| PROFANITY | @*!! | @*!! | @*!! | |
| BABES | 👄 | 👄 | 👄 | |
| COOL CARS | 🚗 | 🚗 | 🚗 | 🚗 |
| HERO WORSHIP | 🚬 | 🚬 | 🚬 | 🚬 |

## WHAT HAPPENS ▰ Just to prove he doesn't believe in vigilante justice, Harry hunts down the killer(s) who is/are shooting mobsters and drug dealers with a Magnum. But don't think that makes him any more popular with the brass than he was before; he still launches a barrage of rude re-

torts whenever they get in his sights. Harry also has to defend his title as the SFPD's best marksman against a trio of young motorcycle cops who are a bit too brash and more than a little too sharp with their Magnums for Harry's comfort. In the end, though, he proves that guns—even big ones—don't kill punks, Harry Callahan does.

**THE CAST** ◾ Clint continues his reliance on Brylcreem to sustain his six-inch-high hair in this movie and adds even more sideburn than he sported in the first *Dirty Harry*. This antiauthoritarian hairstyle sets him in marked contrast to the clean-cut motorcycle cops, played by Tim "Otter" Matheson, Robert "Dan Tanna" Urich, and David "Hutch" Soul. They're guided by the Harry-hatin' Lieutenant Briggs, a role that Hal Holbrook plays with lots of extra grease; before it's over, he gets a headache from Harry that he deserves.

**HONEY, YOU'LL LIKE THIS MOVIE ...** ◾ Because you always thought Hutch was cuter than Starsky.

**DON'T MISS**
- Those few blissful moments of topless frolicking by the pool before the bad cops show up.
- The marksmanship contest: All the clues as to how the movie turns out are in this sequence.

**MEMORABLE LINES**
"A man's got to know his limitations," says Harry, knowing that in his world too few do.

**TRIVIA**

Stare through the glare in that pool scene and you'll see a snatch of Suzanne Somers.

# THE ENFORCER (1976)

## RATINGS

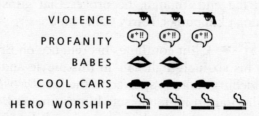

| | |
|---|---|
| VIOLENCE | 🔫 🔫 🔫 |
| PROFANITY | #*!! #*!! #*!! |
| BABES | 👄 👄 |
| COOL CARS | 🚗 🚗 🚗 |
| HERO WORSHIP | 🚬 🚬 🚬 🚬 |

**WHAT HAPPENS** ⚞ You might call Harry's methods extreme—his supervisors certainly do, and he's sent to work in personnel after a particularly excessive incident. During interviews for new detectives, Harry encounters the women's movement in the form of an earnest but wholly inexperienced female cop, whom he grills mercilessly. So, of course, she becomes his new partner when he returns to the streets. Together (or really, with her chasing after him) they pursue a band of criminals who have stolen heavy weapons from an Army depot and who threaten the city of San Francisco with mass destruction. Harry gets them all—including, finally, their leader, who's fried in his own juices.

**THE CAST** ⚞ Insolence is Callahan's main mode in this movie, and Clint fires off his high-powered sarcasm with the same accuracy his Magnum is famous for. His main targets are his captain, played with pencil-necked pusillanimity by Bradford Dillman, and his eager new partner, played by Tyne Daly (before she became the TV cop Marybeth Lacey).

**HONEY, YOU'LL LIKE THIS MOVIE ...** ⚞ Because Harry learns an appreciation for women's roles on the police force.

## DON'T MISS

When a criminal chased across rooftops by Harry crashes through a skylight right into the middle of a porn movie shoot. You get a brief glimpse of full frontal nudity before Harry crashes through, too.

## MEMORABLE LINES

- As Harry hands over his badge to the captain, Harry says, "Here's your seven-point suppository."
- Whenever Harry's partner is explaining herself, he grunts out a simple "Marvelous."

# SUDDEN IMPACT (1983)

## RATINGS

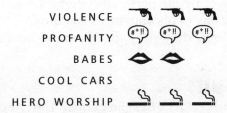

| | |
|---|---|
| VIOLENCE | 🔫 🔫 🔫 |
| PROFANITY | (#*!!) (#*!!) (#*!!) |
| BABES | 👄 👄 |
| COOL CARS | |
| HERO WORSHIP | 🚬 🚬 🚬 |

**WHAT HAPPENS** ▰ Two corpses are found—one in San Francisco and the other in a small coastal town to the north—with similar gunshot wounds to the head and—cover your eyes—groin. Harry is sent north to aggravate the local police chief and gather evidence for the investigation back home. There he meets a soft-spoken blond artist who paints shrieking pictures; a butch redhead with a feel for men and women; and a sadistic creep whose weapon won't fire. Harry breaks up this loveless triangle, solves the mystery, and lets his heart (or his dick; your call) overrule the law.

**THE CAST** ■ In the ten years since we last saw Harry Callahan, Clint's features have definitely softened and his hair has been tamed down to four inches high, but he's still as sarcastic and unyielding as ever. Sondra Locke, Clint's real-life woman at the time, plays the artist as wary and restrained, until she is unleashed in a final frenzy. Bradford Dillman is again his boss. And Albert Popwell has undergone an amazing rehabilitation: In the first *Dirty Harry*, he was a bank robber; in *The Enforcer*, he was the hostile leader of a black militant group. In this movie, he is Harry's partner, Horace.

**HONEY, YOU'LL LIKE THIS MOVIE . . .** ■ Because Clint empowers the woman to help him balance the scales of justice.

## DON'T MISS

- Harry delivering his personal congratulations to a mobster on the day of his daughter's wedding.
- The Las Vegas showgirl with whom the maniac tries his luck.

## MEMORABLE LINES

The one that President Reagan quoted: Harry busts in on a robbery at his favorite coffee shop, and one of the criminals grabs a hostage, pointing a gun at her. When the guy threatens to kill the hostage if Harry doesn't back off, Harry just aims his Magnum at the guy and says through gritted teeth, "Go ahead. Make my day."

# THE DEAD POOL (1988)

## RATINGS

VIOLENCE
PROFANITY
BABES
COOL CARS
HERO WORSHIP

**WHAT HAPPENS** ▬ Here's a cheery little game you can try with your friends: Each player lists celebrities he believes will die within two months; the player with the most dead people named on his list at the end of the game wins. That's exactly what the players of "The Dead Pool" do in this movie, except that someone starts killing off the celebrities on the list belonging to an English horror movie director. Which would be cause enough to involve Homicide Inspector Harry Callahan, but when his name appears on the list, his concern becomes even more urgent. Harry does spare a little of his attention for a TV reporter digging for more than just a scoop on the investigation. The ending, in a bull's-eye shot of self-reference, comes down to how many shots are left in Harry's gun.

**THE CAST** ▬ Clint has aged well—Harry's voice is a little gruffer, his hair is a little grayer, and all those new lines on his face make him look even meaner when he grits his teeth. As the horror movie director, Liam Neeson parries Harry's sarcasm with equally sharp cynical barbs. Goofball comedian Jim Carrey plays the junkie rock star almost straight-faced—which makes the parody that much funnier.

**HONEY, YOU'LL LIKE THIS MOVIE ...** ▰ Because you can picture Irish hunk Liam Neeson in that skirt he wore in *Rob Roy*.

**DON'T MISS**
- How, with a carton of cigarettes, Harry arranges for some protection from a mobster he helped put in jail.
- The miniature Corvette chasing Harry through the streets of San Francisco.

**TRIVIA**

The number of Harry Callahan's partners who are killed or badly wounded (somebody ought to call OSHA!):
*Dirty Harry* 1
*The Enforcer* 2
*Magnum Force* 1
*Sudden Impact* 1
*The Dead Pool* 1

# BILLY BADD (1980)

## RATINGS

| | | | |
|---|---|---|---|
| VIOLENCE | 🔫 | 🔫 | 🔫 |
| PROFANITY | @*!! | @*!! | @*!! | @*!! |
| BABES | 👄 | 👄 | 👄 |
| COOL CARS | 🚗 | 🚗 | 🚗 |
| HERO WORSHIP | 🚬 | | |

**WHAT HAPPENS** ▰ One hundred miles from nowhere (as the opening title reads), hot and horny Zoey and her boyfriend, Frankie, stop by the side of the road to make the beast with two backs. They get the unsettling feeling that they're being watched and, sure enough, as soon as they get back on the road they encounter a wacko on a motorcycle who wants to torture them for laughs. He takes them on a joyride to hell, killing a cop and letting the couple have a look into his warped past.

**THE CAST** ▰ The acting in this movie is so hilariously bad that the only believable action you'll see on the screen is the deaths of the careers any of these people may have once hoped for.

**WHY GUYS LOVE IT** ▰ Billy really is baaaaaad.

**HONEY, YOU'LL LIKE THIS MOVIE . . .** ▰ Because Zoey doesn't abandon Frankie even when good sense tells her she ought to.

**DON'T MISS**
- The opening sequence, when Zoey decides to share her charms with a truck driver.
- Billy relieving himself on the road right in front of their car.

**MEMORABLE LINE**
"You motherfucker," Zoey says to Billy.
 "Brother and sister fucker, too," Billy quickly adds.

# DIE HARD (1988)

**RATINGS**

| VIOLENCE | 🔫 🔫 🔫 🔫 |
| PROFANITY | @*!! @*!! @*!! @*!! |
| BABES | |
| COOL CARS | 🚗 |
| HERO WORSHIP | 🚬 🚬 🚬 🚬 |

**WHAT HAPPENS** ▰ A well-trained troop of professional criminals (presenting themselves as terrorists) take over a Los Angeles office tower during a Christmas party. The only thing the bad guys haven't planned for is the presence of the estranged husband of one employee. The husband is a feisty New York City cop who wages his own guerrilla war against the criminals from inside the office building. The sky-

No one dies harder than Bruce Willis.

20TH CENTURY FOX/SHOOTING STAR

scraper-scale stunts are punctuated with amusing potshots at the press, the FBI, and inept police commanders. The final blows are delivered by the wife and a gun-shy cop.

CAST ▰ Bruce Willis arms the cop, John McClane, with the smart-ass wit that he honed on TV in *Moonlighting* and the subversive style we love most in our heroes. English actor Alan Rickman calls the shots for the criminals with a clipped German accent and a pragmatic self-confidence. Russian ballet dancer Aleksander Godunov, as Henchman #1, performs a vicious pas de deux with McClane at the movie's crescendo. Bonnie Bedelia is the wife, who's not exactly overjoyed to see her husband until he happens to rescue her. Reginald VelJohnson is no braver as the first L.A.

cop on the scene than he is when confronting doofus Steve Urkel on TV's *Family Matters*. William Atherton is Dick the TV reporter without a conscience, a part he prepared for well as Dick the EPA agent in *Ghostbusters*.

## WHY GUYS LOVE IT ☞ Wouldn't you want an entire office building in which to play hide 'n' seek with live ammunition?

## HONEY, YOU'LL LIKE THIS MOVIE ... ☞ Because it's Rapunzel retold: A valiant man rescues his princess trapped in a tower.

## DON'T MISS
- McClane's escape from the rooftop with the help of a fire hose.
- The bonus help the good guys get from the loafing limo driver.

## MEMORABLE LINES
Hang on to this one, because it will resurface: Hans, the chief terrorist, calls McClane "another shallow American raised on John Wayne movies," but McClane states his preference for Roy Rogers, then punctuates his comment with a jaunty "Yippee kai yea, motherfucker."

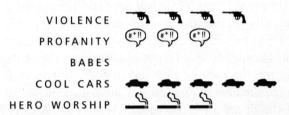

# DIE HARD 2:
# DIE HARDER (1990)

## RATINGS

| | |
|---|---|
| VIOLENCE | 🔫 🔫 🔫 🔫 |
| PROFANITY | (#*!!) (#*!!) (#*!!) |
| BABES | |
| COOL CARS | 🚗 🚗 🚗 🚗 🚗 |
| HERO WORSHIP | 🚬 🚬 🚬 |

**WHAT HAPPENS** ▬ **I**f you see New York City cop John Mc-Clane in a public place, head quickly in the other direction. In this movie, he comes to Dulles Airport in Washington, D.C., to meet his wife's incoming flight, but he cannot help becoming involved when mercenaries with a very complex plan assume command of the airport's control tower so that they can free a prisoner whose plane is arriving at the airport. Though McClane's input is not welcomed by any of the authorities on the scene—the airport management, the police or the Special Forces squad called in to fight the mercenaries—he repeatedly outhustles and outthinks and outwisecracks them. One bad guy gets an up-close look at an icicle, another flies inside an airplane engine. And in the last possible moment, McClane, battered and bruised, cooks the big, bad guy in his own juices. As in the first *Die Hard*, this movie directs its most unforgiving assault on TV news reporters.

**THE CAST** ▬ **M**ost of the originals are back: Bruce Willis as John McClane still veers between sharp-tongued retorts and screaming indignation at the authorities. McClane's wife, played by Bonnie Bedelia, has little to do in this movie except sneer at William Atherton, the Dick TV reporter who happens to be on the same flight as she is. William Sadler (who battles with Steven Seagal in *Hard to Kill*) has the skeletal grin and coldhearted arrogance that is a prerequisite for the job of head mercenary. We've all seen too much of Dennis Franz's butt in his role of Andy Sipowicz on *N.Y.P.D. Blue,* but his familiar impatience and perpetually cranky disposition are welcome in his role as the chief of the airport police. As the airport director, Fred Dalton Thompson reinforces his image as the official Authority Figure, the part he's played in every movie you've seen him in (*In the Line of Fire,* etc.). John Amos shows up as the head of the Special Forces squad. Watch for Robert Patrick, the guy who was the T1000 in *Terminator 2,* or you might miss him.

## WHY GUYS LOVE IT ▰ Any movie that attempts to blow up more big stuff than the first *Die Hard* is worth one hour and forty-five minutes of your time, isn't it?

## HONEY, YOU'LL LIKE THIS MOVIE ... ▰ Because the only reason McClane gets involved is to ensure that his wife arrives safely.

## DON'T MISS
- The snowmobile chase. You just don't see enough of those in the movies.
- The chance to fast-forward through the opening scene, when the head mercenary does his tai chi in the nude— you don't want to see his bony ass any more than you want to see Dennis Franz's chubby one.

## MEMORABLE LINES
Who doesn't remember, "Yippee kai yea, motherfucker"?

# DIE HARD: WITH A VENGEANCE (1995)

## RATINGS

| | |
|---|---|
| VIOLENCE | |
| PROFANITY | |
| BABES | |
| COOL CARS | |
| HERO WORSHIP | |

**WHAT HAPPENS** ◢ **A** mad bomber named Simon threatens to blow up crowded sites in New York City if John McClane doesn't play Simon Says with him. McClane is commanded by the bomber to wear a racially insulting sandwich board in Harlem and is then rescued by a local business owner named Zeus, who thus earns the ire of the bomber, too. Simon runs these two all over the city, along with most of New York City's finest, while he commits a fiendishly clever robbery elsewhere. When McClane and Zeus stop bickering long enough for McClane to apply his already proven capacity to outwit fiendishly clever criminals (see *Die Hard* and *Die Hard 2: Die Harder*), he unravels Simon's scheme and brings him crashing down.

**THE CAST** ◢ **B**ruce Willis plays a grubby McClane who has spiraled downward from his out-of-town triumphs— he's divorced, the N.Y.P.D. has him on suspension, and he's hung over—but he can still fire off a one-liner with lethal accuracy. Samuel L. Jackson gives Zeus a Malcolm X look and a quick tongue to match McClane's. Jeremy Irons stretches his shirt with previously unseen muscles and his accent into a familiar clipped German as Simon. Graham

Greene, the real-life Native American who played the Indian chief in *Dances with Wolves,* is cast out of the cultural straitjacket to play a plausibly heroic New York City cop.

## WHY GUYS LOVE IT ✒ It's the third stop on a tour of exploding major cities.

## HONEY, YOU'LL LIKE THIS MOVIE ... ✒ Because it confronts the issues of race communications in America head on.

## DON'T MISS
Our heroes' cab ride through Central Park.

## MEMORABLE LINES
Stick with what has worked before: "Yippee kai yea, motherfucker."

**TRIVIA**

Believe it or not, an early version of this movie's script was not supposed to be *Die Hard 3* but, rather, *Lethal Weapon 4.*

# FIRST BLOOD (1982)

## RATINGS

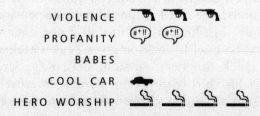

| | |
|---|---|
| VIOLENCE | 🔫 🔫 🔫 |
| PROFANITY | 💬 💬 |
| BABES | |
| COOL CAR | 🚗 |
| HERO WORSHIP | 🚬 🚬 🚬 🚬 |

*Rambo,* the only man more American than Rocky.

SHOOTING STAR

**WHAT HAPPENS** ■ A shaggy-haired Vietnam vet wanders into a small town in the Northwest, where he's picked up by the hard-nosed local sheriff, escorted to the city limits, and told his kind are unwelcome. The vet, John Rambo, declines the sheriff's invitation to leave and he's arrested. In the local jail, Rambo has vivid flashbacks of the prison camp where he was held during the war and his torturers there, and he erupts into jaguar-quick hand-to-hand combat that leads to his escape from the jail and into the woods outside of town. The sheriff and all of his resources (many deputies, National Guard Reserves, dogs) engage in a full-scale duel with the vet—a top-of-his-class Green Beret—and his very large and handy knife, which he uses to build very lethal jungle traps and some nice canvas duds for himself. Before it's over, the vet has wounded most of the deputies, pock-marked the whole town with bullets, and asked America to build the Vietnam Veterans Memorial, so he can have a place to visit with the only real friends he ever had.

**THE CAST** ▬ A presteroids Sylvester Stallone (cowriter of the screenplay) plays John Rambo as hurt, almost pouting, about his mistreatment. That is, until he's pushed too far. Hulking Brian Dennehy has made a career out of playing tough-guy cops who just can't see past their soft underbelly and, as the sheriff here, you can smell his desperation that sours with every failed confrontation with Rambo. Dennehy commands the obedience of his deputies who are quickly less than enthusiastic about pursuing Rambo—especial-ly David Caruso, who acted a lot tougher on TV's *N.Y.P.D. Blue* than he does against Rambo. Richard Crenna shows up as Colonel Trautman, the Army officer who trained Rambo—he comes to talk Rambo down and to warn the sheriff to back off, but he's rooting for Rambo all the way.

**WHY GUYS LOVE IT** ▬ With just a knife and Green Beret training, one real guy can take on a whole army.

**HONEY, YOU'LL LIKE THIS MOVIE ...** ▬ Because it's a classic American tale of the struggle of one man for respect and liberty against the tyranny of the community. And the one man happens to spend a lot of time with his shirt off.

**DON'T MISS**
Rambo's stitching his own wound—talk about your HMOs.

**MEMORABLE LINES**
"Is there any law against me getting something to eat in this town?" asks Rambo.
"Yeah, me," answers the sheriff.

# RAMBO: FIRST BLOOD PART II (1985)

## RATINGS

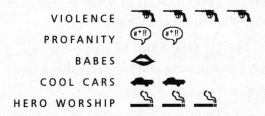

| | |
|---|---|
| VIOLENCE | 🔫 🔫 🔫 🔫 |
| PROFANITY | (#*!!) (#*!!) |
| BABES | 👄 |
| COOL CARS | 🚗 🚗 |
| HERO WORSHIP | 🚬 🚬 🚬 |

**WHAT HAPPENS** ► Our hero, John Rambo, is sprung from prison by his former commander, Colonel Trautman, to go on an unofficial mission to determine if American prisoners of war are still being held in Vietnam. When Rambo finds the POWs, he disregards his orders to merely observe and leave—no, he personally takes on a whole camp full of Vietnamese soldiers and a few Russians, too, with an amazing arsenal (that bow and arrow is no Indian Guides leftover) and the help of an equally disenfranchised (and very attractive) Amer-Asian girl. Rambo does get to right some wrongs by killing the acknowledged enemy with vigor (and a bit of glee), but he's left only to rage and shoot up the office of the true enemy: the American intelligence officers who betray him.

**CAST** ► Sylvester Stallone is back as Rambo, and he's obviously undertaken an intensive weight-lifting program while behind bars. He's still sulking—as he was in *First Blood*—and the chip on his shoulder has grown. Richard Crenna is still Colonel Trautman, who's duped into setting his man up. Charles Napier is suitably sleazy as Murdock, the intelligence officer that assigns Rambo the job of looking for the POWs and then abandons him when the prisoners are found. When the Vietnamese run out of ideas on how to make Rambo suffer after they capture him, they call in a calm, deliberate, and utterly menacing Russian played by Steven Berkoff.

## WHY GUYS LOVE IT ▰ If at first you don't win a war, try, try again—but with bigger weapons.

## HONEY, YOU'LL LIKE THIS MOVIE ... ▰ Because Rambo has even more muscle and less shirt this time.

## MEMORABLE LINES

Rambo asks Trautman, "Do we get to win this time?"

**CHECK OUT**

If you want proof that even nonstop explosions and totally pointless destruction can be boring, watch *Rambo III*.

# LETHAL WEAPON (1987)

## RATINGS

| | |
|---|---|
| VIOLENCE | 🔫 🔫 🔫 |
| PROFANITY | 💬 💬 |
| BABES | 👄 |
| COOL CARS | 🚗 🚗 🚗 |
| HERO WORSHIP | 🚬 🚬 🚬 |

## WHAT HAPPENS ▰ Detective Roger Murtaugh has a lot to live for—a loving family, a nice house, a boat—and he's a

cop because that's a good job he believes in doing well. Detective Martin Riggs can think of nothing to live for and he's a cop because it's the only job where he can use the skills he learned as a Special Forces commando in Vietnam. So, naturally, Roger and Martin are made partners. Their first case together involves Roger's war buddy and a ruthless crew of mercenaries on the wrong side of the drug war. When the mercs kidnap Roger's daughter, he and Martin counterattack, then endure some serious torture, but they get their fair share of the licks in before the fiery finale.

**THE CAST** ▰ Danny Glover is an unsteady Roger Murtaugh, made anxious by the volatility of the calmer Martin Riggs, played by Mel Gibson. They are believable as real partners, because soon enough they are bickering about who drives and about how to handle interrogations. The General's top aide is Gary Busey's Mr. Joshua, another Special Forces alumni who takes special joy in following orders to terminate.

**WHY GUYS LOVE IT** ▰ When a suicidal cop with expertise in death like Riggs squares off with a highly trained killing machine without a conscience (Mr. Joshua), someone's sure to end up hurt.

**HONEY, YOU'LL LIKE THIS MOVIE . . .** ▰ Because it shows real drama in the home lives of police officers.

**DON'T MISS**
- Martin's unconventional strategy for bringing down a guy threatening to jump from a tall building.
- The General's hot test of Mr. Joshua's loyalty.

**MEMORABLE LINES**
- "Have you ever meet anyone you didn't kill?" Roger asks Martin.

- "If you tell me everything you know," Mr. Joshua offers to Martin, "I promise to kill you quickly."

# LETHAL WEAPON 2 (1989)

## RATINGS

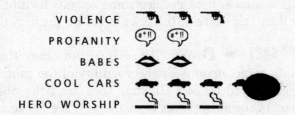

| | |
|---|---|
| VIOLENCE | 🔫 🔫 🔫 |
| PROFANITY | 💬 💬 |
| BABES | 👄 👄 |
| COOL CARS | 🚗 🚗 🚗 ⬤ |
| HERO WORSHIP | 🚬 🚬 🚬 |

**WHAT HAPPENS** ▬ The mismatched cops—edgy Martin Riggs and cautious family man Roger Murtaugh—are back, but instead of being aggravated by each other, they've got Leo Getz, a hyper-happy accountant who is set to testify against the syndicates he laundered money for. Now, Riggs and Murtaugh are supposed to be protecting Getz, but they're too preoccupied with a bund of South African diplomats (especially their secretary, in Riggs's case). So they take Getz along when they raid the Boers' house and use him in their plan to wreak a bit of fun havoc at the embassy. But the boys do pull Getz out before Riggs brings the whole house down.

**THE CAST** ▬ Riggs is still thinking suicide until he meets dainty blond Rika van den Haas (Patsy Kensit), who almost instantly falls for the Mel Gibson charm. After he meets her, he's thinking about a resurrection of his lust. And later, when he learns the dark truth about his past, Riggs thinks nothing but kill. Danny Glover's Roger Murtaugh has his mind on his wife and kids, and the addition to the house. His rear end, however, is on a bomb. Joe Pesci is a warp-speed Leo Getz, who tries too hard to get the boys to like him. Joss Ackland is the chief of the Afrikaners and is as smug and loathsome as any official of the Master Race. His chief henchman, played pure and nasty by Derrick O'Connor, knows lots of Riggs's moves, but not all of them.

## WHY GUYS LOVE IT ▰ The bureaucrats of white South Africa are as close as we can get to the Nazis, the great villains of our fathers.

## HONEY YOU'LL LIKE THIS MOVIE . . . ▰ Because just look at what the Murtaughs are doing with their house.

## DON'T MISS
- Murtaugh nailing one of these guys right between the eyes.
- Murtaugh's appeal for a visa to South Africa downstairs, while Riggs takes his application upstairs.
- The TV debut of Murtaugh's daughter.

## MEMORABLE LINES
- "They fuck you at the drive-thru," Getz philosophizes.
- "Diplomatic immunity," the head South African claims. "Revoked," Murtaugh proclaims.

### CHECH OUT

You can watch *Lethal Weapon 3* without suffering, but everything it has to offer—except the addition of an ass-kicking Internal Affairs babe—has already been done in these first two movies.

# NOWHERE TO RUN (1993)

## RATINGS

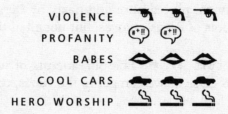

| | | | |
|---|---|---|---|
| VIOLENCE | 🔫 | 🔫 | 🔫 |
| PROFANITY | @*!! | @*!! | |
| BABES | 👄 | 👄 | 👄 |
| COOL CARS | 🚗 | 🚗 | 🚗 |
| HERO WORSHIP | 🚬 | 🚬 | 🚬 |

**WHAT HAPPENS** ▬ **A** busload of convicts is stopped on the road by a reckless driver, the guards are killed, and the prisoners escape. One con hides from the police in the woods, on the property of a terribly lonely young widow and her two children. And the con invades their lives just in time, because the family is being terrorized by a coldhearted developer, his hired strongman, and crooked cops who want the widow to sell her property. She declines their offer. Fortunately, her children strike up a friendship with the con, and he comes to her aid—relieving her loneliness and battling the bad guys without regard for his own safety and freedom. What a guy: He even runs into a burning barn to rescue the neighbor's horses.

**THE CAST** ▬ Jean-Claude Van Damme, the Muscles from Brussels, is the mistakenly convicted hero. As soon as he catches a glimpse of full-frontal nudity from the widow, Rosanna Arquette, he is hooked. Kieran Culkin, brother of Macauley Culkin, is the widow's little boy, who can't wait for her to sleep with his new best friend. And check out the hired gun: It's Ted Levine, the guy who was Jame Gumb, the transvestite psychopath in *The Silence of the Lambs*.

**WHY GUYS LOVE IT** ▰ One look at Rosanna Arquette getting ready for her bath and any of us would violate our unauthorized parole.

**HONEY, YOU'LL LIKE THIS MOVIE** ... ▰ Because this is an equal opportunity film—you'll get to see Van Damme's bare butt, too.

### DON'T MISS

- The heartwarming conversation around the dinner table as the widow and her children discuss the size of Van Damme's penis.
- The vintage Triumph motorcycle he restores and then uses at that most critical of moments.

## CHECK OUT

If you like Van Damme, but . . .
want more gunplay, try *Universal Soldier*
want more fist fighting, try *Kickboxer*
want more romance . . .
how about something with Richard Gere?

# UNDER SIEGE (1992)

### RATINGS

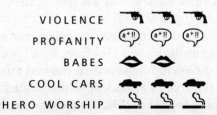

VIOLENCE

PROFANITY

BABES

COOL CARS

HERO WORSHIP

**WHAT HAPPENS** ✦ A surprise party for the captain of the U.S.S. *Missouri* is part of a plot by a rogue CIA operative and an unstable naval officer to seize control of the famous battleship and steal its nuclear missiles. All goes according to diabolical plan but for the ship's cook, who coincidentally is a Navy SEAL—or maybe he's an undercover SEAL who coincidentally knows how to make bouillabaisse. In either case, the cook (with the help of Miss July and a couple guys from the ship's laundry) demonstrates 101 ways to slaughter a mercenary and disrupts the conspirators' elaborate plans. Back home at the Pentagon, the brass stumble around for a response and grill the weaselly CIA manager about how his boy went ballistic. In the end, the psychotic naval officer gets his from a distance, while the operative gone beserk comes to an eye-poppin' finish at close quarters.

**CAST** ✦ We all know that Steven Seagal can punch and chop like a black belt, but who knew that he was an expert in the culinary arts, too? Well, cook Casey Ryback knows quite a few interesting recipes: He can even make a bomb with readily available household chemicals and then detonate it in the microwave. Tommy Lee Jones loses his rudder from the start—veering wildly from cold, calculating CIA agent to recycled hippie caught in the throes of a terminal flashback. Gary Busey's wacko Commander Krill is abusive and bitter, and holds a steady, undefined grudge against our insubordinate hero—everything you'd want in a second-in-command. Erika Eleniak is a very convincing Miss July—and not just because she was *Playboy*'s Miss July 1989. If you want to see the definition of slimy bureacrat, watch Nick Mancuso's CIA middle manager wriggle out of responsibility for Jones's bad attitude. *Star Trek* fans, look for Colm Meaney from *The Next Generation* as one of the bad guys. And who's that playing the role of President of the United States in the movie's opening sequence? Oh, it's George Bush.

**WHY GUYS LOVE IT** ▰ The Navy—It's not just a job, it's a chance to blow away a lot of bad guys on a really cool big boat.

**HONEY, YOU'LL LIKE THIS MOVIE . . .** ▰ Because if it only were broadcast on the Food Channel.

## DON'T MISS
- Busey launch a major hocker into Seagal's soup, just to piss him off (bad idea, Gary).
- Miss July's delirious striptease for no one but Seagal.
- The guys in the welding room get killed by a steel girder, a band saw, and a hand-extracted Adam's apple.

## MEMORABLE LINES
- Jones asks CIA manager (over the phone), "Did you get those two forefingers I sent you in the mail?"
- A cowardly sailor reluctant to help Seagal says, "I spent the Gulf War ironing."

# UNDER SIEGE 2: DARK TERRITORY (1995)

## RATINGS

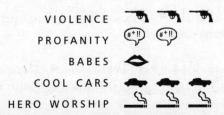

| | |
|---|---|
| VIOLENCE | 🔫 🔫 🔫 |
| PROFANITY | (#*!!) (#*!!) |
| BABES | 👄 |
| COOL CARS | 🚗 🚗 🚗 |
| HERO WORSHIP | 🚬 🚬 🚬 |

**WHAT HAPPENS** ▪ The ass-kickin' cook/Navy SEAL Casey Ryback returns—though he seems to have left the Navy and taken a job as full-time chef since we last saw him. This time he's on a passenger train with his sassy teenage niece when a crew of mercenaries and a disgruntled but brilliant weapons designer board and commandeer the train. These cruelly efficient criminals try to take the Free World hostage and collect billions in user fees from tyrants everywhere with a computer-guided satellite weapon. And these mad bad guys would have succeeded if only they had caught a train that didn't have as a passenger a certain remarkably resourceful cook with an ever-ready recipe for subversion and mammoth explosion.

**THE CAST** ▪ Steven Seagal may have shed the military cover he wore in the first *Under Siege,* but he has hung on to his slightly cross-eyed glare (meant to signify his intensity, no doubt), his vast knowledge of homemade bombs, and his arsenal of nonchalant one-liners. Seagal needs all of those to stop the genius/lunatic portrayed by a wild-eyed Eric Bogosian and his hired hand, another human weapon gone bad, played by Everett McGill. Newcomer Katherine Heigl is Seagal's niece, Sara, and she's got a few moves of her own—most of which she expends on an overeager porter. That porter, played with a nearly plausible degree of reluctance and enthusiasm by Morris Chestnut (from *Boyz N the Hood*), is all the help Ryback needs—though the same admirals and weaselly CIA agent are back from the first movie and are equally futile in their attempts to stop the madman hell-bent on destroying America.

**WHY GUYS LOVE IT** ▪ These villains aren't just greedy or bad; they're crazy and cruel.

**HONEY, YOU'LL LIKE THIS MOVIE ...** ▪ Because Casey is a sensitive guy struggling to communicate with his teenage niece.

## DON'T MISS

- Ryback's idea of a very dry martini . . . it's powder dry.
- The few brief but cool shots of the Stealth in flight.

## MEMORABLE LINES

- "Good evening, ladies and gentleman, this is your captor speaking," Bogosian announces to the passengers.
- "I am not trained for this," Seagal says about dealing with his niece. "This I am trained for," Seagal says when he sees blood on the kitchen floor.

## *Arnold in Action*

Arnold Schwarzenegger is in a class by himself. He really is as big as he seems on the screen—unlike most other action heroes—and he doesn't try to force emotional subtleties into his characters. They are all men of much action and few words. Most of all, he rarely fails to deliver just what we expect: high body counts and stinging one-liners. Here are what I think are the best of Arnold's movies, though all of his movies—even *Kindergarten Cop*—will keep a guy entertained.

# PREDATOR (1987)

## RATINGS

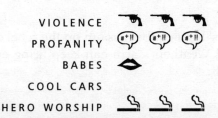

VIOLENCE

PROFANITY

BABES

COOL CARS

HERO WORSHIP

**WHAT HAPPENS** ■ A crew of mercenaries straight from central casting—a Bubba, a little guy with a big mouth, a smart guy, a dark and dangerous African-American, a taciturn Indian tracker, and their extremely muscular leader—arrives in the Latin American jungle to look for lost American operatives. The mercs find a rebel outpost, which they shoot up, and kill everyone in sight except an angry, impoverished young woman (who, thankfully, hasn't been oppressed by American-style underwear). While the mercs are transporting her to their base, they are mysteriously killed off one by one, until finally only the leader and a mysterious, dreadlocked creature from outer space are left for a showdown. The brawny leader ultimately must rely on his brains to stop the Creature-Mon.

**THE CAST** ■ Arnold Schwarzenegger has the muscle to lead the band of tough mercs that includes wrestler Jesse "The Body" Ventura, and he surely has the brains. Carl Weathers (Apollo Creed in *Rocky*) is the group's CIA contact who gets it early and good. The Creature is played by Kevin Peter Hall—not that you can tell.

**WHY GUYS LOVE IT** ■ Arnold Schwarzenegger outsmarting a creature from a race that can reach Earth? It could happen . . .

**HONEY, YOU'LL LIKE THIS MOVIE . . .** ■ Because Arnold has to rely on his wits, which means you get to see why Maria fell for him.

**DON'T MISS**
- The mercs' high-caliber assault on the rebel compound.
- How Carl Weathers's arm can keep firing even after it's hacked off.

## MEMORABLE ARNOLD LINES
- "If it bleeds, we can kill it."
- "You're one ugly mother . . ."

**BEWARE**

In *Predator 2*, the creature comes to the United States, but Arnold is nowhere to be found.

# THE RUNNING MAN (1987)

## RATINGS

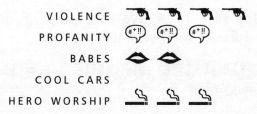

VIOLENCE

PROFANITY

BABES

COOL CARS

HERO WORSHIP

**WHAT HAPPENS** ▬ In the year 2019, a cop refuses to fire on women and children who are rioting for food, and the authorities he defies launch a media campaign depicting him as a mass murderer. He's convicted, he goes to jail, then breaks out and goes to the apartment of a buddy. The buddy is gone, but his hot sister is there and he uses her to help him escape. When they're captured, they're offered their freedom in exchange for participating in a wildly popular game show called *The Running Man*, which ain't exactly a Merv Griffin production. The game involves placing the contestants in an enclosed space with different goons—one is armed with a chain saw, another pair is dressed like hockey goalies with razor-blade sticks—and the audience wagers on when and how they will be killed. The show's host and producer shamelessly promotes the suffering of the contestants to build ratings.

## THE CAST ▰ Arnold Schwarzenegger and Maria Conchita Alonso—the cop and the woman—engage in a battle of crippling accents, but they both look good in the skintight outfits they wear for the game. Richard Dawson plays the game show host—and the survey says, Over the Top. Yaphet Kotto volunteers for the game, too, and he depends on Arnold to carry his keister. Former football player Jim Brown and wrestler Jesse "The Body" Ventura (who also appeared with Arnold in *Predator*) are on the opposing team in the game. Dweezil Zappa and Mick "Fleetwood Mac" Fleetwood show up as rebels who help Arnold when he escapes prison.

## WHY GUYS LOVE IT ▰ We've all imagined our own rules for game shows: You lose, you die.

## HONEY, YOU'LL LIKE THIS MOVIE . . . ▰ Because you loved *Family Feud*.

## DON'T MISS
Maria Conchita Alonso's sheer workout gear.

## MEMORABLE LINES
Arnold says to Dawson, "I'll be back," which we've heard before, but apparently Dawson had not. . . .

# THE TERMINATOR (1984)

## RATINGS

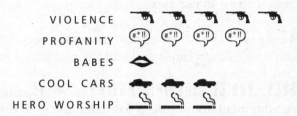

| | |
|---|---|
| VIOLENCE | 🔫🔫🔫🔫🔫 |
| PROFANITY | @*!! @*!! @*!! @*!! |
| BABES | 👄 |
| COOL CARS | 🚗🚗🚗 |
| HERO WORSHIP | 🚬🚬🚬 |

**WHAT HAPPENS** ✒ See if you can follow this: A robotic assassin, The Terminator, is sent back through time by the machines that rule the post-Armageddon future to kill Sarah Connor, a twentieth-century woman who will give birth to John Connor, the leader of the rebel humans of the future. If you can't follow all that, don't worry, because what matters is that an indestructible killing machine with a human face and a severely limited vocabulary pursues a young, very frightened woman relentlessly, undeterred by the damage that puny conventional weapons can inflict upon it. Sarah's only reliable ally is a human soldier sent back from the future by the rebels to protect her. The Terminator trashes a police station, walks out of a flaming truck, and is eventually stripped down to his metal skeleton in his pursuit of her. The movie ends when she gets a crush on him.

**THE CAST** ✒ Arnold Schwarzenegger's looks are pure menace, his movement is plodding, his faintly accented speech is a monotone—just perfect for the part of a nearly human machine. Linda Hamilton (she was the beauty in the *Beauty and Beast* TV series) is wide-eyed and shocked as Sarah Connor, the young woman who finds herself the sole object of The Terminator's interests. Michael Biehn is the other guy from the future and he tries hard to win Sarah's—and the audience's—trust, and he does get his shot in before it's over for him. Veteran actor Paul Winfield plays the cop who takes her in, Dick Miller a shrink who develops an ongoing interest in her case.

## WHY GUYS LOVE IT ▰ The Terminator gets "killed" more than a half dozen times and still the nightmare isn't over.

## HONEY, YOU'LL LIKE THIS MOVIE ... ▰ Because this film is a statement about how a woman must fend for herself in a hostile world.

## DON'T MISS
The Terminator's discreet visit to a local punk club, where some of the regulars offer to do his hair for him.

## MEMORABLE LINES
You surely have found plenty of opportunities to use The Terminator's nonchalant "I'll be back," and his belligerent "Fuck you, asshole" in your daily life.

# TERMINATOR 2: JUDGMENT DAY (1991)

## RATINGS

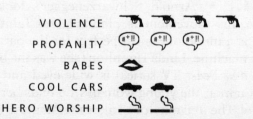

| | |
|---|---|
| VIOLENCE | 🔫 🔫 🔫 🔫 |
| PROFANITY | #*!! #*!! #*!! |
| BABES | 👄 |
| COOL CARS | 🚗 🚗 |
| HERO WORSHIP | 🚬 🚬 |

*Terminator 2:*
He's back.

TRI-STAR/SHOOTING STAR INT'L

**WHAT HAPPENS** ◖ The original Terminator has been re-programmed to protect John Connor, now a thirteen-year-old juvenile delinquent living with foster parents while his mother, Sarah, works on her lats and delts at a mental hospital. A new Terminator (T-1000) hunts the boy, and this one can change himself into whatever appearance he likes—which for most of the movie is a clean-cut, jug-eared cop. The two Terminators go at it—the T-800's fantastic physique versus T-1000's nearly indestructible liquid metal—from start to finish. In the end, the good Terminator sacrifices his present for the future, which raises two important questions: Whether the events we've watched in these movies will be undone by a change of the future (the answer must lie in Einstein's theory of relativity), and whether there's room for a sequel.

**THE CAST** ⬛ Arnold is back as The Terminator, but this time he's a protector not a destructor and is compelled to understand emotions. He learns about them from a kid (played by Edward Furlong) who's an insolent little snot at the start and becomes a thoughtful, generous charmer as soon as his life is threatened. Linda Hamilton is also back as Sarah Connor, who's more fit physically and more out-of-sync mentally than when we left her at the end of the first movie. Robert Patrick is the most persistent of the T-1000's faces, but its most captivating face is computer-generated; neither Patrick nor the computer-generated images have many lines of dialogues.

**WHY GUYS LOVE IT** ⬛ Two, that's two, killing machines for the price of one.

**HONEY, YOU'LL LIKE THIS MOVIE . . .** ⬛ Because it's a real touching boy-loves-machine, machine-loves-boy kind of story.

**DON'T MISS**
- When Arnold goes into a bar to ask the bikers there to borrow some of life's necessities, like clothes and transportation, for himself.
- The movie's first chase, which involves a minibike, a Harley-Davidson, and a tractor-trailer cab on a collision course with each other.

# TOTAL RECALL (1990)

## RATINGS

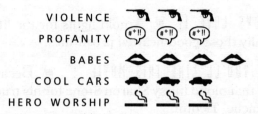

| | |
|---|---|
| VIOLENCE | 🔫 🔫 🔫 |
| PROFANITY | 💬 💬 💬 |
| BABES | 👄 👄 👄 👄 |
| COOL CARS | 🚗 🚗 🚗 |
| HERO WORSHIP | 🚬 🚬 🚬 |

**WHAT HAPPENS** ◤ Quaid is your average lunch pail kind of guy of the future. He works a construction job and he has a good-looking, devoted blond wife at home who wants them to get away for a vacation on Saturn. And he has a recurring dream about being on Mars with another woman. Nothing unusual about that. But when Quaid goes to Rekall—a company that saves you the trouble of traveling by implanting memories of your trip into your brain—he discovers there's more to his dream than he realized. He goes to the troubled planet of Mars, finds the woman in his dream, and discovers he has a complex past he can't fully remember. His past and present embroil him in a struggle between a ruthless and greedy mining company CEO and the planet's many fun-lovin' mutants.

**THE CAST** ◤ Arnold is more human, in many ways, in this movie than he is in his other action movies. It's not his raw strength that makes him the hero—in fact, he appears in drag in one scene—but rather his resentment at being manipulated that propels him into action. That resentment is first targeted at his oh-so-sneaky wife, played by Sharon Stone. She's her usual horny self so long as Quaid is the docile husband, but she turns low and mean—and even more duplicitous—when he discovers her deceit. Better he should stick with Melina, the brunette prostitute on Mars, played by Rachel Ticotin. Ronny Cox adds to his collection of cruel corporate cretins as Cohaagen, the mining company CEO who ultimately brings all the players back to his office for a dressing-down.

### WHY GUYS LOVE IT ■ Arnold fights for the little people, especially those good-hearted prostitutes.

### HONEY, YOU'LL LIKE THIS MOVIE ... ■ Because Arnold dumps that blond hussy Sharon Stone for his true love, brunette Rachel Ticotin.

### DON'T MISS
- Arnold removing the electronic device implanted in his brain. He uses a mechanical nose-picker and pulls the bug out like it was a massive booger.
- The sales savvy prostitute with three breasts—she's sure to be 50 percent more fun.

### MEMORABLE LINES
- "Doug, sweetheart, you wouldn't hurt me, would you? Be reasonable. I am your wife," Sharon Stone pleads with Arnold.

  "Consider that a divorce," he says as he blasts her.
- When Quaid is reunited with dark-haired, exotic Melina, she grabs his little Schwarzenegger and asks him, "What have you been feeding this?"

  "Blondes," he answers.

  "Well, it looks hungry," she observes.

### FOR THE RECORD

More people jump, fall, or are pushed through glass of all kinds in this movie than any other movie ever made.

# THE BIG BRAWL (1980)

## RATINGS

| | |
|---|---|
| VIOLENCE | 🔫 🔫 🔫 |
| PROFANITY | @*!! @*!! |
| BABES | 👄 👄 |
| COOL CARS | 🚗 🚗 🚗 🚗 |
| HERO WORSHIP | 🚬 🚬 🚬 |

**WHAT HAPPENS** ▬ In the 1930s—before pro football, motor sports, and the TV news were able to satisfy the public's blood lust—people went to see organized bare-knuckled fistfights in the streets. The winners took home cash, the losers went home in a box. Most of all, mobsters took in a fortune in gambling profits. When Jerry, an Asian kid living in Chicago, whomps on three thugs trying to shake down his father at the family's Chinese restaurant, a mob boss decides to blackmail Jerry into fighting in a colossal bout called "The Big Brawl" with his backing. Jerry has no choice but to punch, kick, and leap his way into a showdown with the reigning champion—the "Kisser."

**THE CAST** ▰ Jackie Chan—Asia's biggest box-office draw —looks like he's no older than twelve in this movie, which may explain how he can be so quick with his fists and feet, and why he can move like a gymnast. As Jerry, he seems like he's having a good time even when he's surrounded by four guys with weapons. Jose Ferrer plays what must surely be the most genial gangster ever, but Mary Ellen O'Neill as his coldhearted mother more than compensates for his friendliness with an extra dose of sarcasm. Mako plays his part as Jerry's wise and wacky uncle and martial arts teacher.

**WHY GUYS LOVE IT** ▰ What pantywaist outlawed fist-fights to the death, anyway?

**HONEY, YOU'LL LIKE THIS MOVIE . . .** ▰ Because Jerry fights only for his family.

**DON'T MISS**
- The early version of the Roller Derby.
- The uncle's fixation on tubbies.
- The tender, gentle kiss at the end of the first fight.

**MEMORABLE LINES**
"Somebody ought to take out your wad and step on it," says Ferrer's mean, cigar-smokin' mother to one of the goons who got beat by Jerry.

# BLIND FURY (1990)

**RATINGS**

| | |
|---|---|
| VIOLENCE | 🔫 🔫 🔫 |
| PROFANITY | @*!! @*!! |
| BABES | 👄 👄 |
| COOL CARS | |
| HERO WORSHIP | 🚬 🚬 🚬 |

**WHAT HAPPENS** ▬ An American soldier in Vietnam is blinded and left for dead, but he's taken in by a village whose natives undertake his rehabilitation and teach him the martial art of zato-ichi—a sword-fighting skill that seems to demand that he be able to dice fruit tossed through the air. (Why? Your guess is as good as mine.) When Parker (the blind guy) returns to Los Angeles and visits his old Army buddy, he finds himself protecting the friend's wife and son, slicing up unsuspecting bad guys with a razor-sharp blade he keeps in his blind man's cane, and cutting up for laughs from the audience. He even drives a truck on an L.A. freeway (where it is legal for the blind to drive, isn't it?). Parker hacks his way through a couple dozen bad guys, until his showdown with another Blade Master, who is shocked by Parker's skill.

**THE CAST** ▬ Rutger Hauer, who is Parker, may not move as fluidly as other martial arts experts, nor is his delivery of one-liners particularly lethal, but he does appear brave and sure enough to chase bad guys even when he's outnumbered—maybe, especially when he's outnumbered. He takes particular pleasure in cutting mammoth boxer Randall "Tex" Cobb down to size. Meg Foster (who played Hauer's wife in *The Osterman Weekend;* see page 378) is the friend's wife for a short time.

## WHY GUYS LOVE IT ▰ A blind guy who kicks ass reminds us all that we can overcome our limitations—and perhaps even kick a bit of butt ourselves.

## HONEY, YOU'LL LIKE THIS MOVIE . . . ▰ Because it's a story of triumph and rehabilitation for a guy with a handicap.

## DON'T MISS
- Parker slice up no less than ten bad guys in less than three minutes.
- The chance to turn off the movie before the weepy ending with the little boy.

## MEMORABLE LINES
- "I'm gonna put that blind guy in a wheelchair," says one bad guy to another.
- "I also do circumcisions," Parker says to the fat henchman after he trims his eyebrows.

## TRIVIA

Could someone please tell me . . . who came up with the idea to start this videotape with a promo for *Look Who's Talking?* Does some market research show that the audiences for these movies have something in common?

# BLOODSPORT (1987)

## RATINGS

VIOLENCE

PROFANITY

BABES

COOL CARS

HERO WORSHIP

**WHAT HAPPENS** ☛ You may think you've seen every style of martial arts, but until you've seen this movie, you haven't seen it all. You see, at the Kumite (an outlawed international competition held in Hong Kong), anything and everything goes. So the best fighters of every stripe gather to pummel all hell out of each other to see who's the least fair of them all. Two Americans get into the contest—a big Brutus of a guy who works on raw strength and size, and a trained-to-a T kickboxer and Army officer named Frank Dux. The reigning champion, Chong Li, and Dux dispense with their opponents in record times and get on a collision course for the title.

**THE CAST** ☛ Jean-Claude Van Damme is jacked and cut (that is, he's very fit and muscular). He's quick with his feet and hands, and he's not afraid to use his head when it's handy. His defensive end size pal Donald Gibb gets his head used by Chong Li. How Forest Whitaker ended up in this movie is anybody's guess. Oh, the director needed a guy to be one of the FBI agents tracking down Dux, but the part is so slight that Whitaker's sizable skills are wasted.

**WHY GUYS LOVE IT** ▰ More than a dozen guys get whomped and stomped by Li and Dux before we even get to the big match.

**HONEY, YOU'LL LIKE THIS MOVIE . . .** ▰ Because it assesses the merits of ancient Asian art forms.

## DON'T MISS

- The mammoth Asian who hugs his opponents until they beg for mercy (or, perhaps, a date) and the monkey fighter who saunters around on all fours until he leaps into an attack.
- Chong Li's prefight power blow of his nose.
- The lady reporter's look of lust at the match.

## MEMORABLE LINES

"There are three ways to win," says the judge to the competitors. "Knock your opponent out. Throw him off the mat. Or make him cry 'uncle.' " Number three was always a popular choice in my neighborhood.

# ENTER THE DRAGON (1973)

## RATINGS

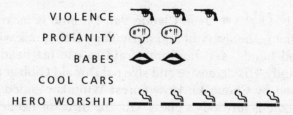

| VIOLENCE | 🔫 🔫 🔫 |
| PROFANITY | (#*!!) (#*!!) |
| BABES | 💋 💋 |
| COOL CARS | |
| HERO WORSHIP | 🚬 🚬 🚬 🚬 🚬 |

**WHAT HAPPENS** ▰ The faint trace of a plot in this movie exists simply to set up just about the most realistic fight

S.S. ARCHIVES/SHOOTING STAR

*Enter the Dragon,* exit a god.

scenes you'll see on film. Anyway, here's the story: Lee, a karate master, is asked by a British agent to infiltrate an invitation-only martial arts tournament held by Han, a suspicious character living on his own island near Hong Kong. Lee is persuaded to take the assignment when he learns that Han's men were responsible for his sister's death. Once there, Lee whips all comers during the day—including a very agile African-American and a tough Anglo-American—and stomps Han's guards at night as he looks for evidence of illicit activities. In the end, Lee wins the tournament, but Han gives himself a hand.

**THE CAST** ✏ This was Bruce Lee's last complete movie before he died at age thirty-two. Lee punched, kicked, and never failed to feint with unmatched style and grace. Watch his every muscle flex—even his eyeballs—and listen to him cry out when he snaps off a sharp swat or kick. Lee staged the fight scenes in the movie, too, and there are no pulled punches. John Saxon (the cop in *Nightmare on Elm Street*) is the Burt Reynolds look-alike who joins forces with Lee for the finale. And most honorable mention goes to Angela Mao Ying, who plays Lee's sister: She kicked around almost as many bad guys as Lee.

**WHY GUYS LOVE IT** ✏ Bruce Lee could maul Chuck Norris, Steven Seagal, Jean-Claude Van Damme, and the stars of the World Wrestling Federation without breaking a sweat.

**HONEY, YOU'LL LIKE THIS MOVIE . . .** ✏ Because the woman who plays Lee's sister could, too.

**DON'T MISS**
- The evening entertainment Han has planned for the contestants.
- Lee fighting off wave after wave of Han's guards armed with every conceivable martial arts weapon for four full minutes of screen time.

# AN EYE FOR AN EYE (1981)

 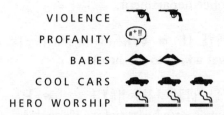
**WHAT HAPPENS** ▰ Sean Kane and his partner, undercover narcs in San Francisco, are ambushed during a meeting with their stoolie, and the partner gets clipped. This really burns Kane, and that's not good for either the dope dealer involved or the bad cop who set them up, because Kane is hell-bent on settling the score and because he has the capacity to do it. Even worse, the dead cop's wife (a TV reporter) is killed, too, and her father just happens to be Kane's martial arts mentor. Kane and his teacher go on an ass-kickin' spree that leads them to a lesson with The Professor, an overweight Asian gimp with the strength to lift Volkswagens and crush windpipes.

**THE CAST** ▰ Chuck Norris is no classically trained actor, but as Sean Kane he delivers all the depth of emotion required for his part: He's sad and angry when his partner is killed, indignant in his dealings with his unsupportive captain, outraged when he learns about the bad cops, and enraged about the wife's murder. More important, he snaps off the quickest high kicks of any of the martial arts stars. This skill is necessary to stop The Professor, aka Professor Toru Tanaka, who proves he can take more than a punch. He's employed by drug kingpin Christopher Lee, doing his diabolical best to be both vicious and highly civilized. Mako takes on his usual role as the mentor, with his typically wise and detached manner broken in this movie by the murder of his daughter. Richard *"Shaft"* Roundtree is the bureaucrat in the police department.

## WHY GUYS LOVE IT ■ When your partner is dead, somebody has to get a kick to the head.

## HONEY, YOU'LL LIKE THIS MOVIE... ■ Because Kane's dog wins the woman's heart before Kane does.

## DON'T MISS
- How Kane has trained his dog to pick up his laundry off the floor.
- The traitor cop getting passed over for recognition . . . by a train.
- What Kane can do with his hands tied behind his back.

## MEMORABLE LINES
"I tried to question him, but he preferred to expire," says Mako about one of the henchmen who attacks them.

# A FORCE OF ONE (1979)

## RATINGS

| | | |
|---|---|---|
| VIOLENCE | 🔫 | 🔫 |
| PROFANITY | @*!! | @*!! |
| BABES | 👄 | |
| COOL CARS | 🚗 | 🚗 |
| HERO WORSHIP | 🚬 | 🚬 |

**WHAT HAPPENS** ☞ After two narcs have their windpipes crushed by a mysterious killer, the cops ask local martial arts teacher and champion kickboxer Matt Logan to give them a few lessons. He agrees, and not only because one of the detectives happens to be a gorgeous but businesslike woman. While Logan is in training for a big bout, he agrees to teach a few lessons and help the hot detective figure out who the killer is. Some of the cops, however, are skeptical of the need to learn martial arts and are more than a little shifty themsevles. Almost every one of them are glad, though, when Logan takes matters into his own hands—and feet—once they discover the killer's identity.

**THE CAST** ☞ You'll have no trouble believing former world karate champion Chuck Norris is champion kick-boxer Matt Logan. He can kick, he can punch, he can get real mad when the bad guys mess with his adopted son. He also can get warm for Detective Mandy Rust, played by demure brunette Jennifer O'Neill. If you were a fan of *Baa-Baa Black Sheep*, you will recognize one of the other cops as James Whitmore Jr., who was J. T. Gutterman, the Black Sheep's second-in-command.

**WHY GUYS LOVE IT** ☞ Chuck is a low-key guy who's slow to get mad, but when he's pissed, y'all better duck.

**HONEY, YOU'LL LIKE THIS MOVIE ...** ☞ Because you loved Jennifer O'Neill in *Summer of '42*.

**DON'T MISS**
The warm-up matches Logan fights or the big match at the end.

**MEMORABLE LINES**
- "You need more than technique," Logan tells his students. "You need attitude." Remember that.

- "After you're done basic karate training, why don't you call me," Logan's opponent says, coming on to O'Neill.

  "I will, as soon as I figure out what to call you," she answers.

# JAGUAR LIVES! (1979)

## RATINGS

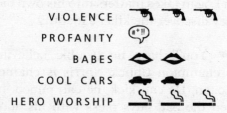

| | |
|---|---|
| VIOLENCE | 🔫 🔫 🔫 |
| PROFANITY | 💬 |
| BABES | 👄 👄 |
| COOL CARS | 🚗 🚗 |
| HERO WORSHIP | 🚬 🚬 🚬 |

**WHAT HAPPENS** ▰ Jaguar wants to live a peaceful life, traveling around with his Native American mentor and kicking only the occasional punk's ass, but his nation needs him. A beautiful government agent asks Jaguar to rescue a shipping magnate who's been kidnapped and blackmailed into letting his fleet be used to smuggle drugs. So Jaguar travels to the Middle East, battles his way through waves of thugs armed with all manner of weapons, until, at last, he catches up with Adam Cain, the kingpin, and a power-crazed Latin American general—both of whom Jaguar knocks down more than a couple pegs.

**THE CAST** ▰ This is surely the greatest cast of real actors ever assembled for what is still essentially a martial arts movie. Joe Lewis, a world karate champion, is Jaguar. On his side are Woody Strode, as his calm and collected Indian sensei; the luscious Barbara Bach as Anna, Jaguar's contact with the government; and John Huston as the blackmailed businessman. Allied against him are the ever-diabolical Christopher Lee as Adam Cain, and Donald Pleasence, the ballistic general.

**WHY GUYS LOVE IT** ■ If you have to stomp face, you might as well do it to please a gorgeous agent.

**HONEY, YOU'LL LIKE THIS MOVIE ...** ■ Because Jaguar stomps face to please a real working woman.

**DON'T MISS:**
- When Jaguar and his friend are cornered by a group of thugs at a remote gas station, watch Jaguar decide who gets a heel to their chin first.
- Jaguar taking on an entire factory full of guys with hand tools.

**MEMORABLE LINES**
"Anna's been looking for you," the Indian tells Jaguar.
   "Let's avoid trouble if we can," Jaguar says.
   "And if we can't?" the Indian asks.
   "Then we'll let Anna pay the hospital bills," Jaguar responds.

# 9 DEATHS OF THE NINJA (1985)

**RATINGS**

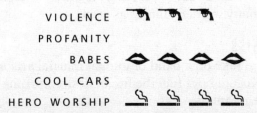

| | |
|---|---|
| VIOLENCE | 🔫 🔫 🔫 |
| PROFANITY | |
| BABES | 👄 👄 👄 👄 |
| COOL CARS | |
| HERO WORSHIP | 🚬 🚬 🚬 🚬 |

**WHAT HAPPENS** ▰ The henchmen of Dr. Cruel, a drool-ing wheelchair-bound psycho who apparently frequents Prince's hair stylist, kidnap a busload of tourists in Manila, and the bad doctor demands the release of one of his men who's been jailed and the withdrawal of all American drug enforcement operations from the Philippines. The U.S. gov-ernment sends two very resourceful guys—one Asian, one Anglo—to find Dr. Cruel and the hostages. To do so, they must stomp somebody every five minutes. And once they find the hostages, they must battle Dr. Cruel's tough security forces—led by Honey Hump, an ass-kickin' African-Ameri-can chick with a two-foot-wide Afro and a minimal ward-robe budget.

**THE CAST** ▰ Sho Kosugi does not have Bruce Lee's smooth-featured good looks or ripplin' muscles, but he is every bit as quick to put foot to face as Lee. Kosugi, who choreographed the fight scenes in this movie, plays the lead character, Spike Shinobi, with an impish smile and a lolli-pop in his mouth throughout the movie. His two sons, Shane and Kane, get into the act, too: As hostages they make mis-chief and deliver a few shots of their own in the climactic fight. Regina Richardson gives her part as Honey Hump real attitude—I'd love to see a showdown between her and Cleo-patra Jones for the title of "Baddest Sistah in the Movies."

**WHY GUYS LOVE IT** ▰ Nobody has more fun beating up five guys at once than Sho Kosugi.

**HONEY, YOU'LL LIKE THIS MOVIE . . .** ▰ Because there are as many women villains as men.

**DON'T MISS**
- Kosugi take on a band of midget martial arts masters.
- The Kosugi boys fuel the fire of desire burning inside one of their captors.

- Kosugi exposing the women who assail him underwater: These babes may be tough, but they're modest.

**CHECK OUT**

Other kick-ass Kosugi to watch:
*Shaolin Drunk Fighter*
*Pray for Death*
*Rage of Honor*
*Journey of Honor*
*Black Eagle*

# THE PERFECT WEAPON (1991)

## RATINGS

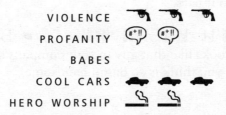

| | |
|---|---|
| VIOLENCE | 🔫 🔫 🔫 |
| PROFANITY | 💬 💬 |
| BABES | |
| COOL CARS | 🚗 🚗 🚗 |
| HERO WORSHIP | 🚬 🚬 |

**WHAT HAPPENS** ◢ There are just three martials arts movie plots, and this movie has one of them: An Asian master and owner of an import store teaches Jeff, the rebellious son of a cop, an ancient discipline. When mobsters try to extort money from the old master, Jeff must kick a few of them around. So the mobsters kill the old master, and that makes Jeff very mad. He tears through the Asian community, beating first and asking questions later, and seals his revenge in a ball of fire. So what makes this movie different from the other martial arts movies with this plot? The ancient discipline is kempo, a Korean style of fighting that uses sticks or bats or rods or something like that. Jeff whips around his sticks, battering wave after wave of thugs with body blows and head shots.

**THE CAST** ■ Three more reasons you can see this movie coming before it arrives: The star, Jeff Speakman, is a former world kempo champion, his character's name is Jeff (just Jeff) and Mako (just Mako, also in *The Big Brawl* and *An Eye for an Eye*) is his mentor. Still, you want to see how swift and sure Jeff is with his sticks. He can punish a half-dozen guys armed with chains, lead pipes, and knives faster than you can say "compound fracture." Except, of course, Professor Toru Tanaka, the Japanese giant who, like Godzilla, crushes everything in his path. To stop him, Jeff must resort to a more pressurized approach.

**WHY GUYS LOVE IT** ■ The sound of wood smacking flesh is music to our ears.

**HONEY, YOU'LL LIKE THIS MOVIE . . .** ■ Because Jeff Speakman looks like that guy in your company's marketing department you think is so damn handsome.

**DON'T MISS**
- The young Jeff deck a football player in full gear—helmet, too.
- The lesson Jeff gives at the karate school to the three guys reluctant to answer his questions.
- The professor take a stun and keep on coming.

**MEMORABLE LINES**
(Cut from the script to leave room for more scenes of Jeff working out with his sticks.)

# RUMBLE IN THE BRONX (1995)

## RATINGS

VIOLENCE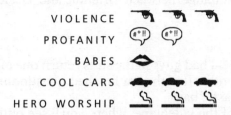

PROFANITY

BABES

COOL CARS

HERO WORSHIP

**WHAT HAPPENS** ▬ As a new immigrant from Hong Kong, Keung is at a great cultural disadvantage: He has no way of knowing that bikers are mean and nasty and shouldn't be provoked, though he might have gotten a clue when he sees their girlfriends motorcrossing over a row of parked cars on a street in the Bronx. This biker gang is at a great disadvantage, too: They're so convinced of their own meanness that they don't see how quick and dangerous Keung is with his hands and feet. All of which propels them into a raging feud that drags in Keung's uncle and his grocery store, a biker babe who takes a shine to Keung, and her wheelchair-bound little brother, and eventually some mobsters and their diamonds. The ending is a series of stunts around New York Harbor that explode into an hilarious finish.

**THE CAST** ▬ With more than 100 movies to his credit, Jackie Chan is as acrobatic as ever and still doing his own stunts. His choreography of the fights and stunts in his movies emphasize fun, and he finds it hard not to smile through this movie, even when he's facing down a room full of bikers. One of the main reasons he's smiling is exotically beautiful Francoise Yip, who plays Nancy, the biker chick with a heart. Her biker beau is the sufficiently cruel Marc Akerstream.

**WHY GUYS LOVE IT** ▰ Bikers versus karate master is no undercard match.

**HONEY, YOU'LL LIKE THIS MOVIE . . .** ▰ Because it's about an exchange between Oriental and Occidental cultures.

**DON'T MISS**

- How the real bad guys in the suits return one of the bikers to his friends after they're finished questioning him—in several plastic bags.
- The end of the videotape, where you'll see outtakes from the stunts and lots of stunt people being driven off in ambulances—including Jackie getting a special cast.

# THE STREET FIGHTER (1975)

**RATINGS**

| | |
|---|---|
| VIOLENCE | 🔫 🔫 🔫 |
| PROFANITY | @*!! @*!! |
| BABES | 👄 |
| COOL CARS | |
| HERO WORSHIP | 🚬 🚬 🚬 |

**WHAT HAPPENS** ▰ This is a Japanese-style karate movie, so it revolves around the notorious Japanese organized crime syndicate, the Yakuza. A sexy, tough woman runs the local chapter and she very nicely asks martial arts expert Terry Sugury to bust up some especially difficult rivals. Terry declines her offer most ungraciously, so she sends some assassins to kill him. They, however, are underarmed because they only have guns and clubs, but he has his own arms and legs. He breaks necks, arms, and legs with his own blend of karate and kickboxing.

**THE CAST** ◢ Sonny Chiba is Terry Sugury—though why an Asian living in an Asian country would have that name is anyone's guess. Chiba is not as acrobatic as Jackie Chan, as lighthearted as Sho Kosugi, or as powerful as Bruce Lee, but he looks fiercer than anyone and he packs more punch in his kicks and kick in his punches. From the side, his shaggy hair and thick sideburns make Chiba resemble Mike "Mannix" Connors.

**WHY GUYS LOVE IT** ◢ You hope in your lifetime to see all the greats, and Sonny Chiba is one of them.

**HONEY, YOU'LL LIKE THIS MOVIE . . .** ◢ Because it proves women can succeed in traditionally male domains, like mob boss.

**DON'T MISS**
- Sonny grinding his way through an entire karate school, only to come face-to-face with the chubby little teacher.
- The guy who tries to take out Sonny by picking up his car and then dropping it.

**MEMORABLE LINES**
"You tell that bitch who sent you," Sonny tells one of the assassins he's about to beat, "how sorry I am that I can no longer be her friend."

**TRIVIA**

Do not confuse this movie with the lame Jean-Claude Van Damme movie with the same title. That one was based on a video game, and believe me, the Muscles from Brussels would sag if he had to square off with Sonny Chiba.

# BLACK SHAMPOO (1976)

## RATINGS

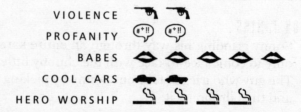

| | |
|---|---|
| VIOLENCE | 🔫 🔫 |
| PROFANITY | (#*!!) (#*!!) |
| BABES | 👄 👄 👄 👄 👄 |
| COOL CARS | 🚗 🚗 |
| HERO WORSHIP | 🚬 🚬 🚬 🚬 |

**WHAT HAPPENS** ▪ Mr. Jonathan runs a full-service salon —especially for his wealthy female customers. And he's very protective of his employees—the boys who cut hair when Mr. Jonathan is busy with a personal beauty consultation, and his receptionist, Brenda, who's the ex of a nasty mobster. When a couple of thugs muss the boys, tear up the salon, and take off with Brenda while Mr. Jonathan is fulfilling a family plan with a mother and her two very competitive daughters, he gets mad. And when Mr. Jonathan is mad, he has to primp and crimp with a 36cc clipper.

**THE CAST** ▪ John Daniels plays Mr. Jonathan unlike any other hairstylist we've ever seen. He's very proud of his ability to make women feel beautiful and humbly does his duty when his appointment book dictates that he do so. But when Mr. Big crosses the line with Brenda, a woman Mr. Jonathan feels very close to, Mr. Jonathan is as mean as a bull. Tanya Boyd plays it both sweet 'n' innocent and ready 'n' rarin'—just the way we (and Mr. Jonathan) like it. Joe Ortiz's Mr. Big also meets all of our expectations for the mob boss with a soft spot for a honey.

## WHY GUYS LIKE IT ▰ We get to see a lot of untrimmed hair, if you know what I'm saying.

## HONEY, YOU'LL LIKE THIS MOVIE... ▰ Because aren't you always telling me how interesting your hairdresser is?

## DON'T MISS
• The bareback barbecue.
• Mr. Big's final cue.

## MEMORABLE LINES
"You're a tough little faggot," a thug says to one of the hairdressers before they start interrogating him with a hot curling iron.

## TRIVIA

This movie has one thing in common with the "white" *Shampoo,* starring Warren Beatty, and it ain't the fact that both movies are about hairdressers. Watch this one instead of the other one because *Black Shampoo* doesn't have some limp-wristed message about society in the final rinse.

# DOLEMITE (1975)

## RATINGS

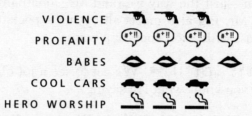

|  |  |
|---|---|
| VIOLENCE | 🔫 🔫 🔫 |
| PROFANITY | 💬 💬 💬 💬 |
| BABES | 👄 👄 👄 👄 |
| COOL CARS | 🚗 🚗 🚗 |
| HERO WORSHIP | 🚬 🚬 🚬 |

**WHAT HAPPENS** ► Dolemite (pronounced dole-a-might), a pimp who knows the martial arts, is sent to prison on trumped-up drug charges. When the drug problem in Dolemite's old neighborhood gets violent, the chief of police sends him back out on the streets to help find the dealers— who, no surprise, are the very cops who set him up. Dolemite kills three men before he's even ejaculated twice, and the whole neighborhood greets him as the returning hero. Fortunately, the madam who worked for Dolemite has kept his girls busy, and not just on their backs. They've learned karate while Dolemite was in prison, and they help him battle the corrupt cops and mayor—to the accompaniment of a vintage seventies funk sound track. In the end, Dolemite helps his rival achieve a change of heart.

**THE CAST** ► Rudy Ray Moore was a popular rappin' comic of the seventies who few people remember. No one else in the movie is even remotely memorable, and it must be noted that none of the many women in this film would be able to work in movies today without getting implants: Such sag you don't see no more.

**WHY GUYS LOVE IT** ► Hookers who know karate . . . what could be better than that?

## HONEY, YOU'LL LIKE THIS MOVIE ...

■ Because these women have empowered themselves economically and physically.

## DON'T MISS

- The climactic brawl in which the hookers give the bad guys a beating, and don't charge them extra.
- Dolemite's impeccably stylish Afro, threads, and big ol' Cadillac that say nothing if not PIMP.

## MEMORABLE LINES

"I'm so bad, I kick my own ass twice a day," says the Hamburger Pimp (don't ask).

# MENACE II SOCIETY (1993)

## RATINGS

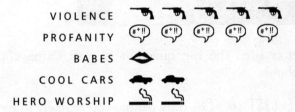

| | | | | | |
|---|---|---|---|---|---|
| VIOLENCE | 🔫 | 🔫 | 🔫 | 🔫 | 🔫 |
| PROFANITY | @*!! | @*!! | @*!! | @*!! | @*!! |
| BABES | 👄 | | | | |
| COOL CARS | 🚗 | 🚗 | | | |
| HERO WORSHIP | 🚬 | 🚬 | | | |

## WHAT HAPPENS

■ Caine and O-Dog grew up together in the same neighborhood in Watts and still like to hang out, and especially to go grab some brews at the local Korean grocery store. What one of them does invariably involves the other. So when O-Dog makes a fatal choice one night in a grocery store and Caine's cousin gets hit by gang bangers, they both have to pay the price. But where O-Dog can't think of anything else he'd rather be doing, Caine is thinking about a sweet young mother who wants him to get a

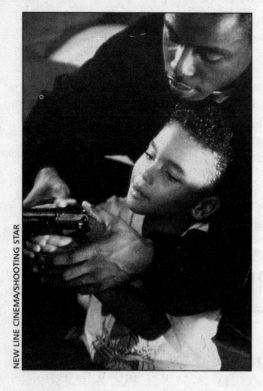

NEW LINE CINEMA/SHOOTING STAR

Passing on what you need to know to be a *Menace II Society*.

better life. The big question is, will Caine choose soon enough.

**THE CAST** ◢ The only people you're likely to recognize in this movie are Charles Dutton, the real ex-convict turned actor who plays the father of one of their friends, and Samuel L. Jackson, Caine's coldblooded stepfather. But all of these relatively unknown actors are convincing people of the street. As Caine, Tyrin Turner wears his doubts in a soft voice and a steady shuffling of his feet. That demeanor contrasts with the smiles and bravado that Larenz Tate makes O-Dog's constant face. The other key contributors to this movie are the Hughes Brothers, Allen and Albert, who cowrote and codirected it.

**WHY GUYS LOVE IT ▪** Nine graphic murders on screen and buckets of spit, puke, and blood flowing out of every victim's mouth.

**HONEY, YOU'LL LIKE THIS MOVIE . . . ▪** Because of its passionate depiction of the plight of troubled inner-city youth.

**DON'T MISS**
- How Caine's stepfather retires a debt—point-blank.
- The cops' generous offer to give a lift to Caine and another buddy . . . right into a Latino neighborhood.

**MEMORABLE LINES**
- "O-Dog was America's nightmare: young, black, and didn't give a fuck," Caine states in a voice-over segment.
- "Do you care whether you live or die?" Caine's grandfather asks him.
  "I don't know," is all the answer Caine has for him.

# SHAFT (1971)

**RATINGS**

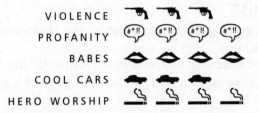

| | | | |
|---|---|---|---|
| VIOLENCE | | | |
| PROFANITY | | | |
| BABES | | | |
| COOL CARS | | | |
| HERO WORSHIP | | | |

**WHAT HAPPENS ▪** Shaft is a cool private eye who takes no guff from the cops or the bad brothers in Harlem. But he does need work, so he takes on a job from a crime boss whose daughter has been kidnapped by the Mafia. With the help of four tough guys hand-chosen by Shaft, he retrieves the girl and hoses down a few nasty thugs. Don't think that Shaft is all work and no play: He's far from a dull boy and he makes sure he stays cooool with several species of fox.

**THE CAST** ◄ Richard Roundtree is Shaft and, as the song says, "he's a bad mother." And when he stands up to the cops or the crooks, he does it not because he has something to prove but because he's already proved it. Moses Gunn (whom you may recognize from *Rollerball* or *Heartbreak Ridge*) plays Bumpy Jones, the Harlem crime boss and father of the kidnapped girl who respects Shaft. Antonio Fargas shows up as Shaft's stoolie, playing it a lot like the dude Huggy Bear he was on *Starsky and Hutch*.

**WHY GUYS LOVE IT** ◄ Shaft has a philosophy we can all relate to: Take no shit and score with a lot of babes, because you never know what's going to happen next.

**HONEY, YOU'LL LIKE THIS MOVIE . . .** ◄ Because everybody wears those seventies fashions that are back in style now.

**DON'T MISS**
- Shaft getting down and clean in the shower with one of his pickups.
- Shaft's reaction to the phoofy waiter in the bar where Shaft goes to watch the Mafia men watch his place.

**MEMORABLE LINES**
- "Where are you going?" a cop asks Shaft.
  "To get laid . . . where you going?" Shaft answers.
- "You're really great in the sack, but you're pretty shitty afterwards," the shower honey tells him.

AWARDS

Funkmaster Isaac Hayes won an Oscar for the title song.

# SUPERFLY (1972)

## RATINGS

| | |
|---|---|
| VIOLENCE | 🔫 🔫 |
| PROFANITY | 💬 💬 💬 |
| BABES | 👄 👄 👄 👄 |
| COOL CARS | 🚗 🚗 🚗 |
| HERO WORSHIP | 🚬 🚬 🚬 🚬 |

**WHAT HAPPENS** ▰ Youngblood Priest is in the making people happy business, but he's tired of it. But to retire and take his sweet, dark lady away from Harlem to live in comfort, Priest wants one more big score—about $1 million worth of happy people powder. So he asks his man Scatter to help him set it up. But some white cops have the idea that they control the business and they take Scatter out of the deal. They want to talk direct to Priest, but he knows what happens to guys who work with them. So Priest sets up a shelter to protect his ass from crooked cops and then rolls out of town.

**THE CAST** ▰ Ron O'Neal is the superfly Youngblood Priest, a laid-back dude who savors his blow and his babes.

He's too clever to threaten or put on—he just lays it on the line because he's got all the angles covered. Sheila Frazier is the mighty fine Georgia he's got on his mind, and Julius Harris is his sorry friend Scatter. Gordon Parks Jr., son of the photographer and director of *Shaft* (Gordon Parks), called the shots for this movie. Curtis Mayfield provided the sound track that makes the movie swing.

## WHY GUYS LOVE IT ⬛ If you ever need a refresher course
in cool, seventies style, skip *Saturday Night Fever* and see what's *Superfly*.

## HONEY, YOU'LL LIKE THIS MOVIE . . . ⬛ Because the
music is just the stuff to get us dancing.

## DON'T MISS
- Priest and Georgia's very heated bath.
- Priest's stylin' El Dorado.

## MEMORABLE LINES
"Some things do go better with coke," observes a naked white babe as Priest lays out a line right on her.

### CHECK OUT

*Superfly T.N.T.* (1973) brings Priest back to help an African bureaucrat, and *The Return of Superfly* (1990) brings back Curtis Mayfield to update the theme song.

# BARB WIRE (1996)

## RATINGS

| | |
|---|---|
| VIOLENCE |  |
| PROFANITY | |
| BABES | |
| COOL CARS | |
| HERO WORSHIP | |

**WHAT HAPPENS** ▰ In the year 2017, America has been taken over by the Congressional Directorate, whose Storm Troopers are fighting a not-so civil war against party-hardy rebels. Barb Wire owns the Hammerhead Lounge, a head-banging bar where most of the people hang out in their underwear, in the safe haven of Steel Harbor. Barb spends most of her time doing contract jobs—bounty hunting, mostly—riding her badass motorcycle and lounging around in her lingerie. Barb's old boyfriend shows up asking for her help in getting a scientist (who happens to be his current wife) past the Storm Troopers. Barb signs on, if only to get even with the Troopers for messing with her brother, and she teaches the colonel in charge the proper way to address women in the twenty-first century.

**THE CAST** ▰ **P**amela Anderson will not be taking parts away from Meryl Streep anytime soon, and that's perfect because it will mean she'll be offered more roles like this one, where we can watch her kick ass in a bustier and fishnet stockings. Homegrown or implanted, it makes no difference when you're watching them on the screen: Bounce and jiggle is bounce and jiggle, no matter what the source. Steve Railsback (who you'll remember as Charles Manson in the TV movie *Helter Skelter*) is the colonel who wants more than information from Barb. Clint Howard (Ron's brother, who played the kid on TV's *Gentle Ben*) has a scene or two as a sleazy bail bondsman, ready to sell out our gal Barb.

**WHY GUYS LOVE IT** ▰ Let me give you two reasons. . . .

**HONEY, YOU'LL LIKE THIS MOVIE . . .** ▰ **B**ecause watching it is like looking at the Victoria's Secret catalog.

**DON'T MISS**
- How Barb handles the heel who heckles her during the opening sequence's striptease act.
- The "hot potato" Big Fatso, Lord of the Unoccupied Zone, catches.

**MEMORABLE LINES**
"Don't call me babe." Don't. The two guys who do are very sorry.

**TRIVIA**

Supposedly this movie is based on *Casablanca*, but nobody in that uptight old film even unbuttons her shirt, let alone strips down to a G-string.

# BLACK WIDOW (1987)

**RATINGS**

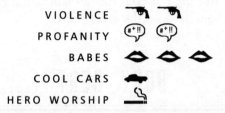

VIOLENCE

PROFANITY

BABES

COOL CARS

HERO WORSHIP

**WHAT HAPPENS** ☛ Three rich guys in different parts of the country die from a rare ailment and leave behind a beautiful wife, Catherine, to whom they've been married for only a short time. A meek Justice Department investigator, Alex, stumbles onto these apparently unrelated cases and becomes suspicious. She tracks down the wife (who happens to be the same woman in each case) in Hawaii, where she's taken up with a hotel tycoon. The cool, confident, seductive widow, Catherine, entrances the guileless Alex and offers to share her man. When Alex falls in love with the hotel tycoon, Catherine's spell over Alex is broken, and Alex must outwit Catherine to ensure her own happy ending.

**THE CAST** ☛ Any one of us would be happy to be caught in Theresa Russell's web. You know she's going to eat you alive, but every bite will be agony and ecstasy. Next to Russell's Catherine, Debra Winger is unusually chaste as Alex. She is as excited to be near Catherine as she is about the chance to bust the big case and earn herself a fairy-tale life. Dennis Hopper is husband number four, blinded by his lust. Writer David Mamet sits in on a hand of poker.

**WHY GUYS LOVE IT** ☛ It's rough stuff, girl style.

**HONEY, YOU'LL LIKE THIS MOVIE . . .** ■ Because a woman cop saves foolish men from a sexy female villain.

**DON'T MISS**
- Catherine doffing her coat for her salivating Hopper.
- The not-so-tender kiss the girls share.

# BODY HEAT (1981)

**RATINGS**

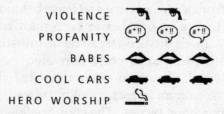

| | |
|---|---|
| VIOLENCE | |
| PROFANITY | |
| BABES | |
| COOL CARS | |
| HERO WORSHIP | |

**WHAT HAPPENS** ■ Lawyer Ned Racine has had his way with the waitresses, nurses, and meter maids in the small Florida town where he lives and he's bored by it. That's the only plausible explanation for why he gets involved with Matty Walker, the wife of a rich man, who is obviously trouble. But involved he gets, and soon she's convinced him to murder her husband in such a way that leaves her with the husband's money. Meanwhile, she works a few shifty legal maneuvers that leaves Ned holding the bag, and you in awe of her brains as well as body.

**THE CAST** ■ William Hurt slicked back his hair and grew a furry little mustache for this movie so we'd have no trouble seeing that Ned Racine thinks of himself as a smooth operator. Ned sustains that illusion long after the rest of us, and even his pals, the district attorney (played nerdy by a heavily toupeed and spectacled Ted Danson) and the detective, see he's been duped. In her first movie role, Kathleen Turner coaxes and pleads with Ned in her breathy voice that comes through to him as pure desperation, while her cold and calculating eyes hide behind long, beautiful blond hair, all of which compounds Matty Walker's mysterious allure. Mickey Rourke takes a minor role as Teddy, one of Ned's former clients who helps him execute the murder, and reveals to us that the none-too-bright one is not Teddy. The husband, Edmund Walker (played by Richard Crenna), is luckier than Ned: Matty only gets him killed.

### WHY GUYS LOVE IT ◄ Who among us wouldn't admit that they've ignored some obvious signals when sex is involved.

### HONEY, YOU'LL LIKE THIS MOVIE . . . ◄ Because after she sleeps with him, *she* jerks *him* around.

### DON'T MISS
- Ned's rear entry . . . through the patio door.
- When Ned mistakenly propositions Matty's high school friend instead of Matty.
- How Edmund's niece describes to the cops the man she catches Matty with.

### MEMORABLE LINES
"You shouldn't dress like that," Ned says to Matty.

"It's a blouse and skirt. I don't know what you're talking about," she responds.

"Maybe you shouldn't wear that body," he tells her.

# CLEOPATRA JONES (1973)

## RATINGS

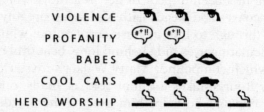

| | |
|---|---|
| VIOLENCE | 🔫 🔫 🔫 |
| PROFANITY | 💬 💬 |
| BABES | 👄 👄 👄 |
| COOL CARS | 🚗 🚗 🚗 |
| HERO WORSHIP | 🚬 🚬 🚬 🚬 |

**WHAT HAPPENS** ▬ Cleo is one tough sister who takes on assignments now and again for the Big Brother, the U.S. government. In this case, she's busting up a drug ring run by a lady-lovin' queenpin who calls herself Mommy. Cleo uses her obvious brains, beauty, and quick-as-a-whip Size 9s (narrow) to stomp on Mommy's heroin trade. Our gal also takes a little time to remind her man that she is all lady.

**THE CAST** ▬ Former model Tamara Dobson is long and lean, swift and mean as Cleopatra Jones. At six feet two, Cleo towers over the little goons Mommy sends to stop her and the puny cops who are of no help to her. As taut and tense as Cleo is, that's how loose and loony Shelley Winters plays Mommy. Be sure to watch as Mommy's wigs change colors, while her refrain remains the same. (In fact, everybody's hairdo except Cleo's exceeds thirty-six inches in diameter.) Antonio Fargas provides himself with a career as a smooth-talkin' hustler in his portrayal of Doodle Bug—he was nearly the same character as Huggy Bear in *Starsky and Hutch*. If you remember other seventies TV actors, you'll also spot Esther Rolle (the mother on *Good Times*) and Teddy Chambers (Earl the mailman from *That's My Mama*) in this movie.

**WHY GUYS LOVE IT** ▰ If you're going to get your ass kicked, it might as well be by a statuesque model.

**HONEY, YOU'LL LIKE THIS MOVIE...** ▰ Because Cleo dresses to kill.

**DON'T MISS**
- Cleo's visit to a hot spot in Turkey in the movie's opening sequence.
- The warm welcome home Mommy arranges for Cleo at the airport.
- The two guys on the street who have it sweet for her.

**MEMORABLE LINES**
"Your head and your body are gonna need separate maintenance," Cleo tells Doodle Bug.

# CRIMES OF PASSION (1984)

**RATINGS**

| | |
|---|---|
| VIOLENCE | 🔫 🔫 🔫 |
| PROFANITY | @*!! @*!! @*!! @*!! |
| BABES | 👄 👄 👄 |
| COOL CARS | |
| HERO WORSHIP | 🚬 |

**WHAT HAPPENS** ▰ China Blue, a streetwalker working the darkest corners of the city, attracts some of the strangest johns and fulfills their bizarre requests. None of them is as disturbed as Father Shayne, a profane priest with a mind to save China's soul. What's even weirder is that during the day the kinky hooker is a successful, tightly wound fashion designer. Her dual identity is discovered by an ordinary guy with a passionless marriage who is moonlighting as a private eye. Together they try to be normal and they get close before the shocking ending that somehow still seems familiar.

**THE CAST** ☛ Kathleen Turner holds nothing back in her performance as China Blue, including her bare body. But, as always, it is her throaty laugh and I-dare-you eyes that both attract and frighten you. Anthony Perkins heads over the top from Father Shayne's first moment on screen and he never looks back. John Laughlin serves perfectly well as Bobby Grady, a guy like any of us, except he's stuck with Annie Potts, whose usual sauciness is completely obscured by the frigidness that's gripped her as Bobby's wife.

**WHY GUYS LOVE IT** ☛ Kinky hooker takes regular guy for a ride, and she likes it.

**HONEY, YOU'LL LIKE THIS MOVIE . . .** ☛ Because it's about a fashion designer.

**DON'T MISS**
- The Statue of Liberty play.
- The kind and considerate wife who brings China home to her dying husband.
- The attention span of the rich couple in the limo.

**MEMORABLE LINES**
- "I never forget a face, especially when I've sat on it," China tells Father Shayne.
- "I am the messenger of God, you little cocksucker," he proclaims to her.
- "There are three things you need to know to be a fifty-dollar hooker," China explains to Bobby. "How to act, how to fuck, and how to count to fifty."

Rick Wakeman, yes, the Yes keyboardist, composed and performed the movie's score. This movie is also known by the title *China Blue*.

# JUNGLE WARRIORS (1984)

## RATINGS

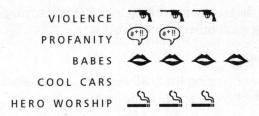

| VIOLENCE | 🔫 🔫 🔫 |
| PROFANITY | 💬 💬 |
| BABES | 👄 👄 👄 👄 |
| COOL CARS | |
| HERO WORSHIP | 🚬 🚬 🚬 |

**WHAT HAPPENS** ▬ Fashion models on a swimsuit shoot in South America are captured by a size XXL drug kingpin and his cruel sister, who are a bit too friendly with each other. The models are imprisoned in the sibling's sixteenth-century Spanish fortress and ravished by their very unkempt security guards. While the bad guys are busy with a major deal, the girls escape their cell and demonstrate that they can handle firearms as well as they apply foundation. American drug enforcement authorities arrive on the scene only after the girls have the situation under their control.

**THE CAST** ▬ Danish actress Nina Van Pallandt is the photographer who turns her focus to rallying the girls and shooting bad guys without hesitation. She's matched by former Playmate of the Year Sybil Danning, who is the sadistic sister. Her beefy brother Caesar is played by Paul L. Smith (he was the heavyweight guard in *Midnight Express*). John

"Dean Wormer" Vernon is trying to cut a deal with them, while Dana Elcar (MacGyver's boss) is the American agent tracking the deal. Woody Strode—the Nubian who squares off with Spartacus—heads Caesar's security team. Last, and certainly not least, the girls are not famous supermodels, but you wouldn't kick the least of them out of bed for eating raw squid.

## WHY GUYS LOVE IT ► What's not to love about models with guns?

## HONEY, YOU'LL LIKE THIS MOVIE . . . ► Because it proves that women working together will triumph over men fighting each other every time.

## DON'T MISS
- Caesar bringing his business with John Vernon to a head.
- The lecherous art director getting a face full.

## MEMORABLE LINES
As the U.S. agents fly overhead in their helicopter, they see the girls below. "Who are they?" the pilot asks.

"I don't know, but I'd sure like to meet them," the agent beside him drools.

# THE LAST SEDUCTION (1994)

## RATINGS

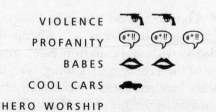

| | |
|---|---|
| VIOLENCE | 🔫 🔫 |
| PROFANITY | 💬 💬 💬 |
| BABES | 👄 👄 |
| COOL CARS | 🚗 |
| HERO WORSHIP | |

**WHAT HAPPENS** ☛ You think you know the woman you marry, but do you really? What if you were a doctor who brought home $700,000 in ill-gotten cash and then left it sitting in the living room while you took a shower? Would your wife take it and run, like Bridget Gregory does? And would she turn some small-town dupe upside down and inside out by using him as her own private pleasure machine, as Bridget does? And would you feel safe, knowing that she could follow Bridget's model and get the dupe to do her dirty work? Watch this spider weave her web and then tell me you trust in love.

**THE CAST** ☛ Sure, you can see that Linda Fiorentino is a dark and dangerous Bridget, but who can resist the temptation of a woman so provocative and direct? Perennial nice-guy Bill Pullman, her doctor husband, sure couldn't—he believes that bringing home the big score for them to live on will satisfy her. Peter Berg must think that his small-town moves dazzled her, but he's the one bedazzled.

**WHY GUYS LOVE IT** ☛ We can live by its motto, "Fuck first and ask questions later."

**HONEY, YOU'LL LIKE THIS MOVIE . . .** ☛ Because this woman takes responsibility for her own orgasm.

**DON'T MISS**
- Watching Bridget straddle the fence about small-town Mike.
- The private dick her husband hires who doesn't know that it's best to keep his dick private around Bridget.

**MEMORABLE LINES**
- "Who's a girl got to suck to get a drink around here?" Bridget asks by way of introducing herself to the friendly folks in the small-town bar.

- "Are you still a lawyer?" she asks her attorney.

   "Yeah," he answers, "and are you still a self-serving bitch?" Fair question.

# LA FEMME NIKITA (1990)
# and
# POINT OF NO RETURN (1993)

## RATINGS

### La Femme Nikita

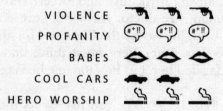

| | |
|---|---|
| VIOLENCE | |
| PROFANITY | |
| BABES | |
| COOL CARS | |
| HERO WORSHIP | |

### Point of No Return

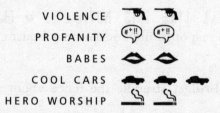

| | |
|---|---|
| VIOLENCE | |
| PROFANITY | |
| BABES | |
| COOL CARS | |
| HERO WORSHIP | |

**WHAT HAPPENS** ▬ You know the musical *My Fair Lady*, about how a stuffy old Englishman takes a poor, dirty girl from the streets and teaches her "how to walk and to talk like a regular lady" to win a bet? Well, forget it. These two nearly identical movies (one French-Italian, the other American; you have to guess which is which) tell how a kindly and buff intelligence agent saves a drug-addled, violent sociopath from court-ordered execution and teaches her how to fight, shoot, and put on mascara like a regular lady agent. Of course, she resists at first, but soon enough handsome Agent Charming wins her over, and she begins to cooperate. Why does he rescue her? So that when the national security interests require a young female assassin, she can be called into service—wherever she is, whomever she's doing. Both Nikita and Maggie (the character in *Point of No Return*) do their best to balance the odd demands of their profession against a healthy, young woman's love life, but it's constantly Agentus Interruptus. Both of them finally get the chance to take control of their own missions and destinies.

THE CAST ► In the French version, Anne Parillaud as Nikita grips your attention with her brutally accurate attacks on the cops and her benefactor, shrieking curses all the way. You can't see who or what's beneath the frizzed hair and contorted face. And that makes her transformation even more stunning, especially after the agency's beauty and manners coach—classy French movie star Jeanne Moreau—gets through with her. In *Point of No Return*, Bridget Fonda's Maggie doesn't come through as vicious as Nikita and she has a harder time hiding her good looks—but she does look great when she's done finishing school with classy American movie star Anne Bancroft. Gabriel Byrne is her mentor, and Harvey Keitel gets in a short shot in the end.

WHY GUYS LOVE THEM ► We like the idea that you can take bad girls off the street and train them to do your bidding.

HONEY, YOU'LL LIKE THESE MOVIES ... ► Because these poor, misguided girls get a second chance to make a contribution by channeling their murderous impulses into service of their countries.

## DON'T MISS

- Nikita driving her point home with the officer who books her.
- Nikita's taste in wall decorations.
- Nikita and Maggie taking aim from the tub.
- How Maggie leaves Harvey Keitel with his motor running.

## MEMORABLE LINES

- "Give us two bottles of water," Nikita tells the waiter in Venice, "because my man and me sweat like pigs when we make love." (Rent the subtitled version if you can—it's so much sexier to hear her say "make love" in French than in unsynchronized dubbed English.)
- The supervisor of Maggie's rehabilitation tells her this joke: A woman takes a duck into a bar. "How could you bring that pig into a bar?" the bartender says.

  The woman replies, "That's no pig, that's a duck," to which the bartender responds, "I was talking to the duck."

Believe it or not, there's a nearly identical Chinese version of these movies called *Black Cat.*

# SAVAGE STREETS (1984)

## RATINGS

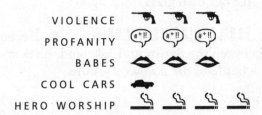

| | | | |
|---|---|---|---|
| VIOLENCE | 🔫 | 🔫 | 🔫 |
| PROFANITY | #*!! | #*!! | #*!! |
| BABES | 👄 | 👄 | 👄 |
| COOL CARS | 🚗 | | |
| HERO WORSHIP | 🚬 | 🚬 | 🚬 | 🚬 |

**WHAT HAPPENS** ☛ Oh, so savage. Brenda is a badass chick and leader of a girl gang called the Satins. But Brenda has a soft spot for her sweet deaf-mute sister Heather. When a mean guy gang (Jake and the Scars) wants revenge on Brenda for a prank she pulls on them, they rape Heather. Then they get real mean, throwing Brenda's friend off a highway bridge. This pisses off Brenda and so she takes a warm bath, dresses to kill, and then lures the Scars into catching Cupid's arrow—fired from her crossbow. When Brenda and Jake are finally alone, she gets him below the belt and then she fuels his fire with paint thinner.

**THE CAST** ☛ Linda Blair has grown quite a bit since she starred in *The Exorcist,* and in mostly the right places. Okay, maybe she was more menacing when she was possessed by the devil—and she snapped off more biting dialogue—but as Brenda she struts it tough in her tight jeans and revealing shirts. Robert Dryer has the mean gleam in his eye and the croaking laugh in his throat, so we know Jake's not going to be satisfied with a harmless prank in return for Brenda's joyride in his car. John "Dean Wormer" Vernon is the blustering principal who clearly likes Brenda more than the prissy cheerleader crying in his office after her kitty fight with Brenda.

## WHY GUYS LOVE IT ☛ We keep tabs on Linda Blair's career . . . for her own good.

## HONEY, YOU'LL LIKE THIS MOVIE . . . ☛ Because a showdown between the Satins and Jake and the Scars has got to be like a battle of the doo-wop groups.

## DON'T MISS
- Brenda's decisive bath—she lays out the whole picture for us.
- The locker-room clash between Brenda and cheerleader Cindy.

## MEMORABLE LINES
- "I wouldn't fuck him if he had the last dick on Earth," Brenda answers Cindy's accusations about stealing her boyfriend.
- "First, I'm gonna fuck you, then I'm gonna slice you into little pieces," one of the Scars says to Brenda.

  "That sounds nice and kinky to me," she shoots back. "Too bad you're not double-jointed."

  "Why?" the guy makes the mistake of asking.

  "Because then you'd be able to bend over and kiss your ass good-bye," she concludes.

# SOMETHING WILD (1986)

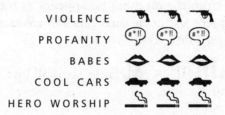
**WHAT HAPPENS** ▪ It starts as one of every guy's fantasies: You're a stockbroker or an actuary or some other boring whatever having lunch in a diner on a typically dull day, when you meet a kooky babe with a breathy voice and big knobs (held only by a very tight black tank top). Before you can say, "May I interest you in 1,000 shares of Amalgamated Preferred," she's seduced you into blowing off the afternoon, getting drunk before sundown, and taking her to a motel. You ignore the facts that she ripped off the liquor store and that she had a pair of handcuffs handy when you got to the motel. So after you spend the night, you two take off on a ride from Manhattan (where those kooky babes breed in captivity, don't they?) to points unknown in Pennsylvania. And then, like all good guilty dreams, things too good to be true begin to unravel. You find yourself at the class reunion from hell, and her ex-con boyfriend appoints himself the master of ceremonies. What started as an edgy but lighthearted romance story devolves into in-your-face mayhem.

**THE CAST** ▪ Jeff Daniels is a perfect stand-in for all of us who have kept our unfettered lusts in the top desk drawer, alongside the Binaca breath spray and the ad for 1-900-

2-HOT-4-U. You won't need to suspend any disbelief to accept the idea that the young Melanie Griffith could command Jeff to do anything. Ray Liotta, all sharp edges with his slicked hair and haw-hawing laugh, plants his boot on your throat from the moment he appears as the boyfriend. Look for cameos by movie directors John Waters (used-car salesman) and John Sayles (cop).

## WHY GUYS LOVE IT ▬ Melanie, we'd all love to be handcuffed by you.

## HONEY, YOU'LL LIKE THIS MOVIE . . . ▬ Because for once, the woman takes the guy for the ride.

## DON'T MISS

- Melanie tearing off (really tearing) that black shirt to reveal two of Hollywood's finest attractions.
- The scene in the coffee shop where Jeff demands his due from Ray and makes him pay for their meal—Jeff's balls grow three sizes in about three minutes.
- Ray's vintage Cadillac convertible.

# THE SPECIALIST (1975)

## RATINGS

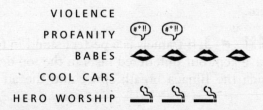

| | |
|---|---|
| VIOLENCE | |
| PROFANITY | @*!! @*!! |
| BABES | ◇ ◇ ◇ ◇ |
| COOL CARS | |
| HERO WORSHIP | 🚬 🚬 🚬 |

**WHAT HAPPENS** ▰ Small-town politics can be sooo interesting. In this case, the president of the local water company fires the shifty lawyer who's been representing the company and hires a new attorney, who appears to be nothing but proper. But the first lawyer isn't going down so easily and he hires a private investigator to help him undermine Attorney Straight Arrow. The plan: to place a hot babe on the jury of a case the attorney is trying who will lure him into imprudent behavior. Before the movie is over, everybody goes down—including her.

**THE CAST** ▰ There was never a superhero more prim and proper than the TV version of Batman—he spurned all three of the enticing babes who played Catwoman—and Adam West brings the same Boy Scout demeanor to his part as the upright attorney. And look for the invariably goofy Alvy Moore, who played the county agent Mr. Kimball on TV's *Green Acres,* as the bailiff.

**WHY GUYS LOVE IT** ▰ Sure, she's dangerous, but the only harm will be to reputations.

**HONEY, YOU'LL LIKE THIS MOVIE . . .** ▰ Because it proves, in the end, that women have all the power.

**DON'T MISS**
• The not-so-still life the bitter lawyer's son is painting.
• The picnic with Adam West and the Specialist.

**MEMORABLE LINES**
"She's an actress," the private investigator tells the lawyer who hires him. "She hasn't been in any movies; she does her acting in real life."

# BARBARELLA (1968)

## RATINGS

VIOLENCE
PROFANITY
BABES ◇ ◇ ◇ ◇ ◇
COOL CARS 🚗 🚗 🚗
HERO WORSHIP 🚬 🚬 🚬

**WHAT HAPPENS** ▰ Okay, I'll explain the plot, though no one has ever watched it for the story, which is based on a French comic strip. Anyway, a fantastic babe of the future is directed by the president of Earth to search the galaxy for a weapons inventor. She travels from planet to planet in her shag-rug-carpeted spacecraft, looking for the guy and getting into dicey situations. Twice she's rescued by men who teach her about the pleasures of the flesh, in place of the pills and psychocardiogram exchanges she's accustomed to. Her revealing space outfits are repeatedly damaged, so she must put on new ones. Finally, she finds the guy she's looking for and does what she's been commanded to do.

**THE CAST** ☛ This is why you want to watch this movie: The title character is played by a young, kittenish Jane Fonda (before workout videos and breast implants), who spends more time without clothes than with. You'll see it all. And she absolutely glows after her first encounter with full-contact sex, and that glow is refueled with every subsequent encounter. There are other people in the movie, including mime Marcel Marceau out of makeup, but nobody watches to see them.

**WHY GUYS LOVE IT** ☛ A young Jane Fonda nude. A lot, a whole lot, enough to make you wish you were Ted Turner.

**HONEY, YOU'LL LIKE THIS MOVIE . . .** ☛ Because Jane's French husband, Roger Vadim, directed it, so it must be about his idolization of her.

**DON'T MISS**
The opening credits: Our Miss Jane does a weightless striptease down to skin.

**MEMORABLE LINES**
Not a single one.

**TRIVIA**

Duran Duran, the preening pop band, took its name from the weapons inventor Jane pursues in this movie.

# CHERRY HILL HIGH (1982)

## RATINGS

VIOLENCE
PROFANITY
BABES
COOL CARS
HERO WORSHIP

**WHAT HAPPENS** ◆ **I** know I dreamed up the premise to this movie during Mrs. Greer's eleventh-grade chemistry class; what I don't know is how the producers of this movie got ahold of my thoroughly detailed fantasy and turned it into *Cherry Hill High*. Anyway, it goes like this: Six high school babes head out on an extracurricular bicycle trip with their seemingly prudish teacher. One night around the campfire the girls confess to each other their inexperience with sex and challenge each other to a contest to see which of them will lose their virginity in the most interesting way. One girl dives into a tank full of sharks with a skin diver; another runs full throttle with a biker chick. Don't squawk when you see the girl who gets laid by a guy in a chicken suit on the set of a game show, nor howl in fright when another is spirited away by a ghost in a haunted mansion. There's nothing unconventional about climbing into the backseat of a car, unless it happens to be a stock car in the midst of a race. Oh yes, and one of the girls tries it in bed.

**THE CAST** ◆ **S**ix young actresses with breasts of various sizes and shapes willing to do what it takes to get a break in Hollywood—or six young actresses with breasts of various sizes and shapes and who have very bad agents. Whichever is the case, none of them were ever seen again.

**WHY GUYS LOVE IT** ✐ We've known for years that girls have these kinds of contests; we're just glad to finally get the truth.

**HONEY, YOU'LL LIKE THIS MOVIE . . .** ✐ Because it'll bring back fond memories of your senior trip—won't it?

**DON'T MISS**
- The teacher spreading a bit of good cheer in a vat of grapes with a vintner.
- The girls' frequent baths in streams along their route—cleanliness is next to godliness.

**MEMORABLE LINES**
There was dialogue?

# HOLLYWOOD HOT TUBS (1984)

**RATINGS**

| | |
|---|---|
| VIOLENCE | |
| PROFANITY | @*!! @*!! |
| BABES | 👄 👄 👄 👄 |
| COOL CARS | |
| HERO WORSHIP | 🚬 🚬 |

**WHAT HAPPENS** ✐ A young guy gets a job working for a plumber who specializes in hot tub repair in the Los Angeles area. One of the job's hazards is that the guy is often sexually harassed by attractive women who feel oppressed at having to wear tops to their bikinis. One of those customers opens a hot tub center, named Hollywood Hot Tubs, where deprived Angelenos who don't have their own Jacuzzis can come to use a public one. The plumbing company's employees attend the grand opening, complete with plenty of kinks and a horror movie monster ending.

**THE CAST** ⬗ Huh? Oh, you might recognize a quick glimpse of classic Hollywood beauty Lauren Bacall (or what must be her evil twin), who just passes through the grand opening to get a glass of champagne and pick up a paycheck.

**WHY GUYS LOVE IT** ⬗ It puts the excitement back into plumbing, a real man's job.

**HONEY, YOU'LL LIKE THIS MOVIE . . .** ⬗ Because there are as many Speedos as there are bikinis.

**DON'T MISS**
- The two repairmen in a tough match against an entire women's soccer team.
- The opportunity to cover your eyes when our hero is sent to repair the tub at Roman Holiday—it's a men's club, if you know what I mean.

# HOT T-SHIRTS (1979)

**RATINGS**

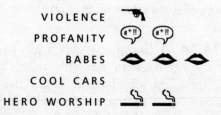

| | | |
|---|---|---|
| VIOLENCE | | |
| PROFANITY | | |
| BABES | | |
| COOL CARS | | |
| HERO WORSHIP | | |

**WHAT HAPPENS** ⬗ Joe owns a bar that's not exactly Cheers. Joe is no Sam Malone, the bar doesn't even have a

Norm, a Cliff, or regulars at all. In fact, Joe has almost no customers. And he's in debt. So how can he lure in guys ready to drop their paychecks night after night? The same way the makers of this movie will lure you into watching it: the promise of breasts of all sizes and shapes on parade. At the suggestion of a horny pal, Joe puts on wet T-shirt contests that attract the local bimbos and the cheerleaders from a nearby college in a hooter-to-hooter showdown for the title of best pair there. With each round, the babes become more, shall we say, enthusiastic in their efforts to score points with the judges—and you. Of course, when the local ladies auxiliary of the Repressed Americans Association finds out about the contest, they organize a protest. But even they cannot dampen the obvious joy of the participants and their fans.

**THE CAST** ► There's Joe, played as every bit the average joe by Ray Holland, whom you may recognize as Norm's college wrestling buddy from a couple episodes of *Cheers*. And I hope you've seen some of the other stars at least once in your life: 32B, 34C, 36D, and the ever-popular 38DD (who must be the cheerleader who identified herself as "Mae East" in the credits).

**WHY GUYS LOVE IT** ► Sure, we believe that participation in organized sports is healthy for women.

**HONEY, YOU'LL LIKE THIS MOVIE . . .** ► Because Joe's sole reason for putting on the contests is to pay off his debts so he can marry his sweetheart, and you won't find a more virtuous motivation for indulging in sleaze than that.

**DON'T MISS**
The brawl that breaks out between the cheerleaders and the townies.

**MEMORABLE LINES**
The tan lines

# IN SEARCH OF THE
# PERFECT 10 (1987)

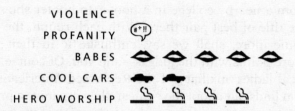
**WHAT HAPPENS** ▬ **W**hat does this movie have in common with that other one of the same number? A keen interest in the ideal woman. But this much more fun movie is a documentary of sorts (parodying the TV series *In Search Of . . .*, hosted by Leonard Nimoy) in which the host employs various strategies to get women to remove their tops so that he can analyze their breasts using his highly sophisticated Mamometer. Along the way there are interviews with guys, and other segments focusing on our favorite topic.

**THE CAST** ▬ **A**ndrew Nichols plays our host Farley Buxton as a guy who might have replaced Danny Terio in the job of emceeing *Dance Fever* if only he had been a better dancer. The rest of the cast is filled out by a pair of 8s, several different sets of 9s, and (I hope this doesn't spoil the suspense for you) a dynamic duo of 10s.

**WHY GUYS LOVE IT** ▬ **F**inally, a movie that addresses our real concerns.

**HONEY, YOU'LL LIKE THIS MOVIE ... ◆** Because it's an up-close and personal documentary about women's anatomy and physiology.

## DON'T MISS
- The informative and revealing visit to the offices of Dr. Heinz Titsling, named, of course, after the inventor of the brassiere.
- The game of Twister.

## MEMORABLE LINES
"Time and gravity are the enemy of all titties!"

# PORKY'S (1981)

## RATINGS

| | |
|---|---|
| VIOLENCE | |
| PROFANITY | |
| BABES | |
| COOL CARS | |
| HERO WORSHIP | |

**WHAT HAPPENS ◆** Kids and teachers at a South Florida high school in the early 1960s are in heat day and night. When the boys are not busy joking and lying about sex, they peep into the girls' locker room, visit a hooker named Cherry Forever, and visit a go-go bar/bordello named Porky's, where they're scammed by the eponymous owner. When one of guys is worked over by Porky's bunch, they band together with the local cops to exact some revenge on

20TH CENTURY FOX/SHOOTING STAR

In *Porky's,* who's that hanging out in the girls' showers?

the porcine pimp. Meanwhile, two of the gym teachers work up a sweat on their own and another spends her time hunting for a student with a tell-tale mole. In the end, nearly everyone is satisfied—one way or another.

**THE CAST** ▰ If you've never seen one of the three *Porky's* movies, you likely won't recognize most of this cast. Dan Monahan is Pee Wee, who keeps a growth chart of his undersized member underneath his bed. Tony Ganios, by contrast, is known as Meat, whose oversized equipment shocks even the hooker. Both Roger Wilson and Scott Colomby are familiar from *ABC Afterschool Specials:* Wilson is Mickey, who gets stomped by Porky, and Colomby is Brian Schwartz, the school's Jewish student who must prove his worth to the rest of the gang. You'll have no trouble figuring out how Chuck Mitchell got cast as Porky. Alex Karras, who terrorized quarterbacks as a defensive lineman for the Detroit Lions before he terrorized TV audiences as Webster's father, turns up as the dopey sheriff and brother of Porky. Kim Cattrall plays the very vocal gym teacher, Miss Honeywell.

## WHY GUYS LOVE IT ▰ So what's wrong with thinking about sex every thirty seconds . . . or more.

## HONEY, YOU'LL LIKE THIS MOVIE . . . ▰ Because it proves your theory that guys think about sex every thirty seconds or more.

## DON'T MISS
- The great gag two of the guys and Cherry Forever play on the rest of the gang.
- Lassie coming home.

## MEMORABLE LINES
"There's so much wool you could knit a sweater," says one peeper to another.

# AN AMERICAN WEREWOLF IN LONDON (1981)

## RATINGS

| | |
|---|---|
| VIOLENCE | 🔫 🔫 🔫 |
| PROFANITY | 💬 💬 |
| BABES | 👄 👄 👄 |
| COOL CARS | |
| HERO WORSHIP | 🚬 🚬 |

**WHAT HAPPENS** ▰ Two American college kids are traveling through the British countryside when one of them is mauled to death and another escapes with just scratches. Jack, the dead one, visits David, the survivor, and tells him that they were attacked by a werewolf and that David will turn into one at the next full moon. David, of course, is skeptical, an attitude reinforced by his exceptionally attentive nurse, who treats him with a personalized therapy program. But Jack keeps showing up, more decomposed with each visit, insisting that David kill himself before he becomes a werewolf. When the moon is full, David is transformed into a werewolf and he kills a few no doubt deserving people. They join Jack in visiting David and in advocating his suicide, until David can take it no longer. In the midst of a traffic jam in Picadilly Circus, the nurse discovers the difference between man and beast.

**THE CAST** ▪ David Naughton is, no surprise, David. Though he's disturbed by the visits from his dead friend and concerned about his sanity, David can hardly contain his eagerness to get his paws on the nurse. She's played by Jenny Agutter, a demure brunette with a soft and entrancing British accent. Griffin Dunne decomposes and delivers one-liners as Jack, whose horniness is uninhibited by death. The people in the pub who warn the boys to stay on the road could not be cast—they must have come with the setting.

**WHY GUYS LOVE IT** ▪ David gets his lust for blood satisfied and sympathy sex from a nurse.

**HONEY, YOU'LL LIKE THIS MOVIE . . .** ▪ Because the nurse believes her love can calm the savage beast.

**DON'T MISS**
The shower scene—you'll never hear Van Morrison's "Moondance" again without picturing it.

**MEMORABLE LINES**
When anyone says to you, "Stay off the moors, stick to the roads," listen to them.

# BLOOD HOOK (1986)

## RATINGS

| | |
|---|---|
| VIOLENCE | 🔫 🔫 🔫 |
| PROFANITY | 💬 💬 |
| BABES | 👄 |
| COOL CARS | |
| HERO WORSHIP | 🚬 |

**WHAT HAPPENS** ► A group of five kids and a family of four come to a lakeside in northern Wisconsin to enter a muskie fishing contest—and one by one they are killed by a fisherman with a very sharp lure and a deadly accurate cast. There are several likely suspects: the bitter old caretaker of a cabin inherited by one of the kids; a slow-talking bait store owner (with an odd resemblence to the older Neil Young); a babbling Vietnam vet with an arsenal of guns; and a zealously competitive fisherman. The end may be no great surprise, but you just don't see this much blood on your average fishing trip.

**THE CAST** ► The kids could have been the cast of *Our Town* from Benjamin Harrison High School in Port Washington, Wisconsin, class of '82, but the scary truth is that no one in this movie has ever been seen or heard from again.

**WHY GUYS LOVE IT** ► Watch it for the mammoth muskies! Watch it for the sympathetic psychos! Watch it for the murders of innocent and annoying people!

**HONEY, YOU'll LIKE THIS MOVIE ...** ► Because it has all the fun of fishin' without the smell.

## DON'T MISS
The New Age lady comfort her bereaved boyfriend with her ample bosom.

## MEMORABLE LINES
"Can you turn that music down—I can't hear myself drink," one kid tells the other.

# CHEERLEADER CAMP (1988)

## RATINGS

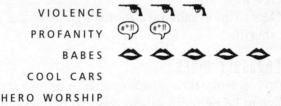

| | |
|---|---|
| VIOLENCE | 🔫 🔫 🔫 |
| PROFANITY | 💬 💬 |
| BABES | 👄 👄 👄 👄 👄 |
| COOL CARS | |
| HERO WORSHIP | |

**WHAT HAPPENS** ◗ The competition at Camp Hurrah is fierce as peppy girls, guys, and mascots battle for the approval of Miss Dee Dee Tipton, camp director, and for the audience's appreciation. So fierce, that some of the kids start turning up dead. This has Alison, dear sweet perfect Alison, especially upset because she keeps having nightmares about other kids' dying. So who is killing the cheerleaders at Camp Hurrah? The answer is not as well masked as you might expect.

**THE CAST** ◗ Leif Garrett once expected he'd be the next Shaun Cassidy, and he might have been but that hasn't prevented him from landing with a distinct thud in this movie as Alison's boyfriend, a high school student with a receding hairline and shorts that are way too short. If you've seen movies like *Avenging Angel, Delta Heat,* or *Private School,* you may recognize brunette Betsy Russell, who weeps well as Alison. Paying those two major talents left little cash in this movie's budget for any other known, ahem, talent.

**WHY GUYS LOVE IT** ► Cheerleaders. Next question.

**HONEY, YOU'LL LIKE THIS MOVIE . . .** ► Because it delves into the pressures on high school girls and the choices it forces them to make.

**DON'T MISS**
- The sunbathing scene, where much of the movie's plot is revealed.
- Miss Tipton reliving a football game of the past with the sheriff.

**MEMORABLE LINES**
"Do you know how it feels to always be on a stage, to always have to be perfect," Alison wails to her very understanding bunkmate, the team mascot. "I just want to be me."

# DEAD RINGERS (1988)

**RATINGS**

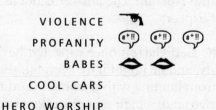

| | |
|---|---|
| VIOLENCE | 🔫 |
| PROFANITY | @*!!  @*!!  @*!! |
| BABES | 👄 👄 |
| COOL CARS | |
| HERO WORSHIP | |

**WHAT HAPPENS** ✒ Identical twin brothers, Elliot and Beverly, are gynecologists. Elliot is a celebrated researcher who's coldhearted but smooth with women. Beverly, the clinician, is more sensitive and awkward. Yet the French woman with the unusual anatomy and the drug habit is seduced by one of them and then can't tell when they've pulled a switch on her. When she does figure out that they have deliberately misled her, she breaks it off, leaving sensitive Beverly with a broken heart and a drug addiction. He plunges himself and his brother into a spiraling descent that will haunt you for days.

**THE CAST** ✒ Jeremy Irons plays the twins absolutely distinct from each other with his posture, tone of voice, and mannerisms. At the same time, he underscores the ties between them and their dependence on each other. And because he's built these characters so completely, the conclusion is all the more chilling. Older and sexy French actress Genevieve Bujold is all the more enticing because of what we know about her character's reproductive system.

**WHY GUYS LOVE IT** ✒ Twins who are experts in the female anatomy share the same woman—what guy wouldn't want to see that?

**HONEY, YOU'LL LIKE THIS MOVIE ...** ✒ Because it deals with the difficulties of modern gynecology.

**DON'T MISS**
- The new instruments Beverly designs for surgery.
- How the boys celebrate their birthday with their favorite cake and prescriptions.

# THE EVIL DEAD (1983)

## RATINGS

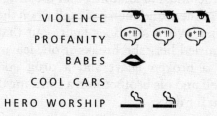

VIOLENCE
PROFANITY
BABES
COOL CARS
HERO WORSHIP

**WHAT HAPPENS** ▬ Five college kids (two guys and three girls) rent an archaeologist's cabin in the mountains for a cheap vacation in the wilderness—and find out why they should have gone to Daytona for spring break. In the professor's basement, they discover his notes and tape recordings on an ancient culture with a demon fetish. One guy plays the tape recordings to spook the girls, and that conjures up an invisible force that possesses the three girls first and then one of the guys. The remaining guy, Ash, battles his zombied friends, dodges the fluids of varying colors and viscosity that are flying everywhere, and eventually decapitates his girlfriend with a shovel—'cause you have to do it sometimes.

**THE CAST** ▬ The senior class officers of Bowling Green University, '81.

**WHY GUYS LOVE IT** ▬ The possessed girls, one notch beyond a nasty case of PMS, scare the pants off the guy, but he gets to live.

**HONEY, YOU'LL LIKE THIS MOVIE . . .** ▬ Because the guys don't get to have all the fun in this horror movie.

## DON'T MISS
A quick glimpse of breast and panty as the first girl is possessed.

# FRANKENHOOKER (1990)

## RATINGS

| | |
|---|---|
| VIOLENCE | 🔫 🔫 🔫 |
| PROFANITY | @*!! @*!! @*!! |
| BABES | 👄 👄 👄 👄 |
| COOL CARS | |
| HERO WORSHIP | 🚬 🚬 🚬 |

**WHAT HAPPENS** ▰ When Jeffrey Franken's fiancée is sliced to pieces by a remote control lawn mower he invented, he is despondent until he devises a plan to rebuild her. Jeffrey, a medical school dropout, employee of the New Jersey Electric Company and a self-described "bioelectric technician," hires an assortment of prostitutes to submit to his inspections so that he can find just the right parts for his remodeled fiancée. Now most of us would have simply salved our grief in the company of a few of the pros, but Jeffrey Franken lets them at some dynamite (literally) crack and then collects their parts in plastic trash bags after it causes them to explode. He reconstructs his fiancée, only she seems to have the hormones of the prostitutes and heads downtown to turn a few lethal tricks. In the end, she has to help him get himself together.

**THE CAST** ▰ The sole recognizable face in this low-budget movie is Louise *"Mary Hartman, Mary Hartman"* Lasser, who was just about the strangest thing in the Woody Allen movies she appeared in, but among this cast of over- and under-actors, she's straight in line.

**WHY GUYS LOVE IT** ▬ Prostitutes in all shapes, colors, and sizes and a mad pseudoscientist who gets to play with their parts.

**HONEY, YOU'LL LIKE THIS MOVIE . . .** ▬ Because it examines the nature of our humanity . . . very, very, closely.

**DON'T MISS**
Jeffrey Franken's personal cure for a pounding morality—a drill to the head.

# HELLRAISER (1987)

**RATINGS**

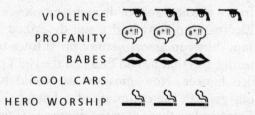

| | | | |
|---|---|---|---|
| VIOLENCE | 🔫 | 🔫 | 🔫 🔫 |
| PROFANITY | @*!! | @*!! | @*!! |
| BABES | 👄 | 👄 | 👄 |
| COOL CARS | | | |
| HERO WORSHIP | 🚬 | 🚬 | 🚬 |

**WHAT HAPPENS** ▬ Frank and Deidre had a hot and dangerous love affair—as the Polaroids we see in the beginning of the movie attest—but he lives a bit too close to the edge and strikes a deal with the wrong folks, if you know what I'm saying, and is gone. Meanwhile, Deidre and her new husband move into the house where she and Frank had lived. When the husband cuts himself and few drops of blood drip on the floor, Frank—or at least part of him—is

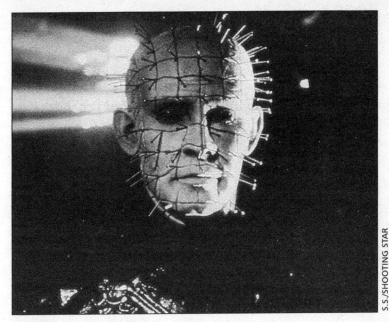

S.S./SHOOTING STAR

In *Hellraiser,* love is pain.

resurrected. Frank tells Deidre he needs more blood to restore himself, so she picks up guys, brings them home, and
kills them for Frank. His taste for blood is insatiable, and
he taps any source he can find, but in the end he has a few
debts to pay that his creditors are persistent in collecting.

**THE CAST** ◾ The only person you may recognize in this
movie is Andrew Robinson, who plays Frank's brother. Robinson was the sadistic killer Scorpio in *Dirty Harry.* More
important than any of the other cast members is horror
writer Clive Barker, who directed this movie (his first at the
helm) from his own story.

**WHY GUYS LOVE IT** ◾ Any woman who will crack a guy
over the head with a hammer so her guy can drink the blood
is a keeper, for sure.

**HONEY, YOU'LL LOVE THIS MOVIE . . .** ◼ Because one look at gruesome Frank and you'll be certain that love conquers all.

**DON'T MISS**
- The acupuncture job on the aptly named cenobite, Pinhead.
- The high-protein diet favored by the creepy homeless guy who follows Deidre's stepdaughter.

**MEMORABLE LINES**
"Every drop of blood you spill puts more flesh on my bones," Frank tells Deidre with a leer, "and we both want that, don't we?"

# THE HOUSE ON
# SORORITY ROW (1983)

**RATINGS**

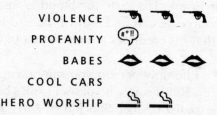

| | |
|---|---|
| VIOLENCE | 🔫 🔫 🔫 |
| PROFANITY | (#*!!) |
| BABES | 👄 👄 👄 |
| COOL CARS | |
| HERO WORSHIP | 🚬 🚬 |

**WHAT HAPPENS** ◼ On graduation eve, the sisters of Giggle Pi plan a party for their last night in the sorority house—in defiance of their creepy old housemother. When she embarrasses one of the girls, they all play a cruel trick on her. Except, of course, the trick is soon enough on them. And, in accordance with the rules dictated by the *Horror Movie Handbook*, the girls meet up with their fate one by one, in varying states of dress, until only the girl with the conscience is left to face down their killer.

**THE CAST** ► All the sisters of Giggle Pi—featuring Vicki, an icy, sharply featured brunette, and Catherine, shorter, softer, and sweeter, and certainly one cheery and chesty blond. Best of all, it appears the girls spent the movie's bra budget on party decorations. Every one else in the movie must remain anonymous—because that's what they are.

**WHY GUYS LOVE IT** ► Eight letters that spell a house full of babes living in close quarters and practicing who knows what kind of initiation rites.

**HONEY, YOU'LL LIKE THIS MOVIE ...** ► Because for once it's a movie about sororities instead of frats.

**DON'T MISS**
- The tidal wave that the housemother lets loose on Vicki's water bed.
- The blonde's quick wardrobe change.

**MEMORABLE LINES**
"I'm really glad this is working out," Catherine's blind date says to her as they hide from the killer.

# THE SHINING (1980)

## RATINGS

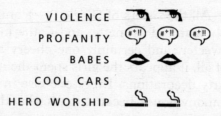

VIOLENCE

PROFANITY

BABES

COOL CARS

HERO WORSHIP

**WHAT HAPPENS** ▬ Jack is writing a book. Jack takes a job as the winter caretaker of a big, old summer resort hotel high in the Rockies. Jack likes the peace and quiet. Jack starts to see people, strange people, people who used to be there. Lots of people. People like the former caretaker who one winter slaughtered his wife and two daughters and then killed himself. Jack's wife, Wendy, and Jack's odd son do their best to stay clear of him. Jack isn't Jack anymore. Jack goes berserk.

**THE CAST** ▬ Jack Nicholson is Jack, and you can see him slipping away, his eyes staring past Wendy in one moment and then boring into her the next. He is full of enthusiasm about the job when they move in, but about the time the snow starts to fall and their isolation is complete, Jack starts reaching out to the spirits around him and cutting himself free of his family. Shelley Duvall is the optimistic, eager-to-please Wendy; Danny Lloyd is their creepy son, Danny, who has an imaginary friend even before they move into the hotel. The only person with a chance of helping them is Scatman Crothers, the summer caretaker whose bad intuition brings him back from his winter roost in Florida.

**WHY GUYS LOVE IT** ◄ When Jack blows a fuse, he brings the whole grid down with him.

**HONEY, YOU'LL LIKE THIS MOVIE . . .** ◄ Because it's based on one of those Stephen King books you're always pushing me to read.

## DON'T MISS
- When Wendy looks at Jack's manuscript; you'll see the most terrifying sentence you can imagine.
- The grisly bathtub scene that appears to Jack.

## MEMORABLE LINES
- "Redrum," says Danny's imaginary friend, "redrum."
- "Wendy, darling, light of my life," Jack croons. "I'm not going to hurt you, Wendy. I'm just gonna bash your brains in. I'm gonna bash them right the fuck in."

**TRIVIA**

The hotel where this movie was filmed is the Stanley Hotel, near Boulder, Colorado; it was owned by the Stanley who invented the Stanley Steamer car.

# TO THE DEVIL—
# A DAUGHTER (1976)
[aka *Child of Satan*]

## RATINGS

|  |  |
|---|---|
| VIOLENCE | 🔫 🔫 🔫 |
| PROFANITY | |
| BABES | 👄 👄 👄 👄 |
| COOL CARS | |
| HERO WORSHIP | 🚬 🚬 |

**WHAT HAPPENS** ▪ You gotta give that Satan guy credit: When he decides to take a wife, it's always a good-looking young girl. In this case, she's a nun in the church of Asteroth, a prehistoric incarnation of the Baddest Guy. Her weak father signed a pact with Him on the day of her birth, but he reconsiders as her eighteenth birthday—the day she is to be given to Asteroth—nears, and he asks a noted occult writer to intervene for her. The writer gets a look at this beautiful, innocent young woman and he takes up her cause. To free her, he must break the powerful spell worked by the excommunicated priest who heads the cult.

**THE CAST** ▪ Nastassja Kinski has the beguiling eyes and pouty lips of Satan's ideal bride (if you can believe what you see in the movies). Veteran horror movie actor Christopher Lee has the entrancing eyes and hypnotic voice that Satan always seems to like in his priests. The writer is tough, no-nonsense Richard Widmark and he takes a mostly chaste interest in Kinski. Her father, played by Denholm Elliott, has less altruistic motives. Honor Blackman ("Pussy Galore" in the James Bond film *Goldfinger*) is a standard-issue middle-aged follower of the Dark Prince, who seems a bit jealous she doesn't get a shot at the Big Guy.

**WHY GUYS LOVE IT** ➥ You can't fault Satan's taste in women.

**HONEY, YOU'LL LIKE THIS MOVIE . . .** ➥ Because if you're scared, you can sit real close to me.

**DON'T MISS**
- Kinski's kinky sexual encounter with the spawn of hell.
- The priest's offer to Widmark to partake of the pleasures of the flesh for himself.

# BACHELOR PARTY (1984)

## RATINGS

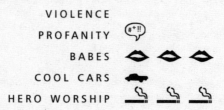

| | |
|---|---|
| VIOLENCE | |
| PROFANITY | #*!! |
| BABES | 👄 👄 👄 |
| COOL CARS | 🚗 |
| HERO WORSHIP | 🚬 🚬 🚬 |

**WHAT HAPPENS** ▰ **R**egular-guy Rick is going to marry rich and gorgeous Debbie, so his buddies plan a night of depravity and debauchery for him, which, of course, Debbie objects to. Her snobby father and ex-boyfriend plot to disrupt the party and catch Rick with his pants down—only he's zipped up tight and they're not. The funniest parts of this movie are in the setup, but still hang on for the ride to the end because justice can be good for a laugh or two, too.

**THE CAST** ▰ **A**s Rick, Tom Hanks is not as wacko as Bill Murray or as much of a smart-ass as Michael Keaton might be in the same part—Hanks is just a likeable cutup who might be found in any bunch of friends. His intended is played by Tawny Kitaen, who is a bachelor party all by her-self. Adrian Zmed, last seen leering at Heather Locklear on TV's *T. J. Hooker,* is one of Rick's buddies. And Wendie Jo Sperber, a regular on *Bosom Buddies* (the TV show that gave Hanks his start), appears here as Debbie's unsatisfied sister-in-law.

## WHY GUYS LOVE IT ➤ Women never understand that we don't go to bachelor parties because we really want to, but because we owe it to our buddy whose life is about to end.

## HONEY, YOU'LL LIKE THIS MOVIE . . . ➤ Because it's about an enduring wedding tradition.

## DON'T MISS

- When the bridal shower turns raunchier than the bache-lor party.
- Debbie trying to trap Rick into infidelity at the party.

## MEMORABLE LINES

"Nothing is going to change our friendship," Rick assures his friends. "We're still going to bowl every Tuesday, play cards every Friday, and wear each other's underwear every Sunday."

# DINER (1982)

## RATINGS

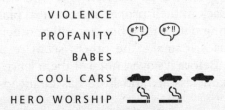

| | |
|---|---|
| VIOLENCE | |
| PROFANITY | 💢 💢 |
| BABES | |
| COOL CARS | 🚗 🚗 🚗 |
| HERO WORSHIP | 🚬 🚬 |

© YORAM KAHANA/SHOOTING STAR

In *Diner*, boys will be boys so they don't have to be men.

**WHAT HAPPENS** ➧ In the late 1950s, six guys do their best to stay one step ahead of creeping adulthood and spend all their free time hanging out at their favorite diner, trying to resolve important questions like, "Who's the best singer to make out to—Frank Sinatra or Johnny Mathis?" One of the guys is set to be married by the end of the week—if his fiancée can get a passing grade on his quiz about the Baltimore Colts. The other guys each grapple with equally weighty concerns—one is already married to a wife who can't put his records back in their proper alphabetical place; another has a mounting debt with a bookie; still another drinks too much and tries to make the others seem responsible by comparison. Before it's over, none of them learn any particularly poignant lessons and little has changed—just as it should be.

**THE CAST** ☛ This movie is a who's who of as-yet undiscovered talent. Mickey Rourke, when he was still trying to be an actor not a boxer, is the group's smoothest operator, but he gets himself in deep with his bookie. Daniel Stern (well before he was the voice of the kid on *The Wonder Years*) badgers his wife, a ripe 'n' ready Ellen Barkin, because she puts a blues record in with the R&B records. Kevin Bacon wants to live on the edge—if only he could see it. Steve Guttenberg loves the Colts first and foremost. Timothy Daly, the nice brother on TV's *Wings,* is as revoltingly sincere and decent in this movie as he is on TV. Comedian Paul Reiser's part is to annoy everyone, especially Guttenberg. Watch for Michael Tucker, the guy who was the unlikely sex god on *L.A. Law.*

**WHY GUYS LOVE IT** ☛ What's not to love about hanging out and arguing about nothing?

**HONEY, YOU'LL LIKE THIS MOVIE ...** ☛ Because Mickey Rourke is well-groomed in it—well, mostly.

**DON'T MISS**
- The great prank Bacon plays on his pals in the movie's first sequence.
- Reiser's comedy routine at Guttenberg's wedding that runs through the closing credits.

**MEMORABLE LINES**
"It was an accident," Rourke explains to his date about the surprise she found in her popcorn.

"Your thing got into a box of popcorn and it was an accident?" she asks.

"I try to come on like I'm cool all the time, but there I am, sitting with a boner ... the pain was killing me, so what I did was open up my fly to loosen everything up, to give it a little air, and it worked, everything got settled ... and that's when Sandra got her leg caught on the bush and it lifted up her dress . . . and it popped right up and went through the bottom of the popcorn box. The force of it just lifted up the flap and I couldn't move the box."

"Well, that's true," says this truly understanding sweetheart. "You couldn't move the box."

### TRIVIA

Can you identify Guttenberg's fiancée? If you can, you've got a future in police work or on the Psychic Friends Network.

# THE LAST DETAIL (1973)

## RATINGS

| | |
|---|---|
| VIOLENCE | 🔫 🔫 |
| PROFANITY | @*!! @*!! @*!! |
| BABES | 👄 👄 |
| COOL CARS | |
| HERO WORSHIP | 🚬 🚬 |

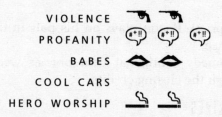

**WHAT HAPPENS** ► **T**wo not-quite-regulation sailors in the Shore Patrol are dispatched to pick up another sailor who's been convicted of stealing on a Navy base and transport him to a military prison. The convict, Meadows, turns out to be a gentle giant who has been given a raw deal by the military court and who has never been drunk or laid or had much fun of any kind. Well, his two escorts can't see any reason why Meadows shouldn't get to live a little before he goes up the river, so they set out to show him a good time on their trip in and make a man of him. On some counts, they even succeed.

**THE CAST** ✏ Jack Nicholson has never been regulation anything, and as one of the Shore Patrol sailors he wears his insolence like a medal of honor throughout the movie. He is particularly incensed that Meadows won't stand up for himself and he goads him from the beginning almost to the end. His partner, Mule (played by Otis Young), is hardly regulation, but he is much more sympathetic to Meadows and certainly more anxious about their unscheduled stops along the way. Randy Quaid is big and stooped, and as Meadows that makes him look like he's been stepped on all his life. He is a bumpkin, but he's no Gomer Pyle, either—he's just accepted his lot as a doormat. On their last stop they get him a waiflike hooker, Carol Kane, who seems as beaten as Quaid's character, and you can imagine that if they had met under other circumstances they could be shy sweethearts who rendezvous at the willow tree in some small Southern town. Michael Moriarty appears at the end as the tough Marine warden of the prison. Watch closely and you'll spot Gilda Radner (pre-*Saturday Night Live*) in a funny part as a member of the weird chanting group the boys stumble onto.

**WHY GUYS LOVE IT** ✏ If you were about to go to prison, wouldn't you hope for a last binge?

**HONEY, YOU'LL LIKE THIS MOVIE . . .** ✏ Because it's about men with compassion for less fortunate men.

**DON'T MISS**
- Nicholson ordering beers at gunpoint from the redneck bartender in Washington, D.C.
- The quick glimpse of Carol Kane nude, talking to Meadows after his quick shot.

## MEMORABLE LINES

- "I used to go to a whore who had a glass eye," Nicholson relates. "She used to take it out and wink people off for a dollar."
- "You're shitting me," Mule says to their commanding officer.

    "I wouldn't shit you," the officer responds, "you're my favorite turd."

# LET'S GET HARRY (1986)
## (aka *The Rescue*)

## RATINGS

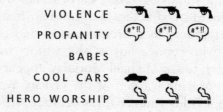

| | | | |
|---|---|---|---|
| VIOLENCE | 🔫 | 🔫 | 🔫 |
| PROFANITY | @*!! | @*!! | @*!! |
| BABES | | | |
| COOL CARS | 🚗 | 🚗 | |
| HERO WORSHIP | 🚬 | 🚬 | 🚬 |

## WHAT HAPPENS ▬ What would you do if your buddy was taken hostage by a scuzball drug dealer in Colombia and the pencil-necked bureaucrats in Washington refused to detach the 82nd Airborne to bring him back? You'd get a group of guys from down the plant and bring him back yourselves, right? Well, that's just what the brother and four friends of Harry do when he and the American ambassador are snatched by a drug lord in South America. The friends of Harry hire a mercenary to lead them into the jungle and in the process discover just how clever and deadly they can be. And what would you do when you successfully com-

pleted the mission? Have a keg party, just like these guys do, of course.

**THE CAST** ▰ Mark Harmon always seems so terminally mellow that you have a hard time imagining he wouldn't just try to talk the terrorists out of taking him hostage, but as Harry he does work up enough fight to become a nuisance to his kidnappers. Robert Duvall's shaved head, goatee, and swagger are just enough to convince the five guys back in Chicago that he's their soldier of fortune. Harry's brother, Corey, is played by Michael Schoeffling (who looks like he would be modeling jeans in the special issue of *GQ* devoted to denim). His pals include Glen Frey (of the Eagles), whose nose leads them straight to the drug lord's compound, and Gary Busey as Smilin' Jack, the used-car salesman, who can't pass up the opportunity to go huntin'. You'll recognize Gregory Sierra, a Colombian gun dealer Duvall knows, from recurring roles on *Barney Miller* and *Sanford & Son*.

**WHY GUYS LOVE IT** ▰ It's what we'd all do for our own buddy, when the time came.

**HONEY, YOU'LL LIKE THIS MOVIE ...** ▰ Because you once told me "Hotel California" was your all-time favorite song and now Glen Frey needs your support for his movie career.

**DON'T MISS**
- Busey's in-your-face approach to asking directions from the natives.

**MEMORABLE LINES**
"You little creep, I'll have you on a stick," says Busey to the bad guy.

# NIGHT SHIFT (1982)

## RATINGS

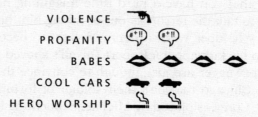

VIOLENCE

PROFANITY

BABES

COOL CARS

HERO WORSHIP

**WHAT HAPPENS** ▰ Who says the overnight shift at the city morgue has to be dull and quiet? What if you brought a little life into the place by, say, using it as the headquarters for a prostitution ring? That's what mild-mannered Chuck Lumley and dopey scam-meister Bill Blazejowski do at the morgue where they work, after the slinky strumpet who lives next door to Chuck loses her manager. And though Chuck and Bill are not professional pimps, the business thrives because Chuck is a financial whiz who invests all of their earnings, and Bill is a natural promotions man. The only glitches in this scenario are: Chuck's fiancée, rival pimps, the police.

**THE CAST** ▰ If you can think of Henry Winkler only as Fonzie, you'll be surprised at how convincing he is as the good-hearted doormat Chuck. Everyone steps on Chuck, and all he wants is to be left in peace. But his compulsive-obsessive fiancée Charlotte, played by Gina Hecht, manipulates him; his boss takes advantage of him; he can't even get his take-out dinner order delivered right. And then comes his new colleague Bill, a party animal with a steady stream of harebrained ideas he treats like inspiration. Michael Keaton has Bill dancin', singin', and jammin' air guitar like he's star of his own show. Shelley Long proves here that she doesn't have to be as uptight as her character Diane on *Cheers*—she is Belinda, Chuck's very friendly neighbor and the only person who treats him with any respect. Comic Richard Belzer appears at the beginning and end as the hatchet man for a competing pimp. Look for Clint Howard (director Ron's brother) in Drawer No. 12. Kevin Costner attends the party, and Shannen Doherty gets a bit of work, too. Think you know your football? Do you recognize the cowboy john who corrals Long? (Hint: He was a linebacker for the Philadelphia Eagles who once entered a glass-eating contest.)

## WHY GUYS LOVE IT ▪ Finally, a movie that depicts the hard-working women of the oldest profession in a positive light.

## HONEY, YOU'LL LIKE THIS MOVIE ... ▪ Because these two guys give the women their due.

### DON'T MISS
- Shelley Long making breakfast in her underpants; I'll have mine over easy, please.
- The frat party at the morgue.

### MEMORABLE LINES
Here are just two of many classics in this movie:
- "Who's this, your wife?" Bill asks Chuck as he looks at a picture on Chuck's desk.
   "Fiancée," Chuck answers.
   "Nice frame," says Bill.
- "You know, maybe it's just me, but I feel a lot of love in this room," Bill tells the girls. "It was here a minute ago and it's beautiful. So at this moment, I think it's important that I see all of your breasts."

**ANSWER**

The football player is Tim Rossovich.

# WATCH IT (1993)

## RATINGS

VIOLENCE
PROFANITY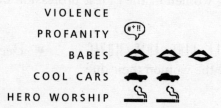
BABES
COOL CARS
HERO WORSHIP

**WHAT HAPPENS** ▪ John visits his cousin Michael's house in Chicago, which Michael shares with two college buddies and where the favorite pastime is a ball-busting contest of practical joking called Watch It! Each of the housemates humiliates John, the new pigeon in the game, and he'd retaliate if he weren't preoccupied by Michael's girlfriend. Conflict erupts between the cousins that dredges up some ugly family business from the past, and the girlfriend is cool to John even though she knows Michael's not exactly faithful to her. So John decides to leave town, leaving the three buddies one last opportunity to prank him—this one, though, involves his mint-condition late sixties Mustang, and it pushes him to his limit. He ambushes each of them with surprises that land right where they live: the last and best of which involves the cousin and a woman in a cloakroom where the girlfriend finds him.

THE CAST ◄ You might not know any of these actors by name, but you'll recognize almost all of them. Peter Gallagher (the pervert yuppie lawyer in *sex, lies, and videotape*) plays John, who's so earnest he could get a part in a Jim Varney movie. Jon Tenney's Michael is suave and arrogant. John C. McGinley (who's had parts in virtually every Oliver Stone movie), and Tom Sizemore (see *Flight of the Intruder* on page 50) are the housemates who've never left the frat house. Blond Suzi Amis is the veterinarian girlfriend who (bonus points) likes the White Sox. She's counseled by her assistant, who's played funky but pragmatic by Lili Taylor. Cynthia Stevenson gets an especially sharp shot at McGinley for his weasely treatment of her.

WHY GUYS LOVE IT ◄ This game is fun!

HONEY, YOU'LL LIKE THIS MOVIE . . . ◄ Because it's sort of a movie about relationships.

DON'T MISS
• The seduction set up for John at the party he goes to the first night.

MEMORABLE LINES
Michael, explaining the game to John, "There's only one rule: You can't get mad; you can only get even."

# THE WILD ONE (1954)

## RATINGS

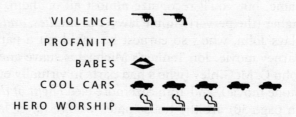

VIOLENCE

PROFANITY

BABES

COOL CARS

HERO WORSHIP

**WHAT HAPPENS** ▬ Of course, not everyone who rides a motorcycle is an outlaw—but it sure does seem that the outlaws have more fun. Just look at this movie, in which the Black Rebel Motorcycle Club is run off from a bike race in one small town and head to a more hospitable little town nearby where they stage their own motorcycle riding events and terrorize the poor people trapped in the dull 1950s. While the club's leader hangs in the café inciting the waitress (and sheriff's daughter) to live dangerously, a rival gang shows up to raise the stakes on the fun and games. Some of the local stiffs do get together to try to drive the hoodlums out of town, but even the sheriff sees that harmless hijinks are not a criminal conspiracy.

**THE CAST** ▬ A young Marlon Brando, already a legend from his performances in *A Streetcar Named Desire* and *On the Waterfront*, is Johnny, the tough and gruff leader of the Black Rebels. But he is not entirely one of them because he's an outlaw by choice, not by nature—he can articulate his disenchantment with the world, while they can't even recognize theirs. The waitress played by Mary Murphy sees this and is turned on by it, probing him to understand why he lives as he does. The rival gang's chief, a grisly-looking young Lee Marvin, is better suited to lead the pack.

**WHY GUYS LOVE IT** ■ Bikers and beer we all hold dear.

**HONEY, YOU'LL LIKE THIS MOVIE . . .** ■ Because the sheriff seems happy to consider the outlaw an in-law.

**DON'T MISS**
- The beer bottle slalom event.
- The satisfied look on the waitress's face after she and Johnny take an all-night ride on his hog.

**MEMORABLE LINES**
"What are you rebelling against?" the waitress asks Johnny. "What have you got?" he answers.

# *Those Darn Kids*

## CLASS OF 1984 (1982)

 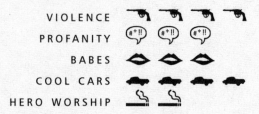
**WHAT HAPPENS** ▰ The first few days of school can be rough on a new teacher unfamiliar with its protocols and mores. For example, may a teacher carry a .45 caliber pistol, or is anything over a .38 considered excessive? And, if a teacher's car is firebombed, can he automatically assume the bad/brilliant leader of the school's ruling gang is responsible? These questions and others like them are the challenges faced by Andy Norris as he adjusts to his new job as a high school music teacher. He gets his answers from Stegman, a punk terrorist who runs drugs and prostitutes and fears no punishment, and a cynical biology teacher named Terry Corrigan. Norris and Stegman are quickly locked into an escalating war that comes to a crashing finale

on the rooftop above the auditorium where the school orchestra is performing a concert.

THE CAST ☛ Perry King (who co-starred with Sylvester Stallone and Henry Winkler in *The Lords of Flatbush*) is an idealistic Andy Norris at the outset, but as his battle with Stegman (Timothy Van Patten) grows more heated, Norris gets tougher and meaner. Stegman is a complete manipulator—of the principal, the cops, his mother—but he grows more desperate when he is confronted by someone who won't be intimidated. As biology teacher and Norris's friend Terry Corrigan, Roddy McDowall starts off jaded, but he is renewed by his discovery of a very effective new teaching technique—the menacing of his inattentive students with a pistol. A chubby Michael J. Fox is one of Norris's students, Arthur the trumpet player.

WHY GUYS LOVE IT ☛ It earns extra credit in Gratuitous Violence.

HONEY, YOU'LL LIKE THIS MOVIE . . . ☛ Because the music teacher cares, really cares, about these kids and their education.

DON'T MISS
• The bunny rabbit and froggy tableau the kiddies set up for Mr. Corrigan.
• Stegman beating himself up in the bathroom and then blaming it on Norris.
• Norris teaching the guys in Stegman's gang about the proper use of shop tools, like the circular saw and the blowtorch.

MEMORABLE LINES
"Life is pain, pain is everything, you will learn," Stegman tells Norris.

# DAZED AND CONFUSED (1993)

## RATINGS

VIOLENCE

PROFANITY

BABES

COOL CARS

HERO WORSHIP

**WHAT HAPPENS** ◆ **All** the good stuff you remember from high school: hanging out, mindless partying, sexual frustration. On the last day of school in 1976, the incoming seniors initiate the incoming freshman—the boys get walloped with wooden paddles, the girls humiliated. The in crowd disdains the outsiders, the outsiders mock the in crowd. And, this being the seventies, everybody must get stoned—they

GRAMERCY PICTURES/SHOOTING STAR

In *Dazed and Confused,* dudes will be dudes.

all seem to end up at a mammoth outdoor party with no cops around for miles. The only major question to be answered is whether the school's star quarterback will sign a pledge to forswear alcohol, drugs, and sex.

**THE CAST** ☛ No recognizable stars, but people who all look familiar to anyone who went to high school after 1968.

**WHY GUYS LOVE IT** ☛ The whole town seems to go along with the idea that for a day the freshman can be abused.

**HONEY, YOU'LL LIKE THIS MOVIE ...** ☛ Because the girls get in their own brand of freshman abuse.

**DON'T MISS**
- Watching the freshman girls go through the car wash.
- The freshmen's revenge on the biggest senior creep.

**MEMORABLE LINE**
"If I ever say these were the best days of my life, remind me to kill myself," says one of the perpetual outsiders.

# FAST TIMES AT
# RIDGEMONT HIGH (1982)

**RATINGS**

| | | | |
|---|---|---|---|
| VIOLENCE | | | |
| PROFANITY | (#*!!) | (#*!!) | (#*!!) |
| BABES | 👄 | 👄 | 👄 |
| COOL CARS | 🚗 | 🚗 | 🚗 |
| HERO WORSHIP | 🚬 | 🚬 | 🚬 |

**WHAT HAPPENS** ▰ High school in the 1980s, California style. The stoned surfer dude disrupts history class, the nerd blows his opportunity with a babe from the pizza place and his smooth-talking friend swoops on her, the guy who works at the fast-food joints is humiliated by the uniforms he's forced to wear. All of them spend their time at the mall contemplating the weighty issues on their minds while sucking down smoothies. But don't worry, nearly every situation has a pay-off that's more about laughs than life.

**THE CAST** ▰ Sean Penn's part as Jeff Spicoli, who lives for nothing but great waves and great weed, is small but unforgettable. Jennifer Jason Leigh is as innocent as she ever was as the pizza place babe who misreads the intentions of Mark Damone, the slick ticket-scalper played by Robert Romanus; she should have stuck with Rat, played by Brian Backer, whose intentions may be the same as Damone's but whose capacity for fulfilling them much less. Her best friend, Phoebe Cates, is luscious and she knows it—she's talking about the college guys she will date. Leigh's brother, played by Judge Reinhold, bounces from the burger palace to the chicken emporium to the fried-fish factory. Ray *"My Favorite Martian"* Walston is the exasperated history teacher who figures a way to pay back Spicoli. And watch for Forrest Whitaker as the football player who wants a little vengeance of his own. Eric Stoltz, Anthony Edwards, and Nicholas Cage (billed under his real name, Nicholas Coppola) all make their movie debuts in small parts, too.

**WHY GUYS LOVE IT** ▰ If you don't have any memories of great high school days misspent, you can borrow these.

**HONEY, YOU'LL LIKE THIS MOVIE . . .** ▰ Because it was directed by a woman who knows how girls wasted their time in high school as well as the boys.

## DON'T MISS

- Judge Reinhold's fantasy about his sister's friend, and what happens to him when he gets too involved with it.
- Spicoli's clever plan for concealing that he destroyed his friend's brother's car.

## MEMORABLE LINES

"Hey, bud, let's party," is Spicoli's general greeting.

# THE LIAR'S CLUB (1993)

## RATINGS

| | |
|---|---|
| VIOLENCE | 🔫 🔫 |
| PROFANITY | #*!! |
| BABES | 👄 👄 |
| COOL CARS | 🚗 |
| HERO WORSHIP | 🚬 🚬 |

**WHAT HAPPENS** — Pat is the star quarterback and the repository of all the hopes of his group of friends: He has a football scholarship. So if on graduation night he gets a little forceful with Marla—who admittedly was flirting aggressively with him—the friends are quick to defend Pat. Jimbo, an offensive lineman who's always supposed to protect the quarterback, gets a bit forceful with Marla, too, but she doesn't just lose her innocence to Jimbo, she loses her life. The other friends rally around Jimbo to protect both guys. Until a couple of them have second thoughts.

**THE CAST** — Wil Wheaton, who was last seen when he was a bit smaller in another dead body movie, *Stand by Me*, is Pat and Jimbo's friend with a conscience. Or maybe he wanted a shot at Marla himself. Either way, he has second thoughts he shares with Pat's regular steady girl, who's pissed at Pat for jumping Marla. Bruce Weitz cleaned himself up from his role as the growling detective in TV's *Hill Street Blues* to play the wise garage owner who employs Jimbo and Wil Wheaton and offers sage advice to Wil when he needs it most.

## WHY GUYS LOVE IT ▰ As the quarterback goes, so goes the team.

## HONEY, YOU'LL LIKE THIS MOVIE... ▰ Because it confronts the complex issue of date rape.

## DON'T MISS
Marla's hot little dance with Pat at the graduation party.

## MEMORABLE LINE
"A lie is not a lie if everyone says it's true," says Pat, demonstrating a remarkable grasp of language theory or shameless self-interest—you decide which.

# RIVER'S EDGE (1986)

## RATINGS

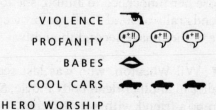

| | |
|---|---|
| VIOLENCE | 🔫 |
| PROFANITY | @*!! @*!! @*!! |
| BABES | 💋 |
| COOL CARS | 🚗 🚗 🚗 |
| HERO WORSHIP | |

**WHAT HAPPENS** ☛ Pop Quiz: 1. A guy you hang out with at school strangles a girl you hang out with at school. Do you, A) Go with him to look at her nude corpse where he left it by the river; B) Listen to your speed-flippin' friend, who says you shouldn't tell anyone about it; C) Drive around, listen to tunes, and get stoned?; D) All of the above. 2. True or False. Taking the guy who killed the girl to the home of a burned-out, one-legged biker and his inflatable old lady for safekeeping sure seems like a good idea at the time. 3. If you pinch two grams of your mother's weed, lay 30 percent of it on your sociopathic eleven-year-old brother, and roll the rest into a joint that you split with the good-looking girl whose father was a rock singer, how much do you actually smoke?

This is an open-book test, spelling counts, and show your work.

**THE CAST** ☛ This is not an advanced-placement class, you know. Matt has Keanu Reeves's cheekbones; he shambles along behind everyone; and he's nice to the girls—his mom, little sister, and Ione Skye, a sweet-faced brunette who's the daughter of Donovan. Layne is fried to a Crispin Glover and he's fired up about loyalty to John or Samson (or Daniel Roebuck), who choked the life out of Jamie because he could. Fortunately, Feck (Dennis Hopper) and his girlfriend, three-input Ellie, will look after John and regale him with tales of the days that used to be until everyone can decide what to do. Still, better for John to be with Feck than Matt's little brother, Tim (Josh Miller), who's armed and loaded.

**WHY GUYS LOVE IT** ☛ The moral is there is no moral.

**HONEY, YOU'LL LIKE THIS MOVIE . . .** ☛ After it's over.

**DON'T MISS**
- Tim's visit to Feck's house.
- Layne's wake-up call.

## MEMORABLE LINES

"I was laying in the gutter and bleeding and shaken, my leg out in the middle of the street next to a beer can," Feck recounts. "And I remember thinking, 'There's my leg, I wonder if there's any beer in that can.' "

**TRIVIA**

Believe it or not, this is based on a true story.

# WEIRD SCIENCE (1985)

## RATINGS

VIOLENCE

PROFANITY

BABES

COOL CARS

HERO WORSHIP

**WHAT HAPPENS** ◾ Two high school dweebs, Gary and Wyatt, use a home computer tapped into the military's system to do what any of us would given the power: create a superbabe programmed to do whatever they ask of her. Lisa, as they've named her, is not only agreeable to doing whatever they want, she has a few ideas of her own. She breaks them out of their dweeb lives by letting a couple of the local cool dudes know what they do with her and by helping our heroes impress two real girls from their school. She even helps them get revenge on Wyatt's bully older brother, Chet.

**THE CAST** ☛ First things first: Kelly LeBrock is an ultimate brunette babe. She has pouty lips, plenty of curves, long legs, a sexy English accent, and she knows how to use all of it so well that even the coolest of dudes stammer in her presence. Anthony Michael Hall has defined Contemporary American Geek in several movies, and in this one he tries his damndest to show us that a geek has a cool dude inside his baggy khakis—if only someone would recognize it. Still, his character, Gary, is much hipper than Wyatt, who's playcd by Ilan Mitchell-Smith. You've met brothers like Chet (maybe you even have one): They punch you in the arm everytime you walk past them, call you scorching nicknames like "butthead," and extort cash or favors from you everytime they catch you doing something you don't want your parents to know about. As Chet, Bill Paxton has a crew cut that makes his forehead jut out like a gorilla's, and he's very simian in his walk and talk. Robert Downey Jr. is one of the guys in their school who thinks he's so cool that he couldn't possibly be cool.

**WHY GUYS LOVE IT** ☛ Look what comes out of their high-density hard drive.

**HONEY, YOU'LL LIKE THIS MOVIE . . .** ☛ Because all these poor boys need is an older woman to help build their confidence and they can win the nice girls away from the cool creeps who take them for granted.

**DON'T MISS**
- Gary and Wyatt's shower with Lisa.
- Their visit to a downtown blues bar and their transformation, after a few bourbons, into jive-talkin' hipsters.

- The big blowout at Wyatt's house . . . everybody will be there, even his grandparents and a few nasty-looking crashers.

## MEMORABLE LINES

- "It'll be the usual teenage orgy," Lisa tells Gary's parents about the party. "You know, sex, drugs, and rock 'n' roll, chips and dip, whips and chains, hundreds of kids running around in their underwear."
- "How about a nice greasy pork sandwich served in a dirty ashtray," Chet says to get Gary to blow chow when the dweebs come home drunk.

# AMAZON WOMEN ON THE MOON (1987)

---

## RATINGS

VIOLENCE

PROFANITY  (#*!!)  (#*!!)

BABES  👄 👄 👄 👄

COOL CARS

HERO WORSHIP

**WHAT HAPPENS** ▰ **A** small TV station broadcasts a B-movie that gives this movie its title—we see parts of the movie, along with commercials and the station's backstage buffoonery. One of the best bits is an ad for a computer system single women can buy to screen potential suitors. After the woman in the ad rejects a blind date whose record with women is poor, she tells him, "It's early, you can still get lucky in a bar," then checking her printout, she adds, "like you did last Thursday." In the opening sequence, a guy is attacked by his apartment. Groucho would be honored by the gag the doctor runs on the couple with the newborn baby. You can relate to the nervous teenager who buys the one millionth Titan condom at the local drugstore. And hang on for the naive beauty queen who gets VD when she goes to New York.

**THE CAST** ■ The opening credits read "Lots of actors," and it's true. Rosanna Arquette and Steve Guttenberg are the blind-date couple. Carrie Fisher is the VD beauty queen. Arsenio Hall gets battered in the first sketch. Look for Michelle Pfeiffer, *SNL* veteran Phil Hartman, comedian Andrew Dice Clay, bluesman B. B. King, and exploitation film director Russ Meyer. The skits were made by several directors and collected by John Landis, who directed several comedy classics, including *Animal House* and *The Blues Brothers*.

**WHY GUYS LOVE IT** ■ It's a no-brainer with nudity.

**HONEY, YOU'LL LIKE THIS MOVIE . . .** ■ Because it's a poignant satire of popular culture.

**DON'T MISS**
The long and very naked "Pethouse" Playmate video.

# BLAZING SADDLES (1973)

**RATINGS**

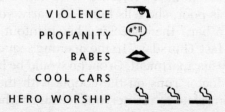

| | |
|---|---|
| VIOLENCE | |
| PROFANITY | |
| BABES | |
| COOL CARS | |
| HERO WORSHIP | |

**WHAT HAPPENS** ▪ The Old West was a lot funnier than you think. There were city-hip black sheriffs policing racist little towns, gunfighters too loaded to shoot straight, scheming railroad barons, insatiable showgirls, and Indian chiefs direct from the Catskills, all of them doing shtick as old as the rocks. They all ride roughshod over movie clichés, and when they have picked the bleached bones of the classic Western clean, they take a few shots at the lavish musical, too.

**THE CAST** ▪ Cleavon Little knows just what to do when the good people of Rock Ridge greet him—their new sheriff, Black Bart—with arms opened: He takes the closest hostage he can find. He does find one friend in Gene Wilder's Jim, known as the Crisco Kid, before he lost a showdown with the bottle. All goes according to the plan of the fiendish Hedley Lamarr ("not Heddy, Hedley"; or is it Harvey as in Korman?), except when it doesn't. Lamarr's plot to use the lewd Lili Von Shtupp, the Teutonic Titwillow (who looks exactly like Madeline Kahn), to break Black Bart backfires when she's tamed by him. Producer–director Mel Brooks gave himself only leading roles: hot and clumsy Governor Lepetomane and a schlemiel of an Indian chief. Ex-Lion Alex Karras surely had an easy time memorizing Mongo's lines and working up his appetite.

**WHY GUYS LOVE IT** ▪ These are not time-release jokes— they start to work as soon as the fizzing stops.

**HONEY, YOU'LL LIKE THIS MOVIE . . .** ▪ Because it's nothing if not multicultural.

**DON'T MISS**
- The Gatling gun fire of gas while the cowboys eat their pork 'n' beans.
- Dom DeLuise directing the choir.

## MEMORABLE LINES

- "Nobody move or the nigger gets it," Black Bart threatens the townfolk. The hostage, of course, is Bart himself.
- "It's twue, it's twue," proclaims Lili after she saw for herself.

**TRIVIA**

Richard Pryor cowrote the screenplay.

# THE BLUES BROTHERS (1980)

## RATINGS

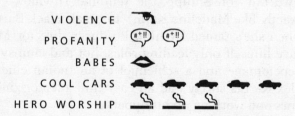

| | |
|---|---|
| VIOLENCE | 🔫 |
| PROFANITY | 💬 💬 |
| BABES | 👄 |
| COOL CARS | 🚗 🚗 🚗 🚗 |
| HERO WORSHIP | 🚬 🚬 🚬 |

**WHAT HAPPENS** ▬ The movie opens and closes with ridiculous car chases—the first includes a tour of a suburban Chicago mall, and the finale occupies the last twenty minutes of screen time and yields an accident every thirty seconds. In between, the movie has great songs performed by Aretha Franklin, James Brown, and Ray Charles, and the brothers themselves, and a sketchy plot about two out-of-touch musicians who are trying to raise money to save the orphanage where they grew up. A mysterious woman with access to heavy weaponry tracks the brothers, as do the state police and a band of Illinois Nazis. The movie evolved out of a recurring skit on *Saturday Night Live,* and because of the music, the stars, or the cars, it is still by far the best of several movies that began as *SNL* acts.

**THE CAST** ✒ John Belushi and Dan Aykroyd are Joliet Jake and Elwood Blues, who dress like 1950s hipsters even though it is the 1980s. Belushi's Jake is antagonistic and deceitful; Aykroyd's Elwood is dim and a petty thief. But they are saved by the advice of the maintenance man at the orphanage, played by Cab Calloway, and the preaching of the Reverend Cleophus James, delivered with a howlin' frenzy by the Godfather of Soul, James Brown. John Candy leads the state police contingent. Princess Leia herself, Carrie Fisher, is the woman with a grudge. *Laugh-In* alum Henry Gibson does the leader of the Nazi Party as cruel and smug. You won't be able to miss seeing Twiggy, supermodel of the 1960s, but you'll have to work a little harder to get a glimpse of Paul Rubens, aka PeeWee Herman. And don't turn off the movie until you've seen Steven Spielberg.

**WHY GUYS LOVE IT** ✒ This was a fun, fun movie to make.

**HONEY, YOU'LL LIKE THIS MOVIE . . .** ✒ Because it's a musical.

**DON'T MISS**
Belushi's trip down the stairs at the orphanage.

**MEMORABLE LINES**
- Best Belushi line: "I had a flat tire, I ran out of gas, I didn't have cab fare, my tux didn't come back from the cleaners, a friend came in from out of town, there was an earthquake, a terrible flood, locusts—it wasn't my fault."
- Best Aykroyd line: "It's 106 miles to Chicago, we have a full tank of gas, a half a pack of cigarettes, it's dark, and we're wearing sunglasses."

# CADDYSHACK (1980)

## RATINGS

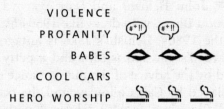

VIOLENCE

PROFANITY

BABES

COOL CARS

HERO WORSHIP

**WHAT HAPPENS** ▬ You'd think that caddying at a posh country club would be a good job, and you'd be right. The caddies at this club get to mock the pompous snob of a judge who runs the place, laugh nervously about the groundskeeper's war on gophers, and savor the insults hurled in every direction by the crass rich guy who joins the club. One caddy, Danny Noonan, plays around with a waitress and the judge's niece, and he wants to play in the club's tournament to win a scholarship sponsored by the judge. Meanwhile, the judge and the loudmouth square off in a high-stakes round of golf.

**THE CAST** ▬ The self-inflating judge played by Ted Knight is begging to be punctured, and Rodney Dangerfield has a sharp pin in his one-liners. Chevy Chase is the slightly off-center playboy son of the club's cofounder, and Bill Murray is the severely off-center groundskeeper on full combat alert for the Varmint Cong. Michael O'Keefe (Mr. Bonnie Raitt) is Danny Noonan, divided by his desire to impress the judge and win a scholarship and his urge to let loose.

**WHY GUYS LOVE IT** ▬ It's eighteen holes worth of great gags and goofy characters.

## HONEY, YOU'LL LIKE THIS MOVIE ...   ◄ Because you've
heard me reciting the lines for years.

## DON'T MISS
- Noonan's nooner with the judge's niece.
- The Baby Ruth that empties the pool.
- Carl the groundskeeper's touching appreciation for women's golf.

## MEMORABLE LINES
- "Is this your wife?" the slob asks the snob. "She must have been something before electricity."
- "I guess I should have yelled 'two,' " says the slob after his ball hits home with the snob.

## BEWARE

Spare yourself the agony of watching *Caddyshack II*. Jackie Mason takes Rodney Dangerfield's role, and the movie is about as funny as a double bogey on a par 4 18th.

# THE CAPTAIN'S PARADISE (1953)

## RATINGS

| | |
|---|---|
| VIOLENCE | 🔫 |
| PROFANITY | |
| BABES | 💋 💋 |
| COOL CARS | |
| HERO WORSHIP | 🚬 🚬 🚬 🚬 |

**WHAT HAPPENS** ◆ When you travel for a living, you have to make wherever you are as much like home as possible. That's what Captain Henry St. James does as he shuttles his steamship back and forth between Gibraltar and Morocco. When he's in Gibraltar, he puts on his slippers and lights his pipe and settles down for a nice home-cooked dinner with Maud, the ever-cheery Mrs. Captain St. James. In Morocco, the captain dances the nights away with Nita, the wild and wanton Mrs. Captain St. James. He keeps both of them happy with proper gifts, and they all celebrate years of anniversaries, until the day when Maud gets a glimpse of Morocco and Nita tires of the endless frolic. Then, the captain's paradise is swept away by a riptide, and he's left standing alone and under the gun.

**THE CAST** ◆ Alec Guinness (Obi-Wan Kenobi himself) is a happy, contented Captain St. James. He has everything he expects in a woman from his two wives and he plays each part he's designed for himself to the full. Maud (Celia Johnson) is a perky and pretty English wife, devoted and dutiful until she gets a few belts under her belt. Nita (Yvonne De Carlo; yes, Lily Munster) is an exotic beauty in love with the captain's dancing and passion, but soon craving a quiet night at home. The captain's story is recounted by his first mate, Chief Officer Ricco (Charles Goldner), who salivates over the captain's perfect achievement.

**WHY GUYS LOVE IT** ◆ The captain is a generous man, sharing his surplus of love and affection with two needy women.

**HONEY, YOU'LL LIKE THIS MOVIE ...** ◆ Because the captain must stand before a firing squad.

**DON'T MISS**
• Or forget the opening scene. You'll need to remember it to see who gets the last laugh.

- The captain's handy midcrossing ritual so he knows where he's headed: to Maud or to Nita.

## MEMORABLE LINES
"May this go on forever," the captain toasts each wife on their anniversary.

# DUMB & DUMBER (1994)

## RATINGS

VIOLENCE

PROFANITY

BABES  👄 👄 👄

COOL CARS  🚗 🚗 🚗 🚗

HERO WORSHIP

**WHAT HAPPENS** ▬ Lloyd, a clueless limo driver on the make, falls madly (and inappropriately) in love with a woman he takes to the airport. She leaves a briefcase with a ransom payment in the airport, which Lloyd sees and believes she's lost. He enlists his roommate, Harry, who is an even more clueless dog groomer, to drive him to Aspen (in his Doggie van) to return the case and win the love of the woman of his dreams. The two dolts are pursued by the gangsters to whom the ransom was due and a couple of tough guys they stiff with their bill in a diner. When they finally get to Aspen, they discover there's money in the briefcase and they spend it all on a luxury hotel, gaudy Western ski wear, and a Ferrari, filling the case with IOUs. The boys then engage in a battle of the vicious pranks over the woman and, sure enough, bungle into helping her catch the bad guy.

**THE CAST** ◾ Comic Jim Carrey grabs the territory left vacant since Jerry Lewis crossed the two-hundred-pound mark. With his buck teeth and page-boy haircut, he seems innocent, but he never misses an opportunity to play a practical joke on his best friend or whomever else is handy. And he has a reserve of misguided pickup lines. Mild-mannered Jeff Daniels is almost as goofy in his role as Harry, the shaggy-haired dog groomer. He's everything a best friend should be: willing to drop everything to help his buddy, and a ready target for any prank. Lauren Holly, beautiful and elegant (and now Mrs. Jim Carrey), is sweet enough as the rich babe to not cruelly dismiss Lloyd, which is all the encouragement he needs. Teri Garr (who took an on-air shower on *Late Night with David Letterman*) plays her snobby friend. You may remember Charles Rocket, who plays the villain, as the guy who was fired from *Saturday Night Live* for ad-libbing "Who the fuck shot J. R.?" at the end of the show one night.

**WHY GUYS LOVE IT** ◾ These guys are masters of the cruel joke.

**HONEY, YOU'LL LIKE THIS MOVIE ...** ◾ Because it's kind of a 'tard love story, like those TV movies you love so much.

**DON'T MISS**
- Harry's snowball fight with the woman.
- Harry and Lloyd's last chance at the end of the movie.

**MEMORABLE LINES**
In the opening minutes, Lloyd asks a woman he's trying to pick up about her accent. When she says she's from Austria, the geographically challenged doofus says, "G'day, mate. Let's throw another shrimp on the Barbie."

**TRIVIA**

Way-out musician Todd Rundgren is credited with the sound track, but his work must appear only on the sound track album. It's almost nonexistent during the movie.

# HOT SHOTS! (1991)

## RATINGS

VIOLENCE

PROFANITY

BABES

COOL CARS

HERO WORSHIP

**WHAT HAPPENS** ▰ If you've seen more than one "flyboy" film (say, *Top Gun*), you know the plot here. This movie parodies them all, and gets in shots at *Dances with Wolves*, *Rocky*, *9½ Weeks*, and lots of other movies, too. The framework is that pilot Sean "Topper" Harley is the son of a decorated flier who made a mistake and left behind a tarnished reputation. Topper hopes to win back his family's good name and prove himself worthy of a gorgeous babe on a mission called Operation Sleepy Weasel. But there is an unethical defense contractor with an interest in seeing Sleepy Weasel nod off. Topper has to deliver his ordnance and his lines without cracking up.

## THE CAST ▰ I always thought Charlie Sheen could give Tom Cruise a run for his money in the Self-Love Sweepstakes, but Sheen proves here that he has a sense of humor—at least about Cruise's career choices. Lloyd Bridges is stuck at altitude as Admiral Tug Benson. Jon Cryer is below sea level as Washout, the pilot with walleyed vision. Longtime TV FBI good guy Efrem Zimbalist Jr. shows he can be good at playing bad as the defense contractor. Jim Abrahams and the Zuckers (Jerry and David) are the masterminds(?) behind this movie, as they were for *Airplane! Top Secret!,* and the *Naked Gun*s.

## WHY GUYS LIKE IT ▰ It's stupid, stupid.

## HONEY, YOU'LL LIKE THIS MOVIE ... ▰ Because it parodies all those stupid movies guys watch all the time.

## DON'T MISS
- The barroom brawl and watch for a couple of real NBA tough guys getting in a few shots.
- The pretty good flight sequences.

## MEMORABLE LINES
"Are you all right, sir?" the admiral's aide asks his c.o. after he bumps his head.

"Of course, I'm all right," the admiral answers. "Why? What have you heard?"

# I'M GONNA GIT YOU SUCHA (1988)

## RATINGS

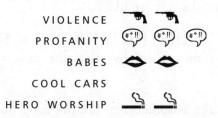

VIOLENCE
PROFANITY
BABES
COOL CARS
HERO WORSHIP

**WHAT HAPPENS** ▬ When June-Bug Spade dies of an O.G (an overdose of gold chains), his brother, Jack, comes home from the Army to find out what led June-Bug to his fatal addiction. Jack enlists the help of his mother's ex-lover, John Slade, who made a name in the 'hood battling bad guys. Together they clean up the streets and bring down Mr. Big. But don't be fooled by the appearance of a substantial plot, because this movie was made by the same guys responsible for *In Living Color,* the funny sketch comedy show from TV, and the plot is just a way to go from gag to gag. Among the funniest are a Youth Gang Competition that in-cludes a car-stripping event, and the Pimp of the Year pag-eant.

**THE CAST** ▬ Keenen Ivory Wayans wrote, directed, and starred in the movie as Jack Spade. His brother Damon Wayans is a thoroughly jive punk working for Mr. Big, played with his glower turned up high by John "Dean Wor-mer" Vernon. You'll see plenty of familiar faces from TV sitcoms like *Good Times* and *A Different World,* too. Football great Jim Brown and singer Isaac Hayes join the crusade against Mr. Big. Even Eve "Jan Brady" Plumb shows up as the wife of the black militant played by Clarence Williams III (Link from *The Mod Squad*). There's a part for Antonio "Huggy Bear" Fargas, too.

## WHY GUYS LOVE IT ▬ The jokes are as juvenile and crude as can be—just the way we like it.

## HONEY, YOU'LL LIKE THIS MOVIE ... ▬ Because the women are stronger—literally—than the men.

## DON'T MISS
The raid on the whorehouse. It's the only nudity in the movie.

## MEMORABLE LINES
- The recurring exit line: "You guys have a choice: You either go out the window or you can take the stairs."
- Whenever anyone sees June-Bug's picture with all of his chains on, they ask, "How did he go to the bathroom with all that stuff on?"

# MAN BITES DOG (1992)

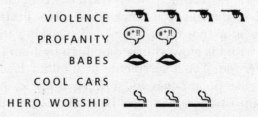

RATINGS

| | | | | |
|---|---|---|---|---|
| VIOLENCE | 🔫 | 🔫 | 🔫 | 🔫 |
| PROFANITY | @*!! | @*!! | | |
| BABES | 👄 | 👄 | | |
| COOL CARS | | | | |
| HERO WORSHIP | 🚬 | 🚬 | 🚬 | |

**WHAT HAPPENS** ◄ A French documentary crew follows a serial killer through his daily rounds, from his Monday murder of a postman to a Friday face-off with vengeful relatives of one of his victims. The crew even meets the killer's family, who reminisce about what a lovable but mischievous little boy he was. Throughout, the killer keeps up a running commentary about a variety of topics, including architecture, social theory, and how to properly dispose of the corpses. When the filmmakers begin to run low on funds, he kills more affluent people to keep the cameras rolling. Eventually, the crew gets even more involved; in fact, a couple sound engineers become more a part of the action than they care to. The ending is abrupt. Oh, did I mention this is satire—more like *This Is Spinal Tap* than *Henry: Portrait of a Serial Killer*.

**THE CAST** ◄ All of the actors are French, which makes sense because this is a French movie. Benôit Poelvoorde, who plays Benôit the killer, looks like a software engineer or a bureaucrat. Rémy Belvaux and André Bonzel are the presences behind the camera—as the director and cameraman, to be specific—and they record their own interactions with Benôit as dutifully as they film his activities. The movie is dedicated to the two sound engineers who are killed during the movie.

**WHY GUYS LOVE IT** ◄ We can all appreciate the hard work and dedication it takes to be a successful serial killer

**HONEY, YOU'LL LIKE THIS MOVIE . . .** ◄ Because it's a French art film—with subtitles and everything.

**DON'T MISS**
- The unique approach to playing the flute by Benôit's girlfriend.

- The couple who use their kitchen table for a late-night snack.

## MEMORABLE LINES
Benôit fancies himself a poet, as well as a philosopher. Here's just one of his inspiring observations: "Love leaves a trail of sulfur, like some lingering smell."

# MONTY PYTHON AND THE HOLY GRAIL (1975)

## RATINGS

| | |
|---|---|
| VIOLENCE | 🔫 🔫 |
| PROFANITY | (@*!!) (@*!!) |
| BABES | 👄 👄 |
| COOL CARS | |
| HERO WORSHIP | |

## WHAT HAPPENS ▪ In the hands of Monty Python's Flying Circus no British tradition is sacred—everything from the monarchy and sheepherding to cross-dressing and Scot-bashing is open to ridicule. In this movie, the Pythons skewer the legends of Camelot, the Knights of the Round Table, and television documentaries about historical events. King Arthur and his knights search for the goblet used at the Last Supper, while fighting off vicious bunny rabbits, taunting Frenchmen, a three-headed knight with strange landscaping ideas, and other perilous threats. The end is quite arresting.

## THE CAST ▪ If you know the Monty Python crew, you'll recognize the late Graham Chapman as King Arthur, John

Cleese as Tim the Enchanter, Eric Idle as Brave Sir Robin, and Michael Palin as Sir Gallahad the Pure. If you don't know Monty Python, you may recognize John Cleese and Michael Palin from *A Fish Called Wanda*.

## WHY GUYS LOVE IT ✏ It's dumb in the most intellectual way possible.

## HONEY, YOU'LL LIKE THIS MOVIE... ✏ Because it shows that chivalry was never all it was cracked up to be.

## DON'T MISS

- King Arthur's one-sided duel with The Black Knight— only one of them walks away.
- Sir Lancelot's rampage through the wedding to rescue a girl in trouble.

## MEMORABLE LINES

- "I fart in your general direction," the French gatekeeper rebuffs King Arthur. "Your mother was a hamster and your father smelled of elderberries. Now go away or I will taunt you a second time."
- "We are but eight score blondes and brunettes, all between the ages of sixteen and nineteen and a half," Zoot tells Sir Gallahad, "stuck in this castle with no one to protect us. Oh, it's a lonely life . . . bathing . . . dressing . . . undressing . . . making exciting underwear."

## TRIVIA

Quote this movie to guys and you're almost certain to get laughs; quote it to a woman and more often than not you'll get the fish-eyed stare.

# THE NAKED GUN: FROM THE FILES OF POLICE SQUAD! (1988)

## RATINGS

| | |
|---|---|
| VIOLENCE | 🔫 🔫 |
| PROFANITY | |
| BABES | 👄 👄 |
| COOL CARS | 🚗 |
| HERO WORSHIP | 🚬 🚬 |

**WHAT HAPPENS** ◾ A failed TV show has enough popular interest to convince its producers to make a feature film about a dense cop bungling his way to arrests and full of the lowest, most obvious humor imaginable. But that's what happened behind the scenes. What happens on screen is rapid-fire sight gags, cheap jokes, and innuendo—all placed in the context of a frame-up of one cop and an investigation into a threat to kill the Queen of England at a baseball game. Like its kin, *Airplane!* and *Hot Shots!*, this movie keeps you busy from start to finish with movie references, a few ridiculous stunts, and plenty of pointless destruction.

**THE CAST** ◾ Leslie Nielsen is Lieutenant Frank Drebin, who's neither bright nor suave. His boss, the captain played by George Kennedy, has the utmost faith in Drebin. Frank is determined to save his partner's reputation, a seemingly impossible dream considering that his partner is O. J. Simpson, who says little and gets stepped on a lot. Ricardo Montalban is the villain who's almost as powerful as *Fantasy Island*'s Mr. Rourke. His assistant, Priscilla Presley, decides she'd rather assist Frank. John Houseman gives driving lessons the same way he taught law. There are plenty of cameos to keep your attention, including: Reggie Jackson, Curt Gowdy, Weird Al Yankovic, Dr. Joyce Brothers, and others.

**WHY GUYS LOVE IT** ▰ It's stupid, stupid. (Did I say that once already? Oh, then it's really stupid, stupid. That's better.)

**HONEY, YOU'LL LIKE THIS MOVIE . . .** ▰ Because you won't have to work hard to get the humor.

**DON'T MISS**
- The student driver quickly learning the lessons of the road.
- The Queen passing hot dogs at Dodger Stadium.

**MEMORABLE LINES**
- "The doctors say he's got a 50-50 chance of living," the captain tells Frank, "but there's only a ten percent chance of that."
- That's a honey of an ankle bracelet," Frank tells Jane, the bad guy's secretary. "Oh, did that thing slip down again," she blushes.

# NATIONAL LAMPOON'S ANIMAL HOUSE (1978)

**RATINGS**

| | | | |
|---|---|---|---|
| VIOLENCE | | | |
| PROFANITY | @*!! | @*!! | @*!! |
| BABES | 👄 | 👄 | |
| COOL CARS | 🚗 | | |
| HERO WORSHIP | 🚬 | 🚬 | 🚬 | 🚬 |

S.S./SHOOTING STAR

*Animal House,* where gestures were never so stupid or futile.

**WHAT HAPPENS** ☛ The hardest partying fraternity at Faber University, the Deltas, go to war with the clean-cut Omegas and the dictator/dean who puts the Delts on "double secret probation." The Delts' major weapons in the war are a total disregard for classes, rules, and decency, and an inspired subversiveness. Which isn't to say that the Delts don't have any fun. They haze their pledges, throw a toga party, put a horse in the dean's office and, when they cross the final line into expulsion, they wreak havoc on the homecoming parade.

**THE CAST** ☛ The main event is John Belushi's Bluto, who has few lines but who expresses the purest Delta spirit: Never let anything get in the way of a good time. More presentable are the frat's officers: Otter, played by Tim Matheson, who never fails to charm a woman, and Peter Riegert, who loves the blues more than he does Karen Allen. Be sure to cover your eyes when you see Donald Sutherland, the dope-smokin' professor, or you'll see more of him than you care to. The pledges are Pinto, played by Tom Hulce, and Flounder, Stephen Furst (the chubby doctor from *St. Elsewhere* and now on *Babylon 5*). John Vernon will forevermore be Dean Wormer. Look for Kevin Bacon's debut in a toga, and singer/songwriter Stephen Bishop singing a song he wrote.

**WHY GUYS LOVE IT** ▰ Deep down, we're all Delts.

**HONEY, YOU'LL LIKE THIS MOVIE . . .** ▰ Because it explains the whole fraternity thing that's always mystified you.

**DON'T MISS**
- Otter's clever scheme to bag himself a date at an all-girls college.
- Bluto's impersonation of a zit.

**MEMORABLE LINES**
- "Food fight!"
- "What we need right now is a stupid, futile gesture on someone's part."

# A SHOT IN THE DARK (1964)

**RATINGS**

| | |
|---|---|
| VIOLENCE | 🔫 |
| PROFANITY | |
| BABES | 👄 |
| COOL CARS | |
| HERO WORSHIP | 🚬 🚬 🚬 |

**WHAT HAPPENS** ▰ French police inspector Jacques Clouseau is either a brilliant criminologist whose appearance as a bungling fool is a clever ruse devised to disarm the most suspicious of criminals, or he's just a lucky buffoon. Either way, only Clouseau sees that a wealthy man's very luscious maid couldn't possibly be guilty of the heinous murders he's investigating—even if all the clues point to her. And so Clouseau sets out to clear her of the charges, and her clothing.

**THE CAST** ▰ No one has ever bumped their head or slammed a drawer on their fingers with more sincerity (and thus more hilarity) than Peter Sellers. And he'll have you imitating Clouseau's exaggerated French accent every time you talk to a waiter in a fancy restaurant. But the funniest part of Sellers's performance as Clouseau are the looks of condescension and exasperation that he aims at his chief and fellow officers who are duped by the evidence. Elke Sommer is everything you and I would like in a French maid: blond and built, just slightly brighter than Clouseau and yet receptive to his clumsy come-ons. Clouseau's number-one supporter is Kato, his houseboy and sparring partner, played by Burt Kwouk. The inspector's number-one enemy (though Clouseau doesn't know it) is Chief Inspector Dreyfus, played (in this and subsequent *Pink Panther* movies) with bug-eyed mania by Herbert Lom. George Sanders, a properly haughty Englishman, is the wealthy man who can't seem to find good help. And one of the actors playing a small part in this movie goes by the name Turk Thrust, which is a handle suitable for a failed porn star or a rhythm guitar player in a heavy metal band.

**WHY GUYS LOVE IT** ▰ Something about that maid's uniform . . .

**HONEY, YOU'LL LIKE THIS MOVIE . . .** ▰ Because it's a comedy without a fart joke.

## DON'T MISS

- Clouseau and the maid visiting Camp Sunshine and their drive through the crowded streets of Paris.
- The bad case of Kato-us Interruptus Clouseau gets hit with.

## MEMORABLE LINES

"Give me ten men like Clouseau," Chief Inspector Dreyfus declares, "and I could destroy the world!"

## CHECK OUT

Peter Sellers starred as Inspector Clouseau in five other *Pink Panther* movies—he did not, however, appear in *Inspector Clouseau*. In that one, Alan Arkin makes the mistake of trying to play the part Sellers had made indelibly his.

# STRIPES (1981)

## RATINGS

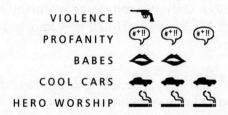

| VIOLENCE | 🔫 | | |
| PROFANITY | @*!! | @*!! | @*!! |
| BABES | 👄 | 👄 | |
| COOL CARS | 🚗 | 🚗 | 🚗 |
| HERO WORSHIP | 🚬 | 🚬 | 🚬 |

**WHAT HAPPENS** ◢ John Winger and Russell Zitsky, two out-of-work guys with no purpose and sliding into their thirties, enlist in the Army to get back in shape. They go through basic training with a hard-ass drill sergeant and a platoon full of defectives of all sorts. Winger gets them all in trouble with his insolence, but when the sergeant is injured, he leads them through the completion of their basic training, though in unorthodox style. This lands them an assignment with the Army's new secret weapon, an RV outfitted with the latest in high-tech munitions. Winger and Zitsky take it for a drive to impress a couple of well-built female officers, and the rest of the platoon finds itself in the middle of the Cold War.

**THE CAST** ◢ Bill Murray is so disheveled, out of shape, and full of wisecracks that he seems unfit for service in the Salvation Army. But the new Army is so eager for recruits that Murray's John Winger and the ectomorph Russell Zitsky—played as straight as possible by Harold Ramis—need only answer a few simple questions and they're in. Still, they're more suitable than Dewey Oxburger, played by John Candy at the height of his weight, who enlists because it's cheaper than signing into a diet center. Judge Reinhold and John Diehl (from *Miami Vice*) have equally valid reasons why they shouldn't be in uniform. For other, more obvious, reasons, neither should Sean Young or P. J. Soles—they're very friendly M.P. women. John Larroquette is the commander who would be stripped of his office if anyone were paying attention. Only Warren Oates is worthy of his uniform—though his Sergeant Hulka gets knocked down off his high tower.

**WHY GUYS LOVE IT** ◢ We love Bill Murray, and I mean that, so get outta here, you knuckleheads.

**HONEY, YOU'LL LIKE THIS MOVIE . . .** ◢ Because the women outrank the men.

## DON'T MISS
- John Larroquette inspecting some of his troops—through binoculars.
- Candy in a down-'n'-dirty mud-wrestling competition.

## MEMORABLE LINES (there are many, so here are three of my favorites):
- "You're a sexual dynamo—I have to read books just to keep up with you," Winger tells his girlfriend as she's walking out on him.
- "Has anyone ever given you the Aunt Jemima treatment?" says Winger to an M.P., proving he really did read those books.
- "I'm a lean, mean, fighting machine," declares Ox.

# THE CINCINNATI KID (1965)

## RATINGS

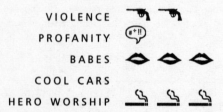

VIOLENCE

PROFANITY

BABES

COOL CARS

HERO WORSHIP

**WHAT HAPPENS** ☛ Anyone who dares to sit at the table with The Man better have nerves of steel or cash to spare. The Man takes on all-comers in all-night poker marathons that leave all the players slumped over, except The Man, whose pockets are bulging with other players' money. Still, when the hotshot Kid gets himself a game with The Man, the cards are stacked in the Kid's favor. But that's a bluff the Kid calls, and he faces The Man fair and square. The game they play is five-card stud—which is just fine with the pair of high-stakes babes watching from the sidelines.

**THE CAST** ☛ Steve McQueen plays it cool as the Kid, but not nearly as cool as Edward G. Robinson as The Man—he's solid ice and all business. Karl Malden is Shooter, who gets squeezed by his foxy wife Ann-Margret and the sore-loser Slade (Rip Torn)—they coerce Shooter into dealing the game between The Man and the Kid dirty. Tuesday Weld tries to get a piece of the Kid's action, too, but he's too focused on beating The Man to give her what she wants. Swingman Cab Calloway gets into the big game, too.

## WHY GUYS LOVE IT  ➧ Poker isn't just a game, it's a way of life.

## HONEY, YOU'LL LIKE THIS MOVIE . . . ➧ Because card games are your idea of a contact sport.

## DON'T MISS
- The girls' visit to the Turkish baths.
- When the Kid takes Shooter's wife to the fights—the cock-fights, that is.

## MEMORABLE LINES
"How did you know I didn't have the king or the queen?" Slade asks The Man after he calls Slade's bluff.

"All you paid was the looking price," The Man answers. "You didn't pay for lessons."

# THE HUSTLER (1961)

## RATINGS

| | |
|---|---|
| VIOLENCE | 🔫 |
| PROFANITY | |
| BABES | 💋 |
| COOL CARS | |
| HERO WORSHIP | 🚬 🚬 🚬 🚬 |

**WHAT HAPPENS** ► Pool is no mere game of sticks and balls any more than poker is just a card game—they're both true tests of a guy's wit and grit. Take Eddie Felson—he can surely shoot pool. Just watch the opening scene when he makes a seemingly impossible shot three times in a row after drinking more than a few shots of his favorite bourbon. But the bigger question is, does he have the nerve and stamina to beat the best, Minnesota Fats? Eddie has a lot to learn about himself, about life, and about death before he's ready to unseat the reigning champion. But don't worry about the movie being a sermon—there's lots of great shots to see along the way.

**THE CAST** ► The young Paul Newman is an unpolished, arrogant Eddie Felson, who's in love with the action more than the money or even the glory. Women always talk about Newman's dreamy blue eyes (which you can't see in this black-and-white movie), but you'll see them flash when he's in the game and then go dull when he's bored. The Great One Himself, Jackie Gleason, fills the role of Minnesota Fats amply, though in this movie he's the complete opposite of Ralph Kramden: he's cool, calm, and classy, with his tie perpetually straight and a fresh carnation in his lapel, even after he's knocked down a few balls and back a few shots. The obvious assumption is that the title of this movie refers to Newman's character, but it more appropriately identifies the professional gambler Bert Gordon, played by George C. Scott. He alternates between backhanded praise and criticism that challenges—both accompanied by a sly smile—that gets Felson hooked and then plays him for a carp. But somewhere along the way Felson learns not to flop—probably from the brainy drunk, Sarah, whom Piper Laurie portrays as painfully divided between carefree and careful. Former middleweight champion Jake LaMotta (subject of *Raging Bull*) shows up as a bartender at the bar where Felson and Sarah meet.

**WHY GUYS LOVE IT ◄** Pool halls are where boys become men, and some men are reduced to boys.

**HONEY, YOU'LL LIKE THIS MOVIE . . . ◄** Because a young Paul Newman learns about love and faithfulness in it, and spends a lot of time in his undershirt.

**DONT MISS**
What happens to Felson when he cons a local hustler on his own turf; your head will ache for him.

**MEMORABLE LINES**
"The game ain't over till the Fat Man says it is," Felson tells his manager.

**CHECH OUT**

In 1986, Paul Newman reappeared as Eddie Felson in *The Color of Money* (directed by Martin Scorsese). In this almost-as-good movie, an older, presumably wiser Eddie Felson stakes a young hot-shot pool shooter (played by Tom Cruise) and takes him and his girlfriend (Mary Elizabeth Mastrantonio) on the road to a big-time pool tournament in Atlantic City. In the end, the Hustle remains the name of the game—which Felson nearly forgets.

# LE MANS (1971)

## RATINGS

VIOLENCE

PROFANITY

BABES 👄

COOL CARS 🚗 🚗 🚗 🚗 🚗

HERO WORSHIP 🚬 🚬 🚬

**WHAT HAPPENS** ▰ Fifty-five cars and 110 drivers do eight-mile loops for twenty-four consecutive hours down country roads and a highway in France. The race includes all kinds of cars, from production models to high-performance machines traveling 230 miles per hour. The movie has some kind of plot going on about a rivalry between an American driver and a German one, and a few racing groupies hanging around, but the only real interest is in watching these guys whip their racing machines through the tight turns of this race and the accidents that slow them down.

**THE CAST** ▰ Steve McQueen actually drove his car in this movie. The only other cast members you're likely to recognize go by the names Porsche and Ferrari.

**WHY GUYS LOVE IT** ▰ I did mention the 230 miles per hour, didn't I?

**HONEY, YOU'LL LIKE THIS MOVIE ...** ▰ Because it's sort of a documentary set in France.

**DON'T MISS**
- The two cars turning 360s in the rain.
- The Italian guy's crash, and McQueen's near miss.

## MEMORABLE LINES

The red line on the speedometer.

# THE LONGEST YARD (1974)

## RATINGS

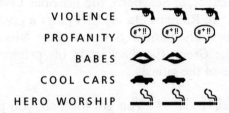

| | |
|---|---|
| VIOLENCE | |
| PROFANITY | |
| BABES | |
| COOL CARS | |
| HERO WORSHIP | |

**WHAT HAPPENS** ▰ Retired football player Paul Crewe runs into trouble with the law and is sentenced to a prison where the warden fields a semipro team. The guards don't like Crewe because he's insolent; the prisoners dislike him because he had been suspected of shaving points when he was a pro. The maniacal warden wants Crewe to help coach the team, and when Crewe declines the warden tries to break Crewe with solitary confinement. Then they make a deal for Crewe and the prisoners to play the guards (ringers who play on the semipro team). Crewe puts together a motley team of prisoners who slobber at the idea of getting a shot at the guards, but when they play the game it is the guards who are underhanded and vicious. Still, the prisoners hit the audience with plenty of hard laughs before the game is over.

**THE CAST** ▰ In most of his movies Burt Reynolds is so in love with himself and fawning to women that no guy can watch him without cringing. But as Paul Crewe, Burt is a wiseass who's tough in the face of guys far meaner than he ever saw on the field. None of them is as frightening and obsessed, however, as the warden played by Eddie Albert; he talks to Crewe in that voice he used when Ebb (his farmhand on *Green Acres*) traded the plow for a rainmaking device from Mr. Hainey. Bernadette Peters has a short but memorable appearance as the warden's secretary, with hair that's in danger of getting caught in the ceiling fan. Michael Conrad (the calm, thoughtful sergeant on *Hill Street Blues*) is the skeptical Nate Scarboro, the prisoner Crewe taps to coach the team. Richard "Jaws" Kiel plays a powerful prisoner appropriately named Samson. Ray Nitschke, who played for the Green Bay Packers in his prime, shows up briefly as one of the guards.

## WHY GUYS LOVE IT ▰ You got football, you got prison, you got a bit of nudity.

## HONEY, YOU'LL LIKE THIS MOVIE . . . ▰ Because you got Burt Reynolds before Loni.

## DON'T MISS
- The opening scene of the movie: It's where the nudity is.
- Crewe's clever play that suckers the captain of the guards . . . twice.

## MEMORABLE LINES
- "I think I broke his fucking neck," says Samson about a particularly brutal clothesline play.
- "You ever do it standing up," Crewe says, apropos of nothing, to the warden's secretary.

# THE NAKED PREY (1966)

## RATINGS

VIOLENCE 🔫 🔫

PROFANITY

BABES 👄

COOL CARS

HERO WORSHIP 🚬 🚬 🚬

**WHAT HAPPENS** ■ You think hunting is a challenge when you're the hunter? You should feel how challenging it is when you're the hunted. A hunter on an African safari sees the whole picture after a band of African tribesmen (and women) capture and torment his entire party and then decide to hunt him. He's set loose in the bush, unclothed and unarmed, so he must lean on his cunning to stay a step ahead of the hunters. Meanwhile, all around him are creatures great and small, pouncing on their entrées.

**THE CAST** ■ Cornel Wilde—producer, director, and lead character—named himself "Man." He needs no other name because he doesn't speak the native tongue and has no one to speak to, anyway. Morrison Gampu, Ken Gampu, Fusi Zazayokwe, Richard Mashiya, Frank Mdhluli, Sandy Nkomo, Jose Sithole, and Joe Diaminl have names that merit mention—they are every bit the warriors.

**WHY GUYS LOVE IT** ■ It answers the age-old question, what is a hunter's favorite game?

**HONEY, YOU'LL LIKE THIS MOVIE . . .** ■ Because it's all-natural.

## DON'T MISS

- The liberated African women who join in the fun.
- Finding out who really sits at the top of the food chain when the hunter bags himself a gazelle that a lion had his heart set on.
- The tasty snake sandwich he settles for.

# RAGING BULL (1980)

## RATINGS

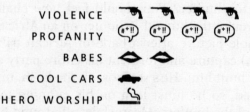

| | |
|---|---|
| VIOLENCE | |
| PROFANITY | |
| BABES | |
| COOL CARS | |
| HERO WORSHIP | |

**WHAT HAPPENS** ▰ In this corner, wearing the green trunks and weighing in at 160 pounds, is a contender for the middleweight championship of the world, Jake LaMotta. In the other corner, wearing blue trunks and weighing a hell of a lot more, is the rest of the world. These are the odds as Jake would have them. In this story based on a real boxer, Jake battles his wives, the guys in his neighborhood, even his brother, accusing them all of disloyalty to him. After Jake meets and marries his second wife, the beautiful blond Vickie, he descends into a paranoia that consumes him faster than he shovels in steaks. For a time he channels that fury in the ring and he takes the title away from Sugar Ray Robinson, a finesse boxer overpowered by Jake's brawling style. But eventually Jake's excessive lifestyle forces him to make compromises and that saps his strength. In the end, he's a bloated, bitter, stand-up comedian, disgraced and alone.

**THE CAST** ☛ Robert De Niro lets his posture communicate Jake's psyche. When he's strong and in control, he leads with his chin, daring anyone to swing on him; when his insecurities get the best of him, he has his head down and his guard up. But he's always a flat-footed fighter, plodding forward in the direction he's set for himself, never reconsidering his attack. No one takes more from him than his brother and manager, Joey, whom Joe Pesci plays in stark contrast to Jake. Joey is light on his feet, always bobbing and weaving, firing a steady stream of exploratory jabs, looking for the soft spot on the people he deals with. Though don't be surprised to see him explode with fury at times. The way Cathy Moriarty looks at Jake in the beginning tells you that Vickie is aroused by the danger of being with him—until being with him is dangerous, and she begins to look at him with contempt. Nicholas Colasanto (the dopey "Coach" from *Cheers*) is Tommy Como, the local mob boss.

**WHY GUYS LOVE IT** ☛ This ain't Rocky—Jake LaMotta was the genuine article—and the fight scenes are the most graphic and realistic ever staged.

**HONEY, YOU'LL LIKE THIS MOVIE . . .** ☛ Because Vickie stands up for herself and breaks away from her abuser.

**DON'T MISS**
- Jake pouring ice water directly on the source when things get a bit hot with Vickie while he's in training.
- Joey using a car door to make his point to a guy who's been talking to Vickie.
- The shower that drenches the judges when Jake lands the punch that wins the title for him.

## MEMORABLE LINES

"He's a good-looking kid," Jake says about one of his opponents. "I don't know whether to fuck him or fight him." Jake answers his own question by taking the first opportunity in the ring to break the kid's nose.

TRIVIA

Vickie Lamotta (the real one) looked great in her November 1981 *Playboy* layout, even though she was older than fifty!

# ROLLERBALL (1975)

## RATINGS

| | |
|---|---|
| VIOLENCE | 🔫🔫🔫🔫 |
| PROFANITY | (#*!!) (#*!!) |
| BABES | 💋 |
| COOL CARS | 🚗🚗 |
| HERO WORSHIP | 🚬🚬🚬🚬 |

WHAT HAPPENS ► Combine the best elements of bowling, basketball, the Roller Derby, and motorcross and you've got Rollerball. In the year 2018, it will be *the* spectator sport for a society riding high on a Prozac-like drug called Big Time. Jonathan E. is like the Michael Jordan of this league, and the directors of the league are tired of him winning all the time, so they ask him to retire. But he declines to go out gracefully, so they stack the odds against him for the championship game, which, like Michael Jordan, makes him that much more determined to win—though in Jordan's case there are rarely weapons involved, unless he's playing the Knicks.

**THE CAST** ━ James Caan has Jonathan E. looking tough during the games, his jaw set and his elbows high, but he keeps a perpetual smug smile on his face when he's off the floor. You can be sure that even a snooty power broker like Bartholomew, played by John Houseman, won't intimidate him (though I did keep expecting him to drill Caan on the case of *Bilitnikoff versus Tatum*). Tasty brunette Maud Adams plays Jonathan's girlfriend, Ella, who helps him relieve the tension of being a star player and forget about the nasty Mr. Houseman. Keep your eye out for Burt "Kato" Kwouk as a courtside doctor.

**WHY GUYS LOVE IT** ━ Now, this is sport!

**HONEY, YOU'LL LIKE THIS MOVIE . . .** ━ Because it's not about football, baseball, basketball, or hockey.

**DON'T MISS**
The guy who doesn't know this game isn't soccer and heads the ball.

**TRIVIA**

Can somebody please tell me . . . why, in the year 2018, everyone is wearing the worst seventies fashions?

# SLAP SHOT (1977)

## RATINGS

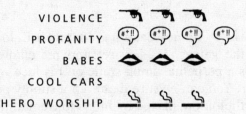

VIOLENCE
PROFANITY
BABES
COOL CARS
HERO WORSHIP

**WHAT HAPPENS** ■ A losing minor league hockey team starts winning when the team acquires the three Hanson brothers—goons who specialize in what's known as the physical side of the game. The aging player/coach rediscovers the fun in the game, the star player complains about the tactics, wishing for a more finessed style of play that will get him noticed by the major league. When the team starts to generate interest, the coach discovers that the owner is shopping the franchise around to buyers in far-flung cities. This is a sports movie, so there's little suspense about how their season turns out. But there's plenty of sex, and because this is hockey, violence, too. And in the finale, even the star player strips away his reservations.

**THE CAST** ■ No one will call this movie the highlight of Paul Newman's career, but he sure does seem to have fun as Reggie Dunlop, the player/coach who's past his playing prime but still plenty able to satisfy certain fans. Even his ex-wife, played by Jennifer Warren, can't turn him down. In contrast, Michael Ontkean (the sheriff from *Twin Peaks*) mopes through the movie as the star player who believes he deserves to be on a better team. That attitude is fueled by his even more miserable wife, played by Lindsay Crouse.

Strother Martin—who appeared with Newman in *Cool Hand Luke* and *Butch Cassidy and the Sundance Kid*—brings his shifty, cover-yer-ass manner to the part of the team's general manager. The three Hanson brothers are played by two brothers named Carlson, Steve and Jeff, and one guy named Hanson (David).

## WHY GUYS LOVE IT
It's proof that in life, as in hockey, force often succeeds where finesse fails.

## HONEY, YOU'LL LIKE THIS MOVIE . . .
Because it's about the personal side of sports, from the Paul Newman perspective.

## DON'T MISS
- Newman's manipulation of an opposing goalie . . . and his wife.
- The Hanson brothers' reverent approach to the national anthem.

## MEMORABLE LINES
"You and I are the only decent items in this place," says bitter Crouse to her nearly as bitter husband Ontkean.

# BAD BOYS (1983)

## RATINGS

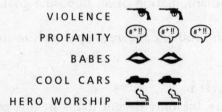

VIOLENCE

PROFANITY

BABES

COOL CARS

HERO WORSHIP

**WHAT HAPPENS** ▰ Out on the streets, two tough kids with grim family situations—Mick O'Brien and Paco Moreno—cross paths during a drug deal gone sour. Mick's buddy and Paco's little brother are killed, and Mick is caught and sent to juvenile prison, where his toughness quickly earns him the title of Top Dog in the joint. That is, until Paco exacts his revenge on O'Brien's girlfriend and is busted and sent to the same prison. Which of them will rule the cell block is decided, finally, by who will be the last man standing in their no-holds-barred showdown.

**THE CAST** ▰ Sean Penn lets his walk show you everything you need to know about Mick's attitude: He swaggers in the face of the worst humiliation. But Penn also lets on how protective he feels of his girlfriend, played by Ally Sheedy, and his cellmate, Horowitz, the overeducated pyromaniac. The too-eager smile Esai Morales keeps on the face of Paco insists that he's joyfully vicious.

## WHY GUYS LOVE IT ▪ Even juveniles know that justice must be settled between two men alone . . . preferably with other inmates laying odds.

## HONEY, YOU'LL LIKE THIS MOVIE ... ▪ Because the ending really isn't as bloody as it could have been.

## DON'T MISS
- Mrs. O'Brien's idea of a night at home with the family that starts in the bathtub with her boyfriend.
- The thoughtful inmate who brings out the flavor of Mick's first meal inside with a seasoning he picked himself.

## MEMORABLE LINES
"Your fellow inmates are murderers, rapists, and mental defectives, just like yourselves," the superintendent says in welcoming Mick to the prison.

# COOL HAND LUKE (1967)

## RATINGS

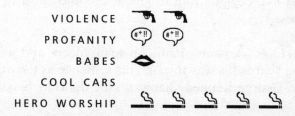

| | |
|---|---|
| VIOLENCE | 🔫 🔫 |
| PROFANITY | (@*!!) (@*!!) |
| BABES | 👄 |
| COOL CARS | |
| HERO WORSHIP | 🚬 🚬 🚬 🚬 🚬 |

S.S./SHOOTING STAR

What they don't seem to understand is, *Cool Hand Luke* has no need to communicate.

**WHAT HAPPENS** ➤ A new inmate at a work farm in the South refuses to submit to the leader of the prisoners, the boredom, the guards, the rules, and most of all, to the tyrannical warden. Sounds like a predictable formula movie, but what we have here is a guy who isn't driven by principle or any other high-minded claptrap—he just knows in his gut that his real imprisonment begins the first moment he doesn't do what he feels like doing when he feels like doing it, even if it's stupid, pointless, or dangerous. Before it's over, you (like the other inmates and even the guards) will feel like begging him to give it up, and cheering when he doesn't.

**CAST** ➤ A young Paul Newman sneers and jeers, burns and yearns his way through his sentence as the title character. George Kennedy hangs on for the ride, playing the inmates' leader, who doesn't realize until too late that no one has any real respect for him. Strother Martin is the warden who believes *he* is the most stubborn guy in the joint. Look for Dennis Hopper and Wayne Rogers (Trapper John from the *M\*A\*S\*H* TV series) among the prisoners. Nearly every actor whose face later became synonymous with Southern law enforcement appears as a guard.

**WHY GUYS LOVE IT** ▰ He eats for glory, he fights out of boredom, he runs to run.

**HONEY, YOU'LL LIKE THIS MOVIE . . .** ▰ Because, you know, Paul Newman is only trying to break out because Joanne has his dinner waiting at home.

**DON'T MISS**
The car wash by the warden's daughter. Prisoners (hell, all of us) are susceptible to the least bit of titillation.

**MEMORABLE LINES**
"What we have here is a failure to communicate." When you've seen the movie, you'll understand.

**TRIVIA**

In the very first episode of *Cheers,* the guys at the bar voted this film "The Sweatiest Movie Ever."

# THE GREAT ESCAPE (1963)

## RATINGS

VIOLENCE 🔫🔫

PROFANITY

BABES

COOL CARS 🚗🚗🚗🚗

HERO WORSHIP 🚬🚬🚬

**WHAT HAPPENS** ▬ The Nazis put all of the captured offi-cers who have attempted escapes from prisoner-of-war

S.S./SHOOTING STAR

In *The Great Escape*, Steve McQueen proves you can't keep a good man down.

camps into one camp with extra protection. So what do these officers do when they are put together? They plan a massive escape attempt. They dig three tunnels, make clothes, and forge papers, and then a slew of them bust out in one shot. The Nazis chase them doggedly and make sure that those they capture will never try to escape again.

**THE CAST** ✒ Sir Richard Attenborough is the senior British officer in charge of escape attempts and he coordinates the joint efforts of an all-star cast of irrepressible escape artists. Steve McQueen is the American airman, Captain Hilts, who escapes and is caught several times but is never deterred by the time he spends in the cooler. He just smiles, gets his baseball and glove, and plays catch against the wall in his cell until it's time to get out and try again. James Garner is The Scrounger and he can score anything from coffee to radios with his sticky fingers and savvy bartering with the guards. Donald Pleasence is an expert forger who's losing his vision; he rooms with Garner, who helps him when the big moment comes. Charles Bronson is the claustrophobic tunnel digger; James Coburn is an Aussie engineer. David McCallum (Illya Kurakin in TV's *The Man from U.N.C.L.E.*) devises their clever plan for getting rid of the tunnel dirt and sacrifices himself in the end.

**WHY GUYS LIKE IT** ✒ Between this movie and *Hogan's Heroes,* you'd think being a prisoner of war was fun.

**HONEY, YOU'LL LIKE THIS MOVIE . . .** ✒ Because there are lots of guys with those English accents you love.

**DON'T MISS**
- The Fourth of July celebration cooked up by The Scrounger and Captain Hilts.
- How Hilts acquires a motorcycle for himself.

## MEMORABLE LINES

"It is the sworn duty of every officer to try to escape," the senior officer of the prisoners tells the camp's commandant. "If they can't, it is their sworn duty to cause the enemy to use an inordinate amount of troops to guard them and their sworn duty to harass the enemy to the best of their ability."

> **TRIVIA**
>
>  James Clavell, author of *Shogun*, wrote the screenplay, which was loosely based on a true story.

# MIDNIGHT EXPRESS (1978)

## RATINGS

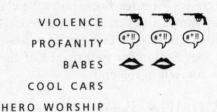

VIOLENCE

PROFANITY

BABES

COOL CARS

HERO WORSHIP

**WHAT HAPPENS** ▰ You don't need to be an expert on international law to know that smuggling drugs out of Third World countries is not a good idea. But any urge you have to try will be quickly squelched when you see what happens to Billy Hayes, an American college student busted at an airport in Turkey with two kilos of hashish taped to his chest. He's sentenced first to four years and then to thirty years in a chaotic and dangerous prison, where he rooms with an English junkie, a half-crazed American, and a Turk who is a bit too friendly with the guards. Eventually we watch Billy slip into insanity, until he gets hung up with the head guard.

**THE CAST** ■ As Billy the amateur smuggler, Brad Davis is so sweaty and twitchy at the airport, you just know he's going to get caught. As Billy the prisoner, he transforms from an indignant innocent (at least about prison life) into a hardened and despairing animal, reacting wildly to what goes on around him. John Hurt won an Academy Award for Best Supporting Actor as the strung-out Max, whose only comfort comes from a kitten and his daily fix. Randy Quaid is a high-strung American prisoner, and his manic, cynical point of view pulls Billy down with him. The one cast member you won't soon forget is Paul Smith—he's the hulking, brutal head of the guards.

**WHY GUYS LOVE IT** ■ There's not a single redeeming quality about anybody in this movie—they all deserve what they get.

**HONEY, YOU'LL LIKE THIS MOVIE . . .** ■ Because even after four years, Billy's girlfriend remains loyal to him and visits him in prison—as I know you would if he were me and you were she.

**DON'T MISS**
- The (tongue)-ectomy Billy performs on his Turk cellmate to end a vicious fight.
- The kind (and teasing) gesture the girlfriend performs for Billy on her visit.

**MEMORABLE LINES**
"I hate you, I hate your nation, I hate your people, and I fuck your sons and daughters because they're pigs. You're a pig, you're all pigs," Billy shrieks at the judge at his second

trial, which Billy's attorney may have explained to him isn't the usual plea for leniency.

**TRIVIA**

Oliver Stone wrote the screenplay for this movie based on William Hayes's book about his experiences.

# THE NAKED CAGE (1986)

**RATINGS**

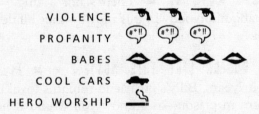

| | |
|---|---|
| VIOLENCE | 🔫 🔫 🔫 |
| PROFANITY | @*!! @*!! @*!! |
| BABES | 👄 👄 👄 👄 |
| COOL CARS | 🚗 |
| HERO WORSHIP | 🚬 |

**WHAT HAPPENS** ▰ A cheap, exploitative presentation of incarcerated women that's certain to offend your sense of good taste. The filmmakers stoop so low as to send a nice, innocent, small-town girl like Michelle to prison for trying to help her ex-husband and a sassy, street-tough chick get away after robbing the bank where Michelle works. But is that the end of the horrors these backstage fiends visit upon poor Michelle? No. The tough chick who turned the ex-hubby bad and who got Michelle busted is sent to the same prison, and every shower turns into a showdown. But don't be surprised if the end is a shock to the tough chick.

**THE CAST** ✒ A suitable selection of girls familiar with the term "exploitation."

**WHY GUYS LOVE IT** ✒ What's in a name? Sometimes, everything you need to know.

**HONEY, YOU'LL LIKE THIS MOVIE ...** ✒ Because it tells us that girls of good character will triumph over floozies in even the most trying situation.

**DON'T MISS**
- The tough chick offering the guy a snort off her breast.
- The warden's personal rehabilitation program.

**MEMORABLE LINES**
"The guards are the zookeepers and you are the animals," the warden tells the new prisoners. (Did the screenwriter think that we'd overlook dialogue that bad just because we see a lot bare flesh? Well, he's absolutely right.)

# PAPILLON (1973)

**RATINGS**

| | |
|---|---|
| VIOLENCE | 🔫 |
| PROFANITY | |
| BABES | 👄 👄 |
| COOL CARS | |
| HERO WORSHIP | 🚬 🚬 🚬 |

**WHAT HAPPENS** ✒ The name of the title character, a French safecracker sentenced to an island prison from which no one escapes, means "butterfly," and every chance he gets, Papillon takes flight. Twice he's caught and spends seven years in solitary confinement, losing weight and his mind, but not his resolve to bust out. He'd be all but dead, except for the help of a counterfeiter whose life he'd saved. The third escape is a charm, sort of. Papillon and Louis Dega, the counterfeiter, escape Devil's Island, only to land at a leper colony. They get separated, and Papillon, aided by several people, manages to elude the authorities for a while, but eventually he's recaptured and sentenced to a not unpleasant prison on the isle of batty old convicts with bad teeth. Do you think Papillon would be content to finish the few remaining days of his life in a quiet little cottage on the island? Or will he attempt one more foolhardy escape?

**THE CAST** ☛ Steve McQueen and Dustin Hoffman must not have bathed for weeks before arriving on the set of this movie. You can almost smell them from the very first scene. In *Papillon*, McQueen avoids the many clichés available to him as the restless prisoner—he doesn't proclaim his innocence, he's not insolent to the guards, or even driven by some romantic ideal of freedom. He just wants out and he won't be deterred by any punishment, even the threat of the guillotine. Hoffman's Dega resembles another of his famous characters, Ratso Rizzo in *Midnight Cowboy*, and not just in the hygiene department—both talk of plans to escape their reality, without truly believing those plans will come to something, and both find ways to survive in their nearly hopeless situations. Eventually, however, Dega resigns himself to his fate, which leaves him thoroughly baffled by his friend, Papillon.

**WHY GUYS LOVE IT** ☛ This is our idea of prison reform—put 'em all on an island near a leper colony and see who dares to escape.

**HONEY, YOU'LL LIKE THIS MOVIE . . .** ☛ Because Papillon and Dega hug each other at the end.

## DON'T MISS

- Papillon supplementing his half rations in solitary with some eight-legged protein.
- The gentle bit of field surgery Papillon performs on Dega's leg after they escape.
- The topless Honduran native girl who nurses Papillon back to health with ocean baths and plenty of oysters.

## MEMORABLE LINES

- When Papillon goes to one of the leper's houses to ask for help, the leper offers Papillon the cigar he's been smoking and Papillon takes it. "How did you know my leprosy wasn't contagious," the leper asks Papillon.

   "I didn't," Papillon answers, which convinces the leper to help him.

- After Papillon describes his plan to throw a raft made of coconuts lashed together off a cliff and then jump onto it, Dega asks, "Do you really think it will work?"

   Papillon's answer sums it all up. "Does it matter?"

# REFORM SCHOOL GIRLS (1986)

## RATINGS

| VIOLENCE | 🔫 🔫 |
| PROFANITY | @*!! @*!! @*!! |
| BABES | 👄 👄 👄 👄 |
| COOL CARS | |
| HERO WORSHIP | 🚬 |

## WHAT HAPPENS

Poor Jenny Williams. She seems like such a nice girl, but she just can't stay away from the wrong people. When her boyfriend is arrested in the midst of a robbery, she's nabbed for driving the getaway car. Jenny is sentenced to the Pridemore Juvenile School, where she wants to serve her time quietly. But she immediately finds herself in conflict with the tyrannical head matron, Edna Dawson, and Charlie, one of the other inmates. Before it's over, Jenny must prove how tough she is and how good she looks in a T-shirt and underpants. But you shouldn't let any of that poignant drama distract you from the shower scenes, the cat fights, and the generous revue of Frederick's of Hollywood sleepwear.

**THE CAST** ✏ When Wendy O. Williams was the star attraction of the punk rock band The Plasmatics, she appeared on *Late Night with David Letterman,* menaced the host with a chain saw, and then called him a "wanker." But as the butch inmate Charlie, she really plays tough. Her raspy voice, jacked muscles, and leather underwear intimidate everyone. Charlie even bosses the sadistic head matron, Edna, who, in her white lab coat and frizzed hair, looks like your school nurse nightmare. Edna is played by Pat Ast, a graduate of the weird Andy Warhol movies of the 1960s. The statuesque former Playmate Sybil Danning, star of many B movies (B as in babes with big breasts), keeps her own body under wraps as the wacko warden—all the other inmates show off bodies that could make them future Playmates or Pets.

**WHY GUYS LOVE IT** ✏ A whole dormitory full of *bad* girls is very, very *good.*

**HONEY, YOU'LL LIKE THIS MOVIE . . .** ✏ Because it brings to light the horrifying abuses of the female penal system.

**DON'T MISS**
- The generous service that the truck driver performs for Jenny and for the good of society.

- When Edna puts her foot down about a contraband kitten in the dormitory.

## MEMORABLE LINES

When a guard brings in the new inmates, Edna looks up from her desk and says, "I thought I smelled fish."

# RUNAWAY TRAIN (1985)

## RATINGS

| VIOLENCE | | | |
| PROFANITY | | | |
| BABES | | | |
| COOL CARS | | | |
| HERO WORSHIP | | | |

## WHAT HAPPENS

You'd think that after three years in solitary with the door welded shut Manny would be content to just hang out in the yard with the rest of the guys, maybe work out a little or catch a boxing match. But just as soon as the judge orders the sadistic warden to unweld Manny's cell, Manny starts plotting his escape. And he does get out of the prison, with help from Buck, the laundry boy who idolizes him and who goes along for the ride through the Alaskan tundra surrounding the prison. The ride, it turns out, is on a train they hop whose engineer keels over from a heart attack just after he sets the train at full throttle. The guys at RR Central try to figure out how to keep the train from destroying everything in its path, the warden hunts for the escapees, and Manny, Buck, and a woman conductor they find on the train watch their lives flying by. The last stop, however, is a duet for just Manny and the warden.

**THE CAST** ✒ One look at Jon Voigt through the window of Manny's solitary cell and you see that he will run the first chance he can. His eyes are opened wide and focused on the place he's headed to. He may be wiser than the younger con, but he's also more dangerous—willing to do whatever is necessary to get where he wants to go. No one could call Buck wiser than any of the other parts Eric Roberts has played; in fact, he's dumb enough to think busting out of a prison in the heart of Alaska with a convicted murderer is a cool adventure. Fortunately, conductor Rebecca DeMornay (looking less than her best) is napping on the train with Manny and Buck—so she can scream a lot and keep Buck warm when Manny goes cold.

**WHY GUYS LOVE IT** ✒ "Choo-choo" were the first words many of us spoke and ever since we've imagined ourselves taking over one someday.

**HONEY, YOU'LL LIKE THIS MOVIE . . .** ✒ Because it is a work of existential philosophy.

**DON'T MISS**
- The warden flushing away any reluctance the whiz kid at RR Central has about helping him.
- Manny's finger-tipped crawl from one train car to another.

**MEMORABLE LINES**
- "You don't want to be around me," Manny warns Buck. "I'm at war with the world and everyone in it."
- "Hey, would you like a really good fuck?" Buck asks the girl, because, let's face it, when you're on an out-of-control train hurtling you to God-knows-what conclusion, you can't waste time on pleasantries, like subtle seduction lines or foreplay.

# STALAG 17 (1953)

## RATINGS

| | |
|---|---|
| VIOLENCE | 🔫 🔫 |
| PROFANITY | |
| BABES | |
| COOL CARS | |
| HERO WORSHIP | 🚬 🚬 🚬 |

**WHAT HAPPENS** ▬ This is no episode of *Hogan's Heroes.* For one thing, all the prisoners don't get along—there's one guy named Sefton who's a master scammer living well off the booty he hustles from the guards and other prisoners, and everyone suspects he's selling information about the prisoners' escape plans to the Nazis, too. Now Sergeant Schultz is, like Hogan's hungry pal, a bit of a bumbler, but the kommandant is no Colonel Klink—he's a cold and stiff career officer and aristocrat who disdains his own men as well as the prisoners. When a new Allied officer is brought to the camp, the POWs keep him on ice until they can find a way to get him out. When the bright lights finally shine down, Sefton is in the clear, and the real spy is left exposed.

**THE CAST** ▬ William Holden won an Academy Award for his portrayal of Sefton and he got it by keeping Sefton from being too likable—he's thoroughly cynical and boldly honest in his self-interests, but that doesn't mean he can't be heroic given the chance. The kommandant played by Otto Preminger will have you saluting him. Before Peter Graves took on *Mission: Impossible,* he showed up here to polish his spying skills.

**WHY GUYS LOVE IT** ◗ You can't judge a man by the contents of his footlocker.

**HONEY, YOU'LL LIKE THIS MOVIE . . .** ◗ Because the guys forgive Sefton, and he nearly forgives them.

## DON'T MISS

- How two prisoners, Shapiro and Animal, sneak onto the side where the Russian women are held.
- The kommandant donning his boots just to click his heels while he's on the telephone to Berlin.

## MEMORABLE LINES

- When the rest of the prisoners beat Sefton because they believe he informed the Germans about two prisoners trying to escape, Sefton tells them, "There's two people who know I didn't do it. Me, and the guy who did it. And when I find the guy who left me holding the stick, he'd better watch out."
- "With Christmas coming I have special treat," the kommandmant rewards them. "You will all be deloused for the holidays." On second thought, Herr Kommandant, I'll be home for Christmas.

# TERMINAL ISLAND (1973)

## RATINGS

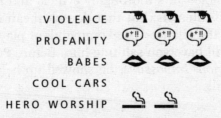

| | |
|---|---|
| VIOLENCE | 🔫 🔫 🔫 |
| PROFANITY | @*!! @*!! @*!! |
| BABES | 👄 👄 👄 |
| COOL CARS | |
| HERO WORSHIP | 🚬 🚬 |

**WHAT HAPPENS** ▬ In the future, capital punishment has been outlawed, so convicted murderers are deposited on an island off the coast of California with no guards and are left to fend for themselves. Here's the catch: The men and women are together. Everyone, men and women, slaves all day in the hot sun—except Bobby, who rules the island, and A. J.'s band of outcasts who live in the woods. But when night falls, the women are doled out to the men—which the women don't like. So one day when the girls are working on the fringes of the camp, they meet up with A. J. and his gang, who invite the women to join them, and they do. Bobby can't have that, so he sends his henchman Monk out with a party to bring them back. They battle with home-made weapons and their wits, which means A. J. and his bunch are better armed.

**THE CAST** ▬ Tom Selleck is a doctor sentenced to the island for a mercy killing—he's a genteel man out of his element, except when he's with the women. Roger E. Mosley, Selleck's cohort from *Magnum P.I.* (he was the helicopter pilot), plays Monk. The women are a well-put-together selection of blacks and whites, willowy and bosomy, tough and demure—just the right mix for a life sentence.

**WHY GUYS LOVE IT** ▬ Brawls and babes, far from anything remotely like authority.

**HONEY, YOU'LL LIKE THIS MOVIE . . .** ▬ Because Tom Selleck is such a good guy—even when he's a murderer, it's out of kindness not cruelty.

**DON'T MISS**
How one of the girls uses a massage of bees' royal jelly to exact her revenge on a guy who jumped her.

## MEMORABLE LINES

- "Anybody want to say a few words?" one of the inmates asks when they're about to bury one of their own.

  "Yeah," somebody pipes up. "Good riddance."
- "What kind of bastards do you have here?" the new girl asks on her first night.

  "We got white bastards, we got black bastards, we got big bastards, we got little bastards. What kind do you want?" one of the others answers her.

# ESCAPE FROM NEW YORK (1981)

## RATINGS

| | |
|---|---|
| VIOLENCE | 🔫 🔫 🔫 |
| PROFANITY | #*!! #*!! #*!! |
| BABES | 👄 |
| COOL CARS | 🚗 🚗 |
| HERO WORSHIP | 🚬 🚬 🚬 |

**WHAT HAPPENS** ● In 1997, Manhattan is a penal colony surrounded by guards outside and ruled inside by twisted, vicious gangs. When the U.S. president's plane is hijacked, he ejects and lands somewhere near Broadway, and then is captured by some of the inmates. Who can get him out? The best choice in those desperate times is Snake Plissken, a Special Forces veteran who is serving time in another prison for unspecified antisocial behavior. The police commissioner offers Snake a pardon if he can retrieve the president within twenty-four hours; if he can't, the police commissioner offers to explode him with a tiny device the cops implant in Snake's body. So Snake takes the job and fights his way through a New York that seems not appreciably

S.S. ARCHIVES/SHOOTING STAR

Snake enjoying a rare quiet moment in *Escape From New York.*

different than you might find it on a hot summer night. He is helped along the way by a guy known as the Brain and a woman who ought to be known as the Breasts.

**THE CAST** ☞ Kurt Russell wears an eye patch, has three days of razor stubble, and looks generally grimy enough to make Snake look not much different than the inmates of New York. But once he accepts the job, he grows into his hero's outfit, registering genuine concern for the people who help him, if not for the president. Harry Dean Stanton is the Brain, which doesn't seem all there; Adrienne Barbeau is his woman, Maggie, who ought to be known as . . . well, you figure it out. The last dependable cabbie in

New York, an extra-friendly Ernest Borgnine, gives Snake a lift. Singer Isaac Hayes rules as the Duke, while Donald Pleasence wimpers as the president. You can't ever tell if the police commissioner, played by Lee Van Cleef (The "Bad" in *The Good, the Bad, and the Ugly*) is rooting for Snake to succeed or not.

**WHY GUYS LOVE IT** ▰ This New York is our kind of town.

**HONEY, YOU'LL LIKE THIS MOVIE . . .** ▰ Because it stars that cute Kurt Russell, who's involved with that cute Goldie Hawn.

**DON'T MISS**
- The freaky inmate displaying the president's finger.
- Snake finding the perfect use for a Ford station wagon—as an armored vehicle.

**MEMORABLE LINES**
- "Snake? I thought you were dead?" several people say.
- "You want to kill me now?" the commissioner asks Snake when it's all over.
  "Not now, I'm tired," Snake answers. "Maybe later."

# MEAN STREETS (1973)

**RATINGS**

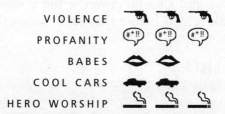

| | | | |
|---|---|---|---|
| VIOLENCE | 🔫 | 🔫 | 🔫 |
| PROFANITY | @*!! | @*!! | @*!! |
| BABES | 👄 | 👄 | |
| COOL CARS | 🚗 | 🚗 | |
| HERO WORSHIP | 🚬 | 🚬 | 🚬 |

**WHAT HAPPENS** ◾ Dopey wiseguy Johnny Boy from New York's Little Italy owes money to the loan sharks, but he can't stop livin' big and talkin' tough. His smarter, smoother cousin, Charlie, with good connections, tries to protect him, but Johnny keeps digging his hole deeper. Charlie tries to give Johnny's sister, Teresa, the benefits of his charms, too. And when the heat is on, they hide out in the cool, dark of movie theaters. Eventually, Johnny Boy's troubles catch up to both of them.

**THE CAST** ◾ A young Robert De Niro is the shaggy-haired Johnny Boy, and Harvey Keitel is his benefactor, Charlie. Johnny Boy's sweet brunette sister, Teresa (Amy Robinson) may be the main reason Charlie looks out for him. The other key person in the cast is behind the camera—Martin Scorsese, the director of several other great guy movies (with De Niro) including *Raging Bull, Taxi Driver,* and *Good-Fellas.* Look for David *"Kung Fu"* Carradine as a sloppy drunk who gets hammered in more ways than one.

**WHY GUYS LOVE IT** ◾ These guys rumble because they don't have anything better to do.

**HONEY, YOU'LL LIKE THIS MOVIE ...** ◾ Because nothing really mean happens to Teresa.

**DON'T MISS**
- The brawl in the bar that rages until the cops show up, then the combatants have a drink, the cops leave, and they resume the brawl.
- Johnny Boy and Charlie covering the gravestones with their handkerchiefs before they sit down on them to talk in the cemetery.

**MEMORABLE LINES**
"Who you calling a mook?" Johnny Boy rages at a guy in the pool hall.

"What's a mook?" Charlie asks him.

"I don't know, but who's he to call me a mook? Make him take it back," Johnny says.

# REPO MAN (1983)

## RATINGS

| | |
|---|---|
| VIOLENCE | 🔫 🔫 🔫 |
| PROFANITY | #*!! #*!! #*!! #*!! |
| BABES | 👄 👄 |
| COOL CARS | 🚗 🚗 🚗 🚗 |
| HERO WORSHIP | 🚬 🚬 |

**WHAT HAPPENS** ▰ Otto works at grocery store during the day and hangs out in the hard-core scene after hours. When he quits his job (with a big "Fuck You" to his boss), he takes a job as a repo man—that is, a guy who repossesses cars from people who fall behind in their loan payments. Of course, since these people don't volunteer to return the cars, there's lots of jump-starting, chasing, and shooting. At the same time, the nastiest of his punker pals get their hands on a car with something mysterious and dangerous in the trunk—which has lots of people interested in it. Their paths inevitably cross in what is a very way-out ending.

**THE CAST** ▰ Emilio Estevez loads Otto up with nervous energy and standard-issue punker disdain for everybody. That energy is channeled into a purpose by his mentor, a veteran repo man played by the ever-weird, but full of philosophy Harry Dean Stanton. Look for The Circle Jerks in the nightclub. And if you're quick, you'll spot Jimmy Buffett and his harp man, Gregg Taylor, among the Blond Agents.

**WHY GUYS LOVE IT** ▰ Getting paid to boost cars is a great way to make a living.

**HONEY, YOU'LL LIKE THIS MOVIE . . .** ▰ Because this irresponsible guy finds himself a solid, respectable job.

## DON'T MISS

- Otto's visit to his religion-addled, doped-out hippie parents.
- The liquor store holdup where lots of blood and bourbon are spilled.

## MEMORABLE LINES

- "Only an asshole gets himself killed over a car," intones Otto's mentor.
- "It happens sometimes—people just explode," pronounces the coroner after inspecting the melted-down body of a dead cop. "Natural causes," he concludes as he writes up his report.

## TRIVIA

Iggy Pop, the godfather of hard core, sings the title song.

# TAXI DRIVER (1976)

## RATINGS

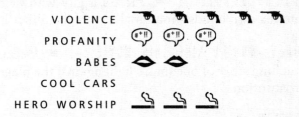

| | |
|---|---|
| VIOLENCE | 🔫 🔫 🔫 🔫 🔫 |
| PROFANITY | #*!! #*!! #*!! |
| BABES | 👄 👄 |
| COOL CARS | |
| HERO WORSHIP | 🚬 🚬 🚬 |

**WHAT HAPPENS** ✏ There are very few moral people left in New York, and cabbie and Vietnam vet Travis Bickle is one of them. He spends a lot of his time picking up fares around seedy Times Square and being appalled by the depravity he sees there. The rest of his time he devotes to watching icy blond Betsy, a campaign aide for a presidential candidate, and trying to get a date with her. When she finally goes out with him, Travis offends her, and she will have nothing to do with him anymore. At about the same time, Travis spots Iris, a teenage prostitute, and decides he must rescue her from her life. Those two women inspire Travis to undertake a crusade that leads him to an unflattering haircut and a bloodbath, and an ending that could very well be his dream.

**THE CAST** ✏ Travis and Iris, Iris and Travis—they are a couple of real innocents doing their best to convince us otherwise. Robert De Niro loads Travis's voice with shock and surprise at the way Iris thinks. Jodie Foster has a sweet, gap-toothed smile and is equally surprised that Travis would care about her. Cool, self-assured Cybill Shepherd has Betsy intrigued and then disgusted by Travis. Albert Brooks is at his weaselly best as a callow colleague of Betsy, who has even less chance with her than Travis. Harvey Keitel is Iris's jukin', jivin' pimp. Director Martin Scorsese gets in front of the camera for a scene as one of Travis's fares who talks of killing his adulterous wife.

## WHY GUYS LOVE IT ▬ Here's a guy who takes matters into his own hands—matters like a high-caliber handgun.

## HONEY, YOU'LL LIKE THIS MOVIE ... ▬ Because it's the touching story of one man's fight against the plague of child prostitution.

## DON'T MISS

- When Travis blasts an armed robber sticking up a convenience store and the store's owner beats the corpse.
- Iris's idea of a complete breakfast: toast topped with jelly and packets of sugar.

## MEMORABLE LINES

- "You talking to me?" Travis says to himself in the mirror—over and over again—as he rehearses before the start of his crusade.
- "Taking me to a movie like this," Betsy tells Travis as she storms out of the porno theater where he takes her on their first date, "is about as exciting to me as saying, 'Let's fuck.' " If she had said that sooner, he could saved himself the fifteen dollars for tickets and popcorn.

## TRIVIA

You may recall that this was the movie that allegedly inspired John Hinckley to send mash notes to Jodie Foster and to shoot President Reagan.

# TRESPASS (1992)

## RATINGS

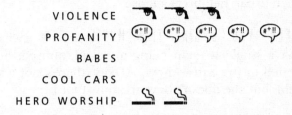

| | |
|---|---|
| VIOLENCE | |
| PROFANITY | |
| BABES | |
| COOL CARS | |
| HERO WORSHIP | |

**WHAT HAPPENS** ☛ Two small-town firemen get a treasure map from a guy they rescue, and the map lures the firemen to an abandoned building in a big-city ghetto. Sure enough, the guys find a stash of stolen gold. The trouble is, the firemen are surrounded by heavily armed drug dealers because they accidentally witnessed an execution they shouldn't have seen. To get out of the building the firemen need all their nerve and their know-how—it's either no cops or no gold. The best news is that the loot lands in the hands of the person most needy.

**THE CAST** ☛ William Sadler (the villain in *Die Harder*) is the fireman who comes down with a bad case of gold fever, while his partner, Bill Paxton (the jerk older brother in *Weird Science*), would rather run than take the money. Homeless Bradlee (Art Evans, the airport engineer in *Die Harder*) could help them out, if only they'd give him a fair share. That's not King James's version of how the standoff will be played out. King James is Ice-T, and he commands his troops not to shoot because the firemen have grabbed his little brother, Lucky. But one of them, rapper Ice Cube, gets bit by the gold bug, too. (Can't keep the Ice men straight? Remember that iced tea is thin, and ice cubes are round, and Ice-T is skinny, and Ice Cube is . . . uh . . . round.) Gold fever proves to be lethal in many cases.

**WHY GUYS LOVE IT** ■ Guts and wits count for something when urban hell breaks loose.

**HONEY, YOU'LL LIKE THIS MOVIE . . .** ■ Because there isn't a single woman being attacked, abused, or even exploited in the entire movie. (Okay, there's not a woman in sight, but she doesn't have to know that.)

**DON'T MISS**
- The old phony cop trick.
- Lucky taking his best shot.

**MEMORABLE LINES**
- "I guess Lucky weren't too lucky," Ice Cube says.
- "Word" is all King James has to say.

**TRIVIA**

*The Looters* was this movie's original title, and it was to be released in the spring of 1992, but because of the riots in L.A. at that time, the movie was renamed and its release postponed until the fall.

# THE WARRIORS (1979)

## RATINGS

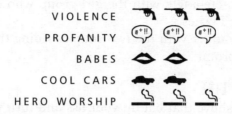

| | |
|---|---|
| VIOLENCE | 🔫 🔫 🔫 |
| PROFANITY | #*!! #*!! #*!! |
| BABES | 👄 👄 |
| COOL CARS | 🚗 🚗 |
| HERO WORSHIP | 🚬 🚬 🚬 |

**WHAT HAPPENS** ▪ Thousands of gang members in the most preposterous costumes from all over New York City gather in the Bronx to listen to Cyrus tell them why they should band under his leadership into one big gang. But Cyrus is shot while giving his pitch, and The Warriors, a particularly plain gang from Coney Island, are wrongly blamed. They must fight their way back to their home turf, battling wave after wave of gangs like the guys in the baseball uniforms, the guys in the overalls, the cops, and, finally, the Rogues, their rivals who actually did kill Cyrus.

**THE CAST** ▪ James Remar is Ajax, the toughest of the Warriors; you've seen him play a psycho in many movies, including *48 Hours*. Michael Beck is the much smarter leader, Swan, who eventually accepts Deborah Van Valkenburgh, the smart-mouth babe who initially provoked The Warriors. You might also recognize Lynne Thigpen: She's the voice of the overnight DJ who gives the play-by-play on the Warriors' progress. But it is the different gangs' "themes" that are the main attraction in this movie.

**WHY GUYS LOVE IT** ▪ There's brawling from one end of New York to the other—oh, what a night.

**HONEY, YOU'LL LIKE THIS MOVIE...** ✏ Because the girls get into the action, too.

## DON'T MISS
- The boys' tête-à-tête with the girl group who call themselves The Lizzies.
- Their encounter with the two couples riding the subway after the prom.

## MEMORABLE LINE
"I'm gonna shove that bat up your ass and turn you into a Popsicle," says Swan to one of the baseball gang members.

# ABRAXAS: GUARDIAN OF THE UNIVERSE (1990)

## RATINGS

| | |
|---|---|
| VIOLENCE |  |
| PROFANITY | |
| BABES | |
| COOL CARS | |
| HERO WORSHIP | |

**WHAT HAPPENS** ▪ Secundas, a big bad guy from the future, comes back to the twentieth century to impregnate a woman so that he can ensure that the "Antilife Equation" that he's carrying will survive into his own era. Abraxas is a good guy from the future who's supposed to kill the woman before she gives birth (so that Secundas doesn't reproduce), but Abraxas can't kill the woman. So he ends up protecting the kid and the mother from Secundas. The kid grows up to have amazing powers, like the ability to make other kids pee in their pants, while the mother hankers for Abraxas, even though he's not a flesh-and-blood human. Abraxas and

Secundas beat each other senseless several times before Abraxas antilifes him.

## THE CAST ▰ Former pro wrestler and auxiliary actor in many movies (*Predator, The Running Man*) Jesse "The Body" Ventura gets his shot at a starring role here as Abraxas. Ventura must have spent a bit too much time with Arnold Schwarzenegger, however, because he uses the Germanic/robotic voice that is Arnold at his best. Still, Ventura has The Body, and it's plenty fun to watch him work it out on the equally built Secundas, played by Sven Ole-Thorson. Marjorie Bransfield is certainly B-movie beautiful as the mother, but she still can't get Abraxas more interested in her than Secundas (or maybe it's just that Abraxas can't stand the idea of picking up Secundas's sloppy seconds). Jim Belushi proves that it is better to work than to not work, by taking the role of the dodo principal of the kids' school.

## WHY GUYS LOVE IT ▰ Ninety-plus minutes of thoroughly pumped and cut behemoths pounding each other is pure fun.

## HONEY, YOU'LL LIKE THIS MOVIE ... ▰ Because Abraxas is a good father figure for the kid.

## DON'T MISS
- Secundas blowing up a big gas station owner.
- Abraxas being lit up for a lamp.

## MEMORABLE LINES
- When Secundas arrives from the twentieth century, he finds a young couple making out in a Firebird. After extracting the guy, Secundas tries out this line on the girl: "Are you a birthing member of the human race? I need your body." Try it sometime; it might work for you, too.

- Secundas evicts a yuppie from his Jeep Cherokee so he can chase Abraxas. The yuppie menaces Secundas with the potent words, "I'm a lawyer; I can litigate."

**WARNING**

As with *The Terminator,* I advise you not to try to puzzle out the implications of people traveling back and forth in time and affecting the past to control the future without a six-pack handy to relieve the brain freeze that can result from this level of thinking.

# AFTER THE FALL OF
# NEW YORK (1983)

**RATINGS**

| | | | |
|---|---|---|---|
| VIOLENCE | 🔫 | 🔫 | 🔫 |
| PROFANITY | @*!! | @*!! | |
| BABES | 👄 | | |
| COOL CARS | 🚗 | 🚗 | 🚗 |
| HERO WORSHIP | 🚬 | 🚬 | 🚬 |

**WHAT HAPPENS** ▪ Twenty years after the nuclear holocaust storm troopers called "Euracs" rule North America, but they are still trying to squelch rebellious humans who have hope for the future. There is one fertile woman left on the planet and she's frozen and kept somewhere in New

York. The leader of the Pan-American Confederacy wants our hero—a demolition derby champion—to find her and do what's necessary to instill hope in the human race. Together with two compatriots, Ratchet and the Claw, the hero gets into the New York City sewer system and finds all manner of people living there, then battles them and the Euracs to find the girl.

**THE CAST** ► Michael Scopkiw is Kurt Russell on a budget with a dash of Michael Pare thrown in. Scopkiw, George Eastman (who plays Big Ape), and everyone else in the cast disappeared in the meltdown that occurred when this movie was released.

**WHY GUYS LIKE IT** ► A postapocalyptic future that still has a place for the demolition derby and Harleys is far from a nightmare.

**HONEY, YOU'LL LIKE THIS MOVIE ...** ► Because it can be reduced to one man's search for one woman.

**DON'T MISS**
• The weapons, which are a bizarre combination of futuristic and medieval styles.
• What "The Claw" can do with his prosthesis.

**MEMORABLE LINES**
When Melissa (the next mother of her people) sees some men being chewed on by rats, she squeals. "What's the matter," Big Ape says to her, "you never saw rats having lunch before?"

# ALIEN (1979)

## RATINGS

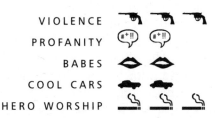

VIOLENCE
PROFANITY
BABES
COOL CARS
HERO WORSHIP

**WHAT HAPPENS** ━ The five-man, two-woman crew of a commercial spaceship is returning home when they receive a distress signal coming from a small planet. They stop to investigate the remains of another ship on the planet, and one of them is mysteriously injured. They take him back to

We'd let Ripley kick our ass anytime.

20TH CENTURY FOX/SHOOTING STAR

their own ship, and the softhearted leader ignores quarantine procedures—which everybody but him knows is a bad idea in a movie like this. The injured man's condition baffles the crew's medical specialist, but the patient seems to be recovering satisfactorily until dinnertime, when a creature with a bulbous head, a long neck, and a squealing laugh comes ripping out of his chest, giving the whole crew wicked indigestion. The Alien escapes into the bowels of the ship, where it grows a lot bigger, eludes capture, and rips apart the crew members one by one, until only one woman is left. She gives it a send-off that only a sequel could rescue it from.

## THE CAST ☛ The usually glamorous Sigourney Weaver shows the truest grit as Ripley, the last woman alive. Tom (*Picket Fences*) Skerritt captains the ship and so must pay, and pay brutally, for his unwillingness to be hard about quarantining the injured man played by John Hurt. Yaphet Kotto and Harry Dean Stanton get in a fair share of complaining as the ship's overburdened mechanics, while Veronica Cartwright just screams and wails a lot. Keep your eye on crew-cut Ian Holm—he's not what he appears to be.

## WHY GUYS LOVE IT ☛ This creature is nasty!

## HONEY, YOU'LL LIKE THIS MOVIE ... ☛ Because Sigourney rescues the cat.

## DON'T MISS
- Ian Holm's heads-up thinking.
- Sigourney stripping down to her skivvies in the last minutes of the movie.

## MEMORABLE LINES
When Sigourney asks the ship's computer (known as "Mother") what to do, the reply is, "Ensure safe return of

the creature for analysis—crew expendable." She finds that answer unacceptable.

# ALIENS (1986)

## RATINGS

| | | | | |
|---|---|---|---|---|
| VIOLENCE | 🔫 | 🔫 | 🔫 | 🔫 |
| PROFANITY | 💬 | 💬 | 💬 | |
| BABES | 👄 | 👄 | 👄 | |
| COOL CARS | 🚗 | 🚗 | | |
| HERO WORSHIP | 🚬 | 🚬 | 🚬 | 🚬 |

**WHAT HAPPENS** ■ If you woke up after fifty-seven years in space, asleep since you battled to the death with a blood-sucking alien parasite that mauled all of your colleagues, would you turn around and head right back out to the planet where you first met up with that alien? No, of course, not, but then again, you're a sensible guy and hardly as tough and determined as Warrant Officer Ripley, whose fine features and slim figure belie her fearlessness and calm in the toothy face of the monsters. Ripley lands on the planet with a troop of heavily armed twenty-first-century Marines and one slimy corporate creep. There they find the mother of all aliens and the last remaining daughter of the humans who had been living there. Once again, Ripley ends up taking on the creatures almost singlehandedly and rescuing the innocent.

**THE CAST** ■ Sigourney Weaver as Ripley isn't exactly eager to go back out, but eventually she's anxious for another shot at the creatures. Paul Reiser's pushy corporate flunky Burke does the persuading, and then pulls a stunt so selfish, he's certain to be a creature's entrée. Michael Biehn (the good guy from the future in *The Terminator*) leads the Marines, including a cowering Bill Paxton. Lance Henrikson redeems androids, because his Bishop hovers into view at just the right moment. Later, he finds himself twice the man (or is it machine) he thought he was.

## DON'T MISS

- Ripley's duct-taped double barrel.
- The final confrontation in the hangar: girl on girl.
- The director's-cut video: It has almost twenty extra minutes and some background on Ripley that helps explain some of her actions.

## MEMORABLE LINES

- "All right, we waste him; no offense," the Marine commander says when they discover Burke's scheme.
- "Come on, you bitch," Ripley hisses at the mother.

## CHECK OUT

*Alien*³ lands Ripley on a penal colony where the inmates are as unsavory as the creatures she left behind . . . or did she? You won't mind watching it, but it doesn't have the nonstop tension that the first two do, and you should consider yourself warned that Ripley shaves her head—a look not everyone can pull off.

# BLADE RUNNER (1982)

## RATINGS

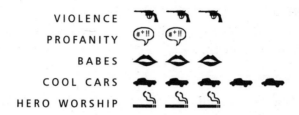

| | | | | |
|---|---|---|---|---|
| VIOLENCE | 🔫 | 🔫 | 🔫 | |
| PROFANITY | 💬 | 💬 | | |
| BABES | 👄 | 👄 | 👄 | |
| COOL CARS | 🚗 | 🚗 | 🚗 | 🚗 |
| HERO WORSHIP | 🚬 | 🚬 | 🚬 | |

**WHAT HAPPENS** — By 2019, the Tyrell Corporation is so successful at manufacturing "replicants" that people have trouble distinguishing humans from them. Replicants are humanlike machines that are handy to have around for doing dangerous work on other planets, but they are not fit for life on Earth. So the police employ "blade runners," who specialize in the identification of and termination of replicants. When four very advanced models show up on the dirty, teeming streets of Los Angeles, the top blade runner, Rick Deckard, is coaxed out of retirement. One by one, he locates the unwelcome replicants and shuts them down.

**THE CAST** — Harrison Ford plays a cool, businesslike Rick Deckard, except when he's near Rachael, the latest in replicants. With Sean Young's curvy figure and provocative demeanor, Rachael distracts Deckard from his mission. But not before he pulls the plug on a sexy snake dancer (Joanna Cassidy), a way-out flower child (Daryl Hannah), and an Aryan warrior (Rutger Hauer). The other humans Deckard deals with seem even less savory than the replicants: M. Emmet Walsh as the bitter, cynical chief of the blade runners, Edward James Olmos as Deckard's origami-crazed ex-partner, and Joe Turkel, the remorseless scientist responsible for the replicants.

## WHY GUYS LOVE IT ▬ The future looks wild.

## HONEY, YOU'LL LIKE THIS MOVIE . . . ▬ Because you're always telling me Harrison Ford is the kind of guy women settle down with.

## DON'T MISS

• The flower child trying to crush Deckard to death with her thighs . . . if you have to go, there are worse ways.
• The Aryan warrior bringing fast, fast relief to Dr. Tyrell's pressure headache

## MEMORABLE LINES

"Give it to Holden, he's good," Deckard says to the chief, trying to reject the assignment.
"I did," the chief answers. "He can breathe pretty good . . . as long as no one unplugs him."

## CHECK OUT

Look for the video of the director's cut in the letter-box format. The director Ridley Scott preferred a more grim (and satisfying) ending than the studio originally released, and the Letter-Box format will let you see more of the vivid and imaginative world he's created for the movie. And it does away with the distracting narration.

# A CLOCKWORK ORANGE (1971)

## RATINGS

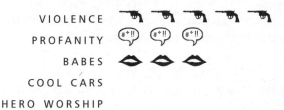

VIOLENCE

PROFANITY

BABES

COOL CARS

HERO WORSHIP

**WHAT HAPPENS** ✒ Are bad boys born or are they made? Who cares, because this movie doesn't waste your time on philosophical questions like that. It just sets loose Alex, a gleefully vicious punk, and his gang (he calls them "droogies") into a grim future in England, where they get pumped on Milk-Plus at the local bar and then head out to engage in their favorite sport, ultraviolence—brawling with other gangs, beating up bums, raping and battering middle-class suburbanites. When the droogies have had enough of Alex's authority over them, they set him up for the police. In prison, Alex is a model prisoner and volunteers for a new program of sex and violence-aversion therapy, which conditions him to be nauseated by violence and sex. Pronounced cured, Alex is released, but he's not exactly welcomed back into the world: His parents have rented his room, and when he meets up with his droogies and his victims, they all are thinking revenge rather than rehabilitation.

**THE CAST** ✒ Alex might be any English high school boy with a healthy interest in reptiles, the dark, brooding music of Beethoven, and sex with teenage girls. The permanent leer on Malcolm McDowell's face lets you know right away that his politeness is a put-on. His white overalls, black combat boots, bowler, and the one false eyelash stuck under one eye are the wrappings of an explosive package inside. Alex can be charming, but even when he's cured you can feel the undertow. The one victim you won't forget (and Alex shouldn't) is the writer Mr. Alexander (Patrick Magee), who is forced to listen to Alex belt out "Singin' in the Rain" while he's being beaten and his wife raped.

## WHY GUYS LOVE IT ◄ We don't want to be around for a future this disturbing, so let's enjoy watching it now.

## HONEY, YOU'LL LIKE THIS MOVIE . . . ◄ Because this movie virtually invented punk style and fashion.

## DON'T MISS
- The sixty seconds of sex with Alex and the two (that's right, two) girls he meets at a record store. They go at it for the full minute on high-speed to the *William Tell Overture* (which you may know as *The Lone Ranger*'s theme).
- Alex crushing the cat lady with her penis sculpture.

## MEMORABLE LINES
- During the demonstration of the results of Alex's sex-and-violence-aversion therapy, the scientists send out a woman wearing nothing but underpants to entice him. "The first thing that flashed into me Gulliver is that I'd like to have her right there on the floor with the old in-out in-out, real savage," we hear Alex saying to himself. Then he upchucks.
- "Moloko Vellocet, Moloko Synthemesc, and Moloko Drencromb" are the names of the Milk-Plus choices on the menu at the milk bar, all dispensed through the nipples of big breast fountains.

# DEMOLITION MAN (1993)

## RATINGS

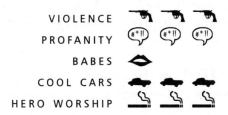

VIOLENCE

PROFANITY

BABES

COOL CARS

HERO WORSHIP

**WHAT HAPPENS** ☛ Cryo-prisons are the answer to over-crowded jails of the future; convicts are kept frozen and are only defrosted for their parole hearings. When Simon Phoenix, a vicious sociopath from the Twentieth century, escapes from his hearing, the pacifist cops of the twenty-first Century are not prepared to deal with him—so they melt down John Spartan, the cop who had arrested Phoenix (who had been frozen himself because his tactics had been deemed "excessive"). Together Phoenix and Spartan have a great time shocking the mellowed-out population of San Angeles while battling each other with weapons both new and old. Before it's over, John Spartan tears the not-so-benevolent mask off this tamed society and gets ahead of Phoenix.

**THE CAST** ☛ As Spartan, Sylvester Stallone lets loose plenty of anger and frustration—directed at his colleagues of the present and future—and lots of bullets and punches at Phoenix, but his real triumph in this movie is that he resists taking himself seriously. He even delivers his line about the Schwarzenegger Presidential Library with good humor. If Dennis Rodman weren't such a nice guy (he is, isn't he?), he would have been perfect to play Simon Phoenix. Instead, Wesley Snipes had to get himself a wacko haircut and develop an insane laugh so that he could be a psycho to remember. Sandra Bullock is a Twenty-first-Century cop with an unhealthy fascination with the Twentieth century and a healthy interest in a certain cop from the earlier times. Fast-talking comic Denis Leary leads the underground resistance. Watch for MTV Sports host Dan Cortese as a lounge singer who revives some of the most memorable tunes of our era.

## WHY GUYS LOVE IT ▰ In a violence-free future, the cops and the criminals of today will seem a whole lot more fun.

## HONEY, YOU'LL LIKE THIS MOVIE . . . ▰ Because together Stallone and Snipes make up one pumped and cut duo.

## DON'T MISS
- Phoenix fooling the prison's eye-scan security lock with the warden's eye.
- The tasty burger Spartan enjoys from an outlaw vendor in the red-meatless future.

## MEMORABLE LINES
- "Be well," everyone says to everyone else.
- When asked what he's rebelling against, Leary fires off this tirade about the homogenized, riskless society he's opted out of. "I'm the kind of guy who likes to sit in the greasy spoon and wonder, 'Do I want the T-bone steak or the jumbo rack of barbecued ribs with a side order of gravy fries?' I like high cholesterol. I want to eat bacon and butter and buckets of cheese. I want to smoke a Cuban cigar the size of Cincinnati in the nonsmoking section. I want to run through the streets naked covered in Jell-O, reading *Playboy* magazine. Why? Because I might suddenly feel the need to."

# LOGAN'S RUN (1976)

## RATINGS

| | |
|---|---|
| VIOLENCE | |
| PROFANITY | |
| BABES | |
| COOL CARS | |
| HERO WORSHIP | |

**WHAT HAPPENS** ■ By the Twenty-third Century, society has progressed enough to recognize that people shouldn't live past thirty. Those fools insistent upon resisting their voluntary "renewal" program after age twenty-nine are chased down by cops called Sandmen. Bras, apparently, have been outlawed, and technology has been developed to facilitate anonymous sex with your choice of partners. Anyway, Logan is a sensitive Sandman who's convinced by a demure twenty-nine-year-old named Jessica to run to a sanctuary and then break out of the domed city and discover the world beyond. Outside, they discover what endures the ravages of time.

**THE CAST** ■ Michael York's Logan is truly an innocent, a do-gooding cop convinced of the righteousness of his work. That is, until he meets up with Jessica, played by Jenny Agutter, who convinces him that women in their thirties can be as sexy as younger women. Farrah Fawcett (actually still Farrah Fawcett-Majors when this movie was made) was thirty herself when the movie came out and, while she hadn't yet developed the acting skills that later won her acclaim, she looks damn fine as the hairdresser's receptionist. English actor Peter Ustinov hams it up as the old coot living outside the domed city who teaches Logan and Jessica a few things about aging.

**WHY GUYS LOVE IT** ▰ This sex without names stuff is a future we can all look forward to.

**HONEY, YOU'LL LIKE THIS MOVIE...** ▰ Because you can see the styles for the fall of 2274 extra early.

**DON'T MISS**
- The laser surgeon's self-induced incision.
- Logan and Jessica's passage through the sex club.

**MEMORABLE LINES**
"One is terminated, one is born. Everything is balanced, logical." This is the motto of all good people of the year 2274.

# MAD MAX (1979)

**RATINGS**

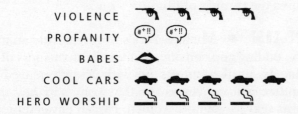

| | | | | |
|---|---|---|---|---|
| VIOLENCE | | | | |
| PROFANITY | | | | |
| BABES | | | | |
| COOL CARS | | | | |
| HERO WORSHIP | | | | |

**WHAT HAPPENS** ▰ "A few years from now" (according to the opening title), reckless drivers in tricked-out cars and motorcycles rule the roads, pursued at equally reckless speeds by hot-roddin' cops. When Officer Max chases one of the road rats—The Nightrider—to a fiery death, his com-

S.S./SHOOTING STAR

Mel Gibson as Max, before he ransomed away his cool.

patriots on motorcycles seek out their revenge on Max. The bikers run down Max's wife and son, and that pins Max's needle in the red zone. He declares war and gives the bikers something more than a traffic citation—and sets in motion a plot that lasts through two sequels.

**THE CAST** ✒ Mel Gibson, looking very young, gets behind the wheel and sets his jaw for action—though he's perfectly believable as the family man, too. The gang of bikers—who have names like Toe-cutter, Mudguts, and Johnny-boy and who wear more eyeliner than the makeover specialist at the Clinique counter at the mall—look like refugees from a Cramps concert.

**WHY GUYS LOVE IT** ✒ Any future that includes plenty of fuel for racing around highways is a good future as far as we're concerned.

### HONEY, YOU'LL LIKE THIS MOVIE . . .

■ Because seeing a young Mel Gibson in tight leather pants will make you remember why you fell for Mel in the first place.

### DON'T MISS

What happens to the guy who dares to lick Max's wife's ice-cream cone.

### MEMORABLE LINES

For some strange reason, this Australian movie was over-dubbed and released on video with Mel speaking a southern American accent.

### TRIVIA

Queen guitarist Brian May composed this movie's sound track.

# THE ROAD WARRIOR
# [MAD MAX 2] (1982)

### RATINGS

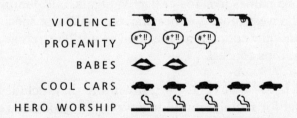

| | |
|---|---|
| VIOLENCE | 🔫 🔫 🔫 🔫 |
| PROFANITY | (#*!!) (#*!!) (#*!!) |
| BABES | 👄 👄 |
| COOL CARS | 🚗 🚗 🚗 🚗 🚗 |
| HERO WORSHIP | 🚬 🚬 🚬 🚬 |

**WHAT HAPPENS** ☛ Just like in *Mad Max*, the first film appearance of our hot-roddin' hero, vicious punks with unruly hair race around the highways of the unspecified future, burning petroleum and eluding the cops. Well, all of the cops except one: Mad Max. With his turbocharged V-8 and his shotgun, Max blasts away at the punks. Max collars one alive, and he shows Max where their refinery is. That's when Max mounts up his Mack truck and lays waste to each and every one of the punks—because that seems to be his job or his mission or something.

**THE CAST** ☛ Mel Gibson is back as Mad Max, but he's a full-tilt warrior this time because he has no family to force him to show his tender side—just a dog that's as vicious as he is. Fortunately, Mel has his brusque Aussie accent back, too; there's no dumb dubbing as there is on the first one. The rest of the cast, no doubt, went on to play important roles in their country's cinema.

**WHY GUYS LOVE IT** ☛ In the future, the only thing that will matter is how fast you're willing to drive.

**HONEY, YOU'LL LIKE THIS MOVIE . . .** ☛ Because Mel Gibson is still young, still dressed in tight clothing, and still stands out among a group of poorly attired youths.

**DON'T MISS**
- Max's idea of a good hot meal—straight from the Alpo can.
- How he keeps punks from stealing his petrol.

## MAD MAX, PIONEER

Movies, of course, are about action—otherwise, they'd be still photography. The first motion picture made to tell a story—*The Great Train Robbery* in 1903—is almost nonstop action for its entire eighteen minutes. Yet sometime in the last fifteen to twenty years, movie studios began producing what are now commonly called "action movies." In them, character, plot, dialogue, theme—in fact, everything—becomes secondary to the staging of the action sequences. Sure, this is true to some degree of many Westerns and just about every martial arts movie. But true action movies today involve more than battles between individuals—they're built around budget-bustin' explosions and stupefying stunts.

I believe that *Mad Max* and *The Road Warrior* are the prototypes for the contemporary action movie. They have very little dialogue, the audience knows nothing about any of the characters except Max, and what we know is insignificant. And as for plot, see if you can't tell your buddies what these movies are about without describing the action itself—you can't. I believe that all truly successful action movies adhere to the simple principles established by *Mad Max*:

1. Everything happens at maximum velocity.
2. People are killed frequently.
3. People are killed in lots of different ways.

# ROBOCOP (1987)

## RATINGS

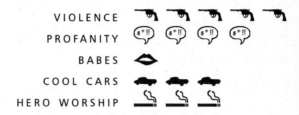

| | |
|---|---|
| VIOLENCE | 🔫 🔫 🔫 🔫 🔫 |
| PROFANITY | #*!! #*!! #*!! #*!! |
| BABES | 👄 |
| COOL CARS | 🚗 🚗 🚗 |
| HERO WORSHIP | 🚬 🚬 🚬 |

**WHAT HAPPENS** ■ In the very dismal future, the city of Detroit is overrun by ruthless gangs who kill cops with glee, though they still do it the old-fashioned way: with automatic weapons. The cops work for a private corporation, whose engineers compete to produce a mechanized cop that will be more durable. When a human cop is shot up and left for dead, one of those engineers gets to implement his plan to create a cyborg cop—one who can make the judgments of a living person, but who is nearly impregnable. The plan veers off course, as they inevitably do, when the Robocop regains some of his memory and goes off to confront the nasty guys who shot him when he was a person. Robocop is helped by his former partner, a babe cop who can kick ass and who seems more attracted to her partner after he is hard-wired. His final confrontation is with Dick Jones, vice president of the company that made him—Robocop fires Dick Jones without consulting the firm's human resources specialists, but nobody files a grievance because he is, after all, Dick Jones.

**THE CAST** ■ Peter Weller portrays the man behind the machine—as a human, he's thoroughly unmoving, but as Robocop, he's strangely sympathetic. Nancy Allen (who appeared most memorably in *Dressed to Kill* before this) is the tough but sexy partner who sees the man behind the metal. Ronny Cox (a perennial movie bad guy who could pass for the Dallas Cowboys' owner Jerry Jones) plays Dick Jones with an emphasis on dick. He is the corporate officer determined to throw a wrench into Robocop and bring down hotshot Miguel Ferrer. He's as conniving if not as nasty as Cox. Kurtwood Smith is plenty vicious as Clarence Boddicker, the gang leader.

## WHY GUYS LOVE IT ■ Maximum mayhem.

## HONEY, YOU'LL LIKE THIS MOVIE . . . ■ Because Robocop would be just another hunk . . . of junk . . . without his woman partner.

## DON'T MISS
- The quick glimpse of bare breasts in the squad room of the police station in the opening minutes of the movie.
- Robocop's well-aimed shot at the rapist.

## MEMORABLE LINES
When the fully robotic cop malfunctions during the demonstration and kills one of the company's employees, Dick Jones says to his boss, "It's just a glitch."

# ROBOCOP 2 (1990)

## RATINGS

| | | | | |
|---|---|---|---|---|
| VIOLENCE | 🔫 | 🔫 | 🔫 | 🔫 |
| PROFANITY | @*!! | @*!! | @*!! | @*!! |
| BABES | 👄 | 👄 | | |
| COOL CARS | 🚗 | 🚗 | | |
| HERO WORSHIP | 🚬 | | | |

**WHAT HAPPENS** ▰ Detroit has deteriorated even more since the end of the first Robocop: A drug called Nuke (that people are injecting into their necks) is all the rage, a twelve-year-old kid controls the streets, and the company that owns the police force and built Robocop is attempting a hostile takeover of the city. And Robocop has been reprogrammed to adhere to regulations and be more passive. Then the company builds Robo-Bad Guy, with the brain of a human criminal and the body of a machine. The rest of the movie involves these two tin men fighting for supremacy, sparks and bullets flying everywhere. Robocop demonstrates a firm grasp of neurophysiology in the climactic moment.

**THE CAST** ▰ Peter Weller returns as Robocop, but all the humanity has been written out of his code. Nancy Allen returns as Robocop's partner, but their relationship has cooled (could it be because of the stainless-steel codpiece he wears?), leaving her very little to do. Daniel O'Herlihy, who was the chairman of the company in both movies, has a bigger part in this movie, and he's sufficiently malevolent. Belinda Bauer is the scheming engineer at the company who gets her boss's ear by starting a bit lower. You've seen Robo-Bad guy Tom Noonan in other movies (*Last Action Hero, Manhunter, Wolfen*) or a guy who looks just like him at Midnight Bowling at your local bowl-a-rama.

**WHY GUYS LOVE IT** ▰ Maximum mayhem revisited.

**HONEY, YOU'LL LIKE THIS MOVIE . . .** ▰ Because it presents a more progressive approach to Robo law enforcement, relying on community policing and positive reinforcement rather than excessive discharge of ammunition unless absolutely necessary.

**DON'T MISS**
The chairman of the board and his able-bodied young executive taking care of business—in the Jacuzzi.

# BLOOD SIMPLE (1984)

## RATINGS

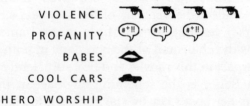

| | |
|---|---|
| VIOLENCE | 🔫 🔫 🔫 🔫 |
| PROFANITY | #*!! #*!! #*!! |
| BABES | 👄 |
| COOL CARS | 🚗 |
| HERO WORSHIP | |

**WHAT HAPPENS** ■ Marty owns a bar in a small town in Texas and he hires a shady private detective to determine if his wife is fooling around with one of the bartenders, which she is. Marty then contracts the P.I. to bring a certain end to their affair; that is, to kill the lovers. The P.I. double-crosses Marty and sets in motion a series of false conclusions that take some blood from everyone. The complex plot is full of surprises, but you'll figure it all out if you remember who can drive away clean.

**THE CAST** ■ This movie belongs to M. Emmet Walsh, the private eye who erupts into guffaws at his own despicability. Dan Hedaya (Carla's crude ex-husband Nick Tortelli on

*Cheers*) is a bitter and remorseless Marty, and Frances Mc-Dormand, the pregnant sheriff in 1996's *Fargo*, is his conniving, manipulative wife. Caught between them is John Getz, who plays the bartender lured in by Mrs. Marty. The brothers who wrote, produced, and directed the movie, Joel and Ethan Coen, provide the off-beat camera angles, brooding atmosphere, and black comedy.

**WHY GUYS LOVE IT** ► We don't need to be talked into watching movies with the word "Blood" in the title.

**HONEY, YOU'LL LIKE THIS MOVIE . . .** ► Because the adulterous couple must take their hits.

**DON'T MISS**
- What happens after the bartender digs himself a hole.
- When the P.I. gets his hand stuck.

**TRIVIA**

Listen carefully to the answering machine to hear the uncredited voice of Holly Hunter.

# BODY DOUBLE (1984)

**RATINGS**

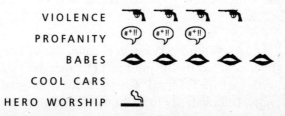

| | | | | |
|---|---|---|---|---|
| VIOLENCE | 🔫 | 🔫 | 🔫 | 🔫 |
| PROFANITY | (#*!!) | (#*!!) | (#*!!) | |
| BABES | 👄 | 👄 | 👄 | 👄 👄 |
| COOL CARS | | | | |
| HERO WORSHIP | 🚬 | | | |

*Body Double:* The more Melanie Griffiths, the merrier.

**WHAT HAPPENS** ▬ Jake, a down-on-his luck B-movie actor with a few troublesome psychological quirks, gets an unexpected break when a new friend offers him an incredible place to stay—complete with a telescopic view of a hot neighbor who performs a nightly solo act. When the woman gets brutally killed, Jake blames himself for his failure to act—until he makes a discovery that suggests things aren't what they seem. His investigation leads him into the porn-film industry and to a direct confrontation with his fears. (If some of the outline seems familiar, it's because elements of the plot have been directly lifted from two much more chaste movies by Alfred Hitchcock: *Vertigo* and *Rear Window.*)

**THE CAST** ▬ Craig Wasson is Jake, the actor–voyeur who is straitjacketed by his phobias. His new best pal, played by smooth-featured blond Gregg Henry, is just a bit too friendly. Deborah Shelton, who did a stint on *Dallas,* is mysterious and magnificent and murdered. You'll love Melanie Griffith as the porn star Holly Body, who's both knowing and innocent. Dennis Franz shows up briefly at the beginning and end as the director of a low-budget horror movie.

**WHY GUYS LOVE IT** ◢ Any legitimate opportunity to look at porn movies and actresses is worth our time.

**HONEY, YOU'LL LIKE THIS MOVIE . . .** ◢ Because Holly proves that even porn stars have standards.

**DON'T MISS**
- The final scene, when they bring in the Body Double.
- A more interesting use of a power drill than Tim Allen ever thought of.

**MEMORABLE LINES**
"What are you, some kind of pervert?" says porn-star Holly to Jake when he asks her to look through his telescope.

# CHINATOWN (1974)

**RATINGS**

| | | | |
|---|---|---|---|
| VIOLENCE | 🔫 | 🔫 | 🔫 |
| PROFANITY | #*!! | #*!! | |
| BABES | 👄 | 👄 | 👄 |
| COOL CARS | 🚗 | 🚗 | 🚗 🚗 |
| HERO WORSHIP | 🚬 | 🚬 | 🚬 |

**WHAT HAPPENS** ◢ Adultery was good business in the 1930s for a private detective like Jake Gittes. He's hired by jilted spouses to document the affairs and then he steps out of the way, leaving the couples to settle their own problems. But Jake can't get away clean when his pictures of a young girl with Hollis Mulray, an engineer for the Los Angeles Water Department, are published and lead to Mulray's death. Lured into deeper water than he usually swims by the sad siren song (and endless legs) of the wife, Evelyn Mulray, Jake finds himself immersed in a quicksand plot of power and corruption, resources stolen and sold, mistaken identities, and twisted family relationships. Most troubling for Jake is that all trails lead to the site of his gnawing failure, Chinatown.

**THE CAST** ▰ Jake Gittes is as cool and unflappable as Jack Nicholson in a room full of models, having a little wicked fun but out before there's any harm done. Until Jake meets Faye Dunaway's Evelyn Mulray. Yes, she has cheekbones and proportions that would make Claudia/Cindy/Elle/Naomi cry with envy, but it is what Jake doesn't see, what he can only sense, that flusters him. Evelyn's father, a frosty Noah Cross, played by John Huston, contacts Jake to find the mysterious girl and leaves Jake stammering, too. Diane Ladd is a woman hired to claim she's Evelyn Mulray—the first cheap shot at Jake.

**WHY GUYS LOVE IT** ▰ Mystery babes is one of our favorite games.

**HONEY, YOU'LL LIKE THIS MOVIE . . .** ▰ Because it brings the shadowy secrets of families out into the dark streets where everyone can gape at them.

**DON'T MISS**
- A close look at the photos Jake gives to his first client, whose wife is barking up the wrong tree.
- Look at everyone's eyes. That's where you'll see all the clues.

## MEMORABLE LINES

- Director Roman Polanski takes responsibility for the movie's most memorable cut, which he delivers with the words, "You're a nosy fellow. You know what happens to nosy fellows? They lose their noses."
- "Most people never have to face the fact," Noah Cross tells Gittes, "that at the right time, in the right place, they are capable of anything."

## CHECK OUT

The sequel to this movie, *The Two Jakes*, was directed by Jack Nicholson and released in 1990. It has some great dialogue and Harvey Keitel, Meg Tilly, and Madeleine Stowe, but you'll need a compass and map to follow the plot.

# F/X (1986)

## RATINGS

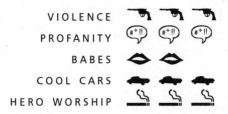

| | | | |
|---|---|---|---|
| VIOLENCE | 🔫 | 🔫 | 🔫 |
| PROFANITY | (#*!!) | (#*!!) | (#*!!) |
| BABES | 👄 | 👄 | |
| COOL CARS | 🚗 | 🚗 | 🚗 |
| HERO WORSHIP | 🚬 | 🚬 | 🚬 |

**WHAT HAPPENS** ▰ A federal agent recruits Rollie Tyler, a top-notch movie special effects expert, to help fake the death of a mobster turned witness so that no one else will try to assassinate him before the trial. Rollie reluctantly agrees to do the work, but when it goes down, nothing is as he expects it to be. He discovers that there's a lot more that's fake than the shots he's fired and he has to dig deep into his bag of special effects and use all of his cunning to evade the killers hunting him. Before the finale, he has staged his stunts so well, he has created an illusion that fools everyone but a persistent city homicide detective.

THE CAST ⬛ Australian Bryan Brown stays just on the near side of panic as Rollie, wary from the start and calm and in control, even when he realizes he's playing with pros. Brian Dennehy is the city detective who never thinks twice about following his hunch at the cost of his job. Jerry Orbach (from TV's *Law & Order*) has the high hair, hunch, and harried look of a guy who has spent too much of his life in the mob. Mason Adams is the head Fed, Colonel Mason, and he's too polite and congenial to be trusted. Diane Venora is Rollie's girlfriend, and she has the sophisticated, sexy look in her sleepwear. Is that Angela Bassett as the TV reporter? It is, it is.

WHY GUYS LOVE IT ⬛ You see, watching lots of movies with great special effects can teach you stuff that could save your life someday.

HONEY, YOU'LL LIKE THIS MOVIE . . . ⬛ Because Rollie relies on his loyal assistant, played by Martha Gehman, to bail him out of a tight spot or two.

DON'T MISS
- How Rollie encourages one of the Feds to tell him Mason's whereabouts by backing up a car into bridge abutments with the Fed in the trunk.
- Rollie's clever ploy for losing the cop chasing him by dropping a dummy on the road in front of the cop car.

## MEMORABLE LINES

"That's strictly confidential," retorts Mason's secretary when Dennehy asks for Mason's home address.

"Lady, I don't give a shit if it's tattooed on your ass. I want it," he insists.

# MARATHON MAN (1976)

## RATINGS

| | |
|---|---|
| VIOLENCE | 🔫 🔫 |
| PROFANITY | |
| BABES | 👄 |
| COOL CARS | 🚗 🚗 🚗 |
| HERO WORSHIP | 🚬 🚬 🚬 |

## WHAT HAPPENS ☛ Babe Levy spends his time minding his own business, working on his graduate degree in history, and training for the Olympic Marathon around New York City's Central Park. But all that changes very quickly when Levy's brother shows up one day for an unannounced visit and is then killed by some unsavory colleagues of his. The brother dies in Levy's arms, and the guys who terminated him—ex-Nazis and American spooks—think Levy knows something about their business. They capture Levy while he's taking a bath (the fiends!) and press him to 'fess up using means both brutally direct and cruelly covert. But Levy runs away (and runs and runs), until he confronts his tormentors and his family's past. The conclusion gets everyone all choked up.

**THE CAST** ◄ From the start of the movie, Dustin Hoffman has Babe Levy defensive about his father's political associations and his brother's career choice. So that by the time his brother, played by Roy Scheider, arrives, Hoffman has already prepared us for a less than warm family reunion. And Scheider is shifty enough to keep us from warming up to him, even as his body is cooling off. Chillier still is Szell, the death camp dentist played by Laurence Olivier, whose shaved head, steely eyes behind steel glasses, and stiff cordiality have Levy shivering with fright. William Devane, an American agent, and Marthe Keller, a German babe Levy meets at the library, seem trustworthy enough. . . .

**WHY GUYS LOVE IT** ◄ You know all that working out could someday come in handy.

**HONEY, YOU'LL LIKE THIS MOVIE . . .** ◄ Because it is about complicated family relationships.

**DON'T MISS**
- The opening sequence involving two typical New York drivers battling for one lane through traffic; it concludes with a blast.
- Levy's clever plan for retrieving an important piece of property from his apartment and the nice neighborhood kids who so kindly help him.
- The handy little bracelet Szell wears and shows to an old acquaintance he meets on the street.

**MEMORABLE LINES**
You'll never sit back in a dentist's chair again without thinking, "Is it safe?"

# MIDNIGHT RUN (1988)

## RATINGS

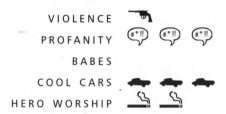

VIOLENCE

PROFANITY

BABES

COOL CARS

HERO WORSHIP

**WHAT HAPPENS** ▪ Everyone wants Jonathan "the Duke" Mardukas. He's an accountant for the mob who embezzled a fortune from a kingpin, Jimmy Serrano, and who was arrested and then jumped bail. Jimmy wants the Duke dead, and the FBI wants him alive to testify against his former boss. And the bailbondsman wants the Duke back to keep from losing the bail money, so the bondsman sends Jack Walsh to retrieve the Duke. From New York to Los Angeles, Jack and the Duke evade hitmen, cops, and a rival bounty hunter. The only thing they can't seem to get away from is each other's character flaws.

**THE CAST** ▪ Jack Walsh doesn't seem like many other characters we've seen Robert De Niro play: He's not a violent, borderline psychotic with a hair trigger. Rather, he is low-key and not what you'd call a quick study. But he does get his job done because he is steady and determined to prove himself. Jonathan Mardukas is a lot like the characters Charles Grodin typically plays (even on his own talk show). Yes, he did rip off the mob—a mortality risk ranked somewhere ahead of excessive consumption of fried foods, but otherwise he is a cautious, hypersensitive nudge. Walsh and the Duke spend most of their time reminding each other of their foolish choices. Yaphet Kotto is an angry FBI agent who chases them both with a growing frustration, Dennis Farina (from *Crime Story*) is the blustery mobster Jimmy Serrano, whose threats grow more preposterous with every step closer that the Duke gets to L.A. Along for the ride is John Ashton, who plays a competing bounty hunter with a bag of clever pranks to pull on Jack.

## WHY GUYS LOVE IT

This bounty hunting, it's a job you can get paid to do?

## HONEY, YOU'LL LIKE THIS MOVIE . . .

Because it has Robert De Niro and yet nobody gets shot, beaten, or even bitten in the entire movie.

## DON'T MISS

- Mardukas's clever "fake twenties" hustle.
- The tense moments in the casino with Serrano.

## MEMORABLE LINES

"Here are two words for you," Jack says to Mardukas. "Shut the fuck up."

# THE MIGHTY QUINN (1989)

## RATINGS

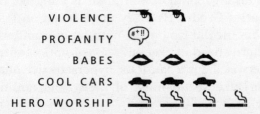

| | |
|---|---|
| VIOLENCE | 🔫 🔫 |
| PROFANITY | 💬 |
| BABES | 👄 👄 👄 |
| COOL CARS | 🚗 🚗 🚗 |
| HERO WORSHIP | 🚬 🚬 🚬 🚬 |

**WHAT HAPPENS** ✦ When a white man is killed at a businessman's house on a Caribbean island, all the evidence suggests that a fun-lovin' black man and local folk hero named Maubee did the deed in the midst of a robbery. But Xavier Quinn, Maubee's boyhood buddy and the island's police chief, has doubts and he begins to dig a bit deeper into the mystery. To find the truth, Quinn has to penetrate the shadowy business of international espionage and the weird world of voodoo, and resolve his own friendship with Maubee. And there are also the pressing matters of Quinn's ex-wife, a very voluptuous other woman, and the elegantly alluring wife of the businessman.

**THE CAST** ✦ Denzel Washington makes Quinn self-righteous, but not humorless or without doubts about his own motivations. He blends those conflicting stances—determined yet reflective, honorable though horny—into a character whose tale we'd like to hear while sipping a Red Stripe at the bar. But when we're in the mood for fun till the sun comes up, we'd rather hang with Rastaman Maubee—and not just because he could hook us up with some of the island's finest agricultural product. As comic Robert Townsend plays him, Maubee runs in high gear all the time, is as slippery as a rainbow trout, and afraid of nothing (including false accusations). Character actor M. Emmet Walsh is the ugly American with a few too many questions, and Esther Rolle (Florida Evans, the mother from *Good Times*) is the scary auntie of Maubee's girlfriend. Mimi Rogers plays it hot and cold as the businessman's wife.

**WHY GUYS LOVE IT** ✦ Any guy ought to give his buddy—even a suspicious one—the benefit of the doubt.

**HONEY, YOU'LL LIKE THIS MOVIE . . .** ✦ Because Denzel is a good man who happens to look very good in his little white shorts.

## DON'T MISS

- The guy who drinks a Red Stripe and spliff roach cocktail to win a bet.
- Denzel singing (yes, he's really singing) Taj Mahal's "Cakewalk Blues."

**TRIVIA**

Irie, irie mon: Rita Marley (Bob Marley's wife and one of the I-Threes), Cedelia Marley, and Sharon Marley Pendergast (who must be relatives) all appear in this movie.

# THE OSTERMAN WEEKEND (1983)

## RATINGS

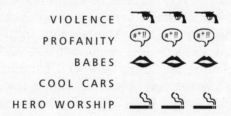

| | | | |
|---|---|---|---|
| VIOLENCE | 🔫 | 🔫 | 🔫 |
| PROFANITY | #*!! | #*!! | #*!! |
| BABES | 👄 | 👄 | 👄 |
| COOL CARS | | | |
| HERO WORSHIP | 🚬 | 🚬 | 🚬 |

**WHAT HAPPENS** ■ Four old friends and their wives gather at Tanner's home for a reunion weekend. Before the friends arrive, Tanner is told by CIA agents that the others work for the KGB. The CIA convinces Tanner to let them set up surveillance in his house for the weekend. All of this stirs the patriotic spirit of Tanner, who is the host of a controversial political talk show on TV. When the friends arrive, the CIA agent in charge sets in motion his complex plan to exact revenge for the mysterious death of his own wife, while he indulges his taste for voyeurism. Tanner and the friends fight each other and then the CIA agent. In the end, Tanner uses his TV show and the agent's own ploys to outsmart him.

## THE CAST ☛ Rutger Hauer is Tanner, incredulous that his friends are not what they seem and indignant enough to go along with the plan of the CIA agent played by John Hurt. Craig T. Nelson, aka "Coach," is Bernie Osterman, the friend who seems most untrustworthy. Most innocent is the friend played (against type) by Dennis Hopper, who's usually the most dangerous man in every movie he's in. His wife is the high and horny Helen Shaver, who wants everyone to get along and get naked. Chris Sarandon, the third friend, bickers with Tanner and heightens Tanner's suspicions. Meg Foster, a sturdy and attractive brunette, is Tanner's wife, and she is fortunately quite handy with a crossbow. Authority figure Burt Lancaster shows up in the beginning and end as the head of the CIA.

## WHY GUYS LOVE IT ☛ Four buddies fight each other and then come together to nail the true enemy—a happy ending if we ever saw one.

## HONEY, YOU'LL LIKE THIS MOVIE ... ☛ Because the CIA agent goes ga-ga when his wife is killed.

## DON'T MISS
- The opening scene with Hurt's wife, who can't seem to get enough.
- Shaver's underwear.

## MEMORABLE LINES
"The truth is a lie that hasn't been found out yet," says Osterman to Tanner.

TRIVIA

This was the last film directed by Sam Peckinpah.

# THE SPY WITHIN (1995)

RATINGS

VIOLENCE

PROFANITY

BABES

COOL CARS

HERO WORSHIP

**WHAT HAPPENS** ◄ **W**ill Rickman is just sitting in the bar, minding his own business, when a saucy brunette comes in to the use the phone. She's followed by two guys, who steal her bag and play rough with her. Being a regular guy, Will steps in to help her and before he knows it, he and the woman, Mary Ann, are balancing on various pieces of furniture in his house—presumably to avoid getting rug burn. The next day, he's so enthralled that he willingly goes along for the ride when she's pursued by a whole team of professionals with a vague connection to the U.S. government. Will hangs on as best he can (as you must, too) while she explains the complicated mess she's in and her plan to extricate them. Watch out, he has to loose his toenails before the plot runs its course.

**THE CAST** ☛ Scott Glenn sits comfortably in well-worn jeans and beat-up Bronco, looking just as you would expect a demolition expert like Will Rickman to look. Glenn is a reactive actor—making his move after the other actors show what they're about—and that works just right here, saving his anger and indignation until he's in way too deep. Theresa Russell is Mary Ann, code name "The Dove," though as always she's anything but passive. You can't ever be sure whether it's him she wants or just a partner to help her out. It's the measured, controlled danger of J. B., played by Terence Knox, that she needs help with. He's her former employer and lover. Katherine Helmond (Jessica Tate from *Soap*) appears briefly as Mary Ann's shrink, before she gets tied up with other things.

**WHY GUYS LOVE IT** ☛ A woman who writes you a note in lipstick on your ass on the first date is worth another night—even if you're chaperoned by trained assassins.

**HONEY, YOU'LL LIKE THIS MOVIE . . .** ☛ Because *she* hatches the clever scheme to outsmart the bad guys.

**DON'T MISS**
- The opening sequence, where Mary Ann gives the coroner a taste of gentle coercion.
- The private dental lab Mary Ann has in the basement of her cabin.

**MEMORABLE LINES**
- "You served your country on your back," Will accuses her.
    "No," she shoots back, "on my knees, and sometimes standing up."
- "Is it true you have no regard for human life?" a lawyer asks Will.
    "Do you mean that if a plane full of lawyers crashed would I be upset? No!" Will answers.

# The Best of Bondage

James Bond is without a doubt the guy-est English guy, mostly because he has a code we can all admire: Stay cool when the heat is on, never pass up a babe—no matter which side she's on—and always be ready to place your drink order at the bar ("Dry martini, gently shaken, not stirred"). Bond invariably has a tricked-up car to drive and a few gadgets devised by Q and the other boys in the lab, but his most fearsome weapons are his license to kill, his Walther PPK pistol, and his razor-sharp wit.

Sean Connery and his toupee were the best of the five guys to play James Bond; the others were George Lazenby (1 film), Roger Moore (7), Timothy Dalton (2), and Pierce Brosnan (1, so far). You can get an argument going about which is the best Bond movie, but from a guy's perspective it has to be *From Russia with Love*, slightly nudging out *Goldfinger*, because *FRWL*'s plot revolves around nothing but Bond's insatiable sexual appetites. And if your woman ever wonders why she'd want to watch a Bond movie, tell her everyone always goes formal, no matter what the occasion or hour of the day.

# FROM RUSSIA WITH LOVE (1963)

## RATINGS

VIOLENCE

PROFANITY

BABES

COOL CARS

HERO WORSHIP

**WHAT HAPPENS** ▰ Bond is lured to Istanbul, Turkey, with an offer from a beautiful Russian agent to defect with a much-sought-after decoding machine. The agent is taking orders from a brutally butch Russian officer who has secretly joined up with SPECTRE, an underworld syndicate bent on world domination. Though Bond knows he's being set up, he meets and beds the Russian babe. The plan gets disrupted because she's won over by his charm and high-caliber weapon. When they make off with the decoder, they are pursued by SPECTRE's Aryan killing machine, who is ultimately outmaneuvered in a small railroad cabin by the ever-resourceful Bond. Comrade Butch catches up to the amorous agents in Venice and shows them her very sensible footwear—a shoe that conceals a venom-tipped knife.

**THE CAST** ▰ Connery's Bond was always contained in his eyebrows—raising them when he spots an object of desire, cocking them as he moves in for the kill—and it's in this movie that he perfects the persona. Daniela Bianchi is the icy blond Russian agent, whose cold heart is thawed by Bond's afterburners. Not since your eighth-grade English teacher have you seen a woman as hard and mean as Rosa Klebb, played by German singer and actress Lotte Lenya. Robert Shaw (who was the shark expert in *Jaws*) is pure and simple as the well-programmed assassin. All the regulars appear in this, the second, Bond movie: Bernard Lee is a classic British bureaucrat as Bond's boss M, and Lois Maxwell is the sturdy but unsensational secretary Miss Moneypenny, terminally devoted to and unrequited by Bond.

## DON'T MISS

- The briefest glimpse of Agent Babe nude through a sheer curtain as she climbs into Bond's bed.
- The fight in the gypsy camp between two women who want to marry the chief's son. The protocol among these gypsy women, apparently, is to dress in tight shorts and short shirts when they're due for some no-holds-barred wrestling.

Guys will not go wrong watching almost any of the other Bond movies. Here are highlights from the best of the rest:

# DR. NO (1962)

## RATINGS

VIOLENCE ·

PROFANITY

BABES · · ·

COOL CARS · ·

HERO WORSHIP · · ·

**WHAT HAPPENS** ▪ When Agent 006 is killed in Jamaica, our man 007, Bond, is dispatched to the island to find out what happened to him. Bond discovers what 006 found out—that a mad scientist named Dr. No has appropriated a small nearby island from which he plans to execute the plot

The best Bond: Sean Connery in *Dr. No.*

for world domination by the Special Executive for Counter-intelligence, Terrorism, Revenge, and Extortion, or SPECTRE. His plan involves launching simultaneous missile strikes at the United States and the Soviet Union, sparking a nuclear war that would leave SPECTRE the only remaining power. But, of course, Bond gets onto the island, scoops up Dr. No's lovely babe Honey Forever, and pulls the plug on Dr. No's operation.

**THE CAST** ■ This is Sean Connery's first time out as James Bond, but right off he has the easy wit, the slight smile of seduction, and the unflappable charm—with both babes and baddies—that became the hallmarks of Bond's character. Joseph Wiseman is the evil Dr. No—not the most dastardly of Bond villains, but a low-key mad scientist. The delicious Ursula Andress is the Honey in the white bikini Bond bumps into on the beach and takes along for the rest of the movie because he likes having her around. (Do you think there's a dating service where sociopathic geniuses meet great-looking women who are not bound up by the conventional thinking on insanity? Must I devise a plan to dominate the world if I want to join?) Bond's CIA contact Felix Leiter is played by Jack Lord, whose hair had not yet reached the heights it did when he was the all-powerful Steve McGarrett on *Hawaii Five-O*.

## DON'T MISS

- The elegant woman Bond takes to the cleaners at the baccarat table, who comes to his suite to earn a measure of retribution.
- The hairy moment when Bond awakes to find a giant tarantula crawling up his leg.
- When Bond's Jamaican cohort gets hot under the collar—and everywhere else.

# GOLDFINGER (1964)

## RATINGS

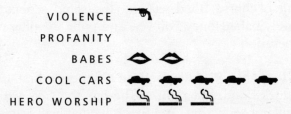

| | |
|---|---|
| VIOLENCE | 🔫 |
| PROFANITY | |
| BABES | 👄 👄 |
| COOL CARS | 🚗 🚗 🚗 🚗 🚗 |
| HERO WORSHIP | 🚬 🚬 🚬 |

**WHAT HAPPENS** ▰ While on holiday in Miami, Bond encounters an international gold smuggler and card cheat, Goldfinger, who plots to contaminate all the gold in Fort Knox so that his gold will be more valuable. To do the job, Goldfinger enlists the help of a group of women stunt pilots led by one Pussy Galore. She, like Goldfinger's assistant, falls for Bond and she helps him thwart Goldfinger's plot. But before Bond can finish the job, he has to elude the deadly hat of Goldfinger's henchman, Oddjob, and give Mr. 'Finger a boost at 20,000 feet.

**THE CAST** ➤ Sean Connery has to lay on the charm and pressure pretty thick to tempt Goldfinger's girls away from him. But Connery's Bond has plenty of suave for the job, though he's not beyond using judo to sway Pussy to do as he likes. And Honor Blackman's Pussy Galore is tough enough to enjoy being tossed around by Bond before she gives in. German Gert Frobe gives Goldfinger the accent and beady eyes that always say "villain," but it's Oddjob, played by Harold Sakata, around whom you'd best keep your head.

## DON'T MISS
- How Goldfinger rewards his secretary for her dedicated service.
- Bond's Astin-Martin, complete with oil slick, machine guns, and passenger ejector seat.

## MEMORABLE LINES
"I'm so glad it's just the car and not you," Bond says to a woman he's accidentally run off the road. "You don't look like a woman who should be ditched."

**TRIVIA**

This must be the first movie to have merchandise marketed with it. I had a toy replica of the Astin-Martin with real ejector seat.

# THUNDERBALL (1965)

## RATINGS

| | |
|---|---|
| VIOLENCE | 🔫 🔫 🔫 |
| PROFANITY | |
| BABES | 👄 👄 |
| COOL CARS | 🚗 🚗 🚗 |
| HERO WORSHIP | 🚬 🚬 |

**WHAT HAPPENS** — The fiends at SPECTRE hold the world hostage with a stolen nuclear weapon, which they get by substituting a lookalike pilot for an English flier in a test of a new airplane. All of the 00 agents are called in on this one, and our man 007 is given an assignment that fits his expertise perfectly. His job is to connect with Domino, the beautiful sister of the pilot who was replaced and mistress of Largos, the SPECTRE operative who plotted the plot. Of course, Bond carries out his duties with vigor and, after surviving undersea attacks by SPECTRE frogmen and a hazardous coupling with an exotic beauty, he helps Domino pinpoint her revenge and then carries her off into the wild blue yonder.

**THE CAST** — Sean Connery lets Bond's sense of humor take over in this movie, knowing that irreverance hasn't scared off a babe yet. For this movie, he has fair-haired Domino, played by Claudine Auger, and the evil, raven-tressed Fione Volpe. Adolfo Celi is SPECTRE's No. 2 (Largos), his eyepatch and craggy face furnishing all the menace necessary for a role with minmal lines.

## DON'T MISS

- When Bond comes upon Fione in the bathtub, she asks for something to put on—being the gent that he is, he offers her a pair of shoes.
- Bond battling a grieving woman in the movie's opening sequence.

## MEMORABLE LINES

- "I did it for King and Country," Bond tells Fione—and you can tell he means it because he remained at attention throughout the whole act.
- "My, what sharp little eyes you have," Domino says to Bond when he spots her name on an anklet before she's introduced herself. "Wait till you get to my teeth," he shoots back.

# ON HER MAJESTY'S SECRET SERVICE (1969)

## RATINGS

| | |
|---|---|
| VIOLENCE | 🔫 🔫 🔫 |
| PROFANITY | |
| BABES | 👄 👄 👄 |
| COOL CARS | 🚗 🚗 🚗 🚗 |
| HERO WORSHIP | 🚬 🚬 🚬 |

**WHAT HAPPENS** ☛ Bond gets married—but it's all right because he's not the real Bond we know and love and she doesn't last. Okay, that out of the way, I can tell you the plot is set in Switzerland and it involves SPECTRE trying to unleash a germ assault on the entire world. Mostly, though, it revolves around ski and snowmobile chases, and Bond bedding down Mrs. Bond in her lush furs.

**THE CAST** ✒ When Connery first bowed out of the Bond series, Australian George Lazenby took a turn as 007—and his square chin fits the mold very well. But he lacked Connery's comedic sense and so this movie has more action than attitude. Diana Rigg—who's best remembered as Mrs. Peale from the TV adventure show *The Avengers*—is a sexy and serious Mrs. Bond; no bimbos get to carry the Bond name. Telly "Kojak" Savalas takes a turn as the infamous Ernst Stavro Blofeld.

**DON'T MISS**
The ice-rink car chase.

# DIAMONDS ARE FOREVER (1971)

**RATINGS**

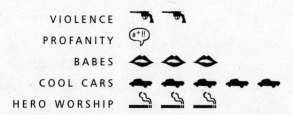

| | |
|---|---|
| VIOLENCE | 🔫 🔫 |
| PROFANITY | 💬 |
| BABES | 👄 👄 👄 |
| COOL CARS | 🚗 🚗 🚗 🚗 🚗 |
| HERO WORSHIP | 🚬 🚬 🚬 |

**WHAT HAPPENS** ✒ The scene is Vegas, where Bond catches the scent of SPECTRE's plot to kidnap a reclusive billionaire named Willard Whyte, smuggle diamonds from South Africa, and destroy Washington with a satellite laser weapon. He climbs to the top of the town, rewrites a few traffic laws on the strip in a candy-apple red Mustang Mach II, survives a perilous fight with two very flexible babes in bikinis, Bambi and Thumper, and frees Whyte. After thwarting the plans of SPECTRE boss Blofeld, Bond settles down for a celebration dinner with the delicious Tiffany Case, but he can't get to dessert until he finishes off Mr. Wint and Mr. Kidd, a pair of Afrikaners a bit too polite for his tastes.

**THE CAST** ▰ Sean Connery took the then record-setting sum of $1 million to come back for one more appearance as Bond. By now we know all the moves and all the moods that Connery brought to the role, but the girls still rev his motor and he knows the stunts are stupendous. Jill St. John as Tiffany Case clearly enjoys the game as much as Bond does. Jimmy Dean, the singer turned sausage salesman, is the mysterious Willard Whyte; shapely Lana Wood is the well-named showgirl, Plenty O'Toole.

**DON'T MISS**
- Bond helping his informant tighten her bikini top.
- Watching where Bond slips the crucial cassette tape to Tiffany.

**MEMORABLE LINES**
- A thug throws Tiffany (wearing only her underpants) out a hotel window from twenty stories up right into the pool and Bond says to him, "Exceptionally good shot."
    The guy answers, "I didn't know there was a pool down there."
- After Tiffany changes from a blond to a brunette, she asks Bond which he prefers. "I don't care," he answers, "as long as the collars and cuffs match."

# LIVE AND LET DIE (1973)

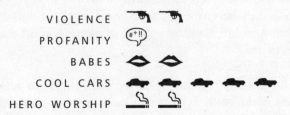
**WHAT HAPPENS** ▪ A Central American dictator, Dr. Kananga, and a New York heroin distributor, Mr. Big, appear to have a lot in common: They both believe in voodoo, spend a lot of time with an exotic brunette named Solitaire, frequent Fillet of Soul restaurants, and are tracked by James Bond for information about the death of another agent. Bond gets down among the black people of Harlem, New Orleans, and Haiti to catch the killers and bust up a scheme to dominate the world's heroin trade. And Bond proves that he's no racist in his own special way by crossing the color line with Rosie, a double agent posing as his wife. He also plays a couple hands of Solitaire himself, inflates Kananga past the recommend p.s.i., and then gives the Claw a final shock.

**THE CAST** ▪ Roger Moore takes his first turn as Bond, and while he's not as physically imposing as Sean Connery, he's almost as cool under pressure and he sure does love the ladies. Even after Kananga orders Bond killed, he stops to make a pass at the soothsayer, Solitaire. She's played by Jane Seymour before (or is it 100 years after?) she hung out her shingle as *"Dr. Quinn, Medicine Woman."* Yaphet Kotto is plenty big enough to be both Dr. Kananga and Mr. Big. Clifton James also makes his first appearance in a Bond movie—as the mush-mouthed, chaw-chewin' Sheriff J. W. Pepper, a part he reprised in *The Man with the Golden Gun*. Julius Harris is Tee Hee, the one-armed–one-clawed henchman, and Geoffrey Holder (the 7-UP cola nut guy) is the voodoo priest with the last laugh.

## DON'T MISS

- The best speedboat chase ever filmed—when Bond's boat cleared a causeway, it landed in the record books for the longest boat jump ever.
- Bond's chance to feed the alligators.

## MEMORABLE LINES

- In the opening sequence, a guy standing on a street corner in New Orleans, watching a ragtime procession, asks a passerby, "Whose funeral is it?" The answer will stick in your mind.
- "You wouldn't, you couldn't after what we just did," Rosie pleads with Bond when he threatens her with his gun after their interlude.

    "I certainly wouldn't have killed you before," he replies.

## TRIVIA

You should know that Paul McCartney's title song was a Top 10 hit when the movie was released—long before it was mangled into another hit by Guns N' Roses.

# THE MAN WITH THE GOLDEN GUN (1974)

## RATINGS

| | |
|---|---|
| VIOLENCE | 🔫 🔫 |
| PROFANITY | |
| BABES | 👄 👄 👄 |
| COOL CARS | 🚗 🚗 🚗 |
| HERO WORSHIP | 🚬 🚬 |

**WHAT HAPPENS** ■ A thin plot about a stolen piece of military technology is contrived simply so that a first-rate assassin can entice Bond to his island lair for a duel in his special constructed playground. The assassin, Scaramanga, kid-

Moore's Bond was no saint in *The Man with the Golden Gun.*

S.S. ARCHIVES/SHOOTING STAR

naps Bond's fellow agent Mary Goodnight in Hong Kong, evades Bond in a high-speed chase, flies off in a car converted into a plane, and waits for Bond to land. Then his little henchman, Nick Nack, starts the contest that only one can win.

**THE CAST** ▬ Roger Moore is back and he's got two treats he has his eye on: brunette Maud Adams (she later resurfaces as Octopussy) and blond Britt Ekland (Mary Goodnight). Herve Villechaize (the dwarf, Tattoo, from TV's *Fantasy Island*) is Nick Nack, who runs the game for the assassin with the anatomical oddity, Scaramanga (rendered tranquilly diabolical by the always evil Christopher Lee).

## DON'T MISS

- The only high-speed chase ever filmed with two vehicles made by the now-defunct American Motors Corporation (creators of the Gremlin and the Pacer).
- The nieces of Bond's Hong Kong contact demonstrating what they've learned in finishing school.

## MEMORABLE LINES

"Good night, Goodnight."

# MOONRAKER (1979)

## RATINGS

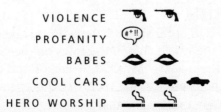

| | |
|---|---|
| VIOLENCE | |
| PROFANITY | |
| BABES | |
| COOL CARS | |
| HERO WORSHIP | |

**WHAT HAPPENS** ► This is the high-tech, special-effects Bond movie, and it revolves around a stolen space shuttle and a renegade space station. You'll have trouble finding fault with the madman in this one, because his diabolical plot is focused on wiping out the human race and then re-populating Earth with his personally selected astronauts. The case takes Bond to Venice, Rio, San Francisco, and, finally, outer space.

**THE CAST** ► Roger Moore tries to snooze through this one and let the pyrotechnics carry the load, but he does wake up on occasion to pay some attention to several babes, most importantly Dr. Holly Goodhead, the perky physicist played by Lois Chiles. French actor Michael Lonsdale is fiendish enough as Drax, the maniac who runs the company that builds the space shuttle and who wants to rebuild the planet, but he still must rely on Richard "Jaws" Kiel for the physical work of taking on Bond. All of the original Bond compatriots are in this movie for the last time—Bernard "M" Lee died in 1981.

**DON'T MISS**
- The amazing free fall before the opening credits.
- Bond going facedown in Dr. Goodhead's lap during a fight in an ambulance.
- Jaws flossing his stainless steel choppers with cable car wire.

**MEMORABLE LINES**
When his work in outer space is done, Bond takes Dr. Good-head around the world. When the folks on the ground get a peek, one of them asks, "My God, what is Bond doing?"

"I believe he is attempting reentry," Q quips.

# FOR YOUR EYES ONLY (1981)

## RATINGS

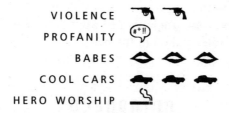

VIOLENCE

PROFANITY

BABES

COOL CARS

HERO WORSHIP

**WHAT HAPPENS** ☛ This installment is a simple spy story about a decoder lost at sea that the British government can't allow to fall into the hands of anyone else. To get it back, Bond must outmaneuver a Russian spy babe and her comrades with the help of a salvage specialist's feisty daughter, and he has to break into an impregnable (well, almost) mountain fortress. He also has to fend off an aggressively amorous figure skater.

**THE CAST** ☛ Roger Moore barely seems to have the energy anymore to rise to the challenge of the many troubled women the script sends his way. Not Chanel No. 5 model Carole Bouquet, who is the dark and delicious Melina, the salvager's daughter. Not Cassandra Harris, who is Lisl, the Russian agent. Not even Lynn-Holly Johnson, the little blond ice skater Bibi, who is determined to go international. In fact, Lois Maxwell's ever-steady Miss Moneypenny seems about the right speed for Bond—at least they could talk to each other about chin tucks. Topol serves well as the bad guy Columbo, and Charles Dance as his muscle. You'll do a double take when you see Janet Brown as the Prime Minister—you'll swear she's ol' Maggie herself.

## DON'T MISS

- The hat trick Bond scores on the hockey players.
- Bond and Melina getting in a bit of waterskiing together, very together.

## MEMORABLE LINES

"I don't think your uncle would approve," Bond tells Bibi when he finds her naked in his bed.

"Oh, him," she replies, "he thinks I'm still a virgin."

# OCTOPUSSY (1983)

## RATINGS

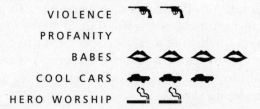

| | |
|---|---|
| VIOLENCE | 🔫 🔫 |
| PROFANITY | |
| BABES | 👄 👄 👄 👄 |
| COOL CARS | 🚗 🚗 🚗 |
| HERO WORSHIP | 🚬 🚬 |

**WHAT HAPPENS** ◢ The burning question is, what's in a name? And the answer here, unfortunately, is not what you'd hope. The title refers to a shapely brunette with an eye-catching tattoo who runs an international jewel-smuggling operation. She conducts her business behind the front of a circus, and, boy, you'll love the group of hench-honeys she assembles to help her. In fact, this is the last Bond movie that is unashamed about sending wave upon wave of beauties at him; it seems that feminism or political correctness or good taste infected the producers after this and all the subsequent movies dole out the babes one at a time. The rest of the plot involves a Frenchman helping a rogue Russian general who wants to launch a nuclear war or something.

**THE CAST** ◆ Roger Moore goes around the world and back to find this Octopussy, even dressing as a clown to get close to her. Maud Adams (who had a small part in *The Man with the Golden Gun*) is the title character who's not quite as diabolical as most of the other villainesses Bond has confronted. But she does have that tattoo. Louis Jourdan is more like the typically cultured and evil Bond bad guys. As General Orlov, Steven Berkoff (who was villain Victor in *Beverly Hills Cop*) has the dead-eye stare and clenched jaw to convince you that he's as cruel as they come. If you know professional tennis from the seventies, you'll recognize Vijay Amritraj as, surprise, Vijay, Bond's Indian cohort.

## DON'T MISS
- The delicious stuffed sheephead Bond is served . . . mmm, mmm, that's good eyeball.
- The circular saw yo-yo.

## MEMORABLE LINES
"We've got company," Bond says to Vijay as they putt along in their motorized rickshaw.

"No problem, this is a company car," Vijay says as he switches on the turbo and pops a wheelie.

# NEVER SAY NEVER AGAIN (1983)

## RATINGS

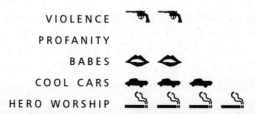

| | |
|---|---|
| VIOLENCE | 🔫 🔫 |
| PROFANITY | |
| BABES | 👄 👄 |
| COOL CARS | 🚗 🚗 🚗 |
| HERO WORSHIP | 🚬 🚬 🚬 🚬 |

**WHAT HAPPENS** ■ The basic story is very familiar—maybe because it's identical to the plot of *Thunderball*—and many of the action scenes are very similar (though updated), but the wrinkles are worth checking out. The babes, Domino and Fatima Blush, are played by two well-known beauties, and the evil one has an especially nasty streak. The villain, again named Largos, is a perfect match to Bond's gentility. And Bond drives a supremely cool motorcycle.

**THE CAST** ■ Sean Connery returned to do Bond once more—that's what the title refers to—and you can bet it was the chance to score with Kim Basinger (and her perfect body) and Barbara Carrera, the deliciously vicious Fatima. But the real winner here is Klaus Maria Brandauer, the malevolently polite and cheerful Largos. Max Von Sydow pets the obligatory cat as the headless head of SPECTRE.

**DON'T MISS**
- The shocking video game Largos and Bond play.
- Bond blinding the SPECTRE agent at the spa with his urine sample.

**MEMORABLE LINES**
- "You know that making love to Fatima Blush was the greatest pleasure of your life," Fatima demands of Bond at gunpoint.

    "Well, to be perfectly honest, there was this girl in Philadelphia," he answers.
- "Do you serve men here?" Bond asks the receptionist at the spa.

    "Some men more than others," she answers.

# A VIEW TO A KILL (1985)

## RATINGS

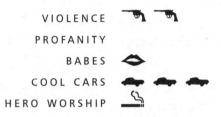

| | |
|---|---|
| VIOLENCE | |
| PROFANITY | |
| BABES | |
| COOL CARS | |
| HERO WORSHIP | |

**WHAT HAPPENS** ▬ Zorin, the product of Nazi genetic experiments and Europe's leading manufacturer of computer microchips, schemes to destroy Silicon Valley so that he can dominate the world's market—which isn't quite as ambitious as destroying the world, but it's a goal. To stop him, Bond must get past Zorin's strong and sexy bodyguard, May Day. Bond enlists a girl named Stacey to help him.

**THE CAST** ▬ Roger Moore is halfway out the door in this, his last appearance as James Bond. He does seem intrigued—and perhaps a bit frightened—by Grace Jones, who's portrayal of May Day is indistinguishable from her own strange persona. As always, Christopher Walken can chill you with his smile. Tanya Roberts is certainly Hollywood beautiful, but she's such a lightweight that you're afraid the Bond charm will crush the life out of her. Patrick Macnee does not deserve to be Roger Moore's flunky in this movie; as Steed in the great TV series *The Avengers,* Macnee handled men far more dangerous than Moore ever has without getting so much as a wrinkle in his suit.

## DON'T MISS
- Bond calling for May Day.
- Bond driving the Peugeot like a French cab driver.

# THE LIVING DAYLIGHTS (1987)

## RATINGS

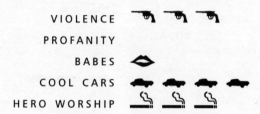

| | |
|---|---|
| VIOLENCE | 🔫 🔫 🔫 |
| PROFANITY | |
| BABES | 👄 |
| COOL CARS | 🚗 🚗 🚗 🚗 |
| HERO WORSHIP | 🚬 🚬 🚬 |

**WHAT HAPPENS** ✏ Those sneaky Russians are at it again, this time posing a high-level scientist as a defector to fool the British into revealing too much about their operations. The only thing the Russkies don't account for is the power of James Bond's determination and his sense of chilvary focused on a beautiful Czech cellist. He gets the girl, uncovers a wacko American arms dealer, and brings down a scheming Russian general—all without wrinkling his tuxedo.

**THE CAST** ✏ In his first Bond movie, Timothy Dalton restores a bit of the credibility that had been slipping away with the collagen in Roger Moore's face—it had been getting harder and harder to believe that Bond could free-fall from airplanes, punch out thugs, chase other spies through crowded streets, and still have the energy to . . . um . . . interrogate female operatives without getting a B12 shot from Q every hour. Dalton is certainly athletic-looking enough and plenty dashing to do all of those things. His only failing is that he doesn't have Sean Connery's cool, detached sense of humor under fire. The cellist, Maryam D'Abo, is a refined beauty, like the best Bond babes. Joe Don Baker as the arms dealer has more than a business interest in military hardware.

## DON'T MISS

- The milkman's lethal pasteurized, homogenized, and highly explosive moo juice.
- Bond's car. It's one of his coolest vehicles, with outriggers, a rocket-grade turbocharger, missiles, a laser weapon, and a self-destruct.
- The new, smarter Moneypenny, who's more than just a secretary and not as easily overlooked as the old one.

# LICENCE TO KILL (1989)

## RATINGS

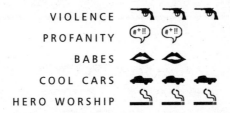

| | |
|---|---|
| VIOLENCE | 🔫 🔫 🔫 |
| PROFANITY | #*!! #*!! |
| BABES | 👄 👄 |
| COOL CARS | 🚗 🚗 🚗 |
| HERO WORSHIP | 🚬 🚬 🚬 |

**WHAT HAPPENS** ☛ Felix Leiter, Bond's long-time American counterpart, is killed on his wedding night by a smug Colombian drug lord, which incites our man 007 to an all-out war against the killer. When Bond is ordered by his superiors to leave the case to U.S. authorities, he resigns and proceeds on his own, wreaking havoc throughout the New World.

**THE CAST** ☛ Timothy Dalton returns for his second go at Bond and this time he's more interested in action that involves multivehicle chases than multibabe chases. Still, he brings along smart Pam Bouvier (Carey Lowell) and he gets a boost from the drug lord's moll (Talisa Soto). Bad skin and slick hair let you know that Robert Davi is a bad, bad guy. Everett McGill, the brutal henchman in *Under Siege 2*, and Benicio Del Toro, the mean mumbler in *The Usual Suspects*, take their futile shots at Bond. Sports fans: Keep your eyes open for Rafer Johnson, who won the Olympic decathlon in 1968. Schmaltzy entertainment fans: Don't miss Wayne Newton in a brief cameo.

## DON'T MISS
- Bond and Felix dropping in at the wedding.
- Bond bobbing to the surface of the shark tank.

# GOLDEN-EYE (1996)

## RATINGS

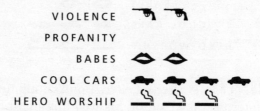

| | |
|---|---|
| VIOLENCE | 🔫 🔫 |
| PROFANITY | |
| BABES | 👄 👄 |
| COOL CARS | 🚗 🚗 🚗 🚗 |
| HERO WORSHIP | 🚬 🚬 🚬 |

**WHAT HAPPENS** ▰ Bond is back after an extended hiatus and he once again has a certifiably suspenseful plot to go along with the usual babes, cars, gadgets, and far-fetched stunts. In this case, Bond is in pursuit of a hot but nasty Russian Agent Babe, who steals an experimental British attack helicopter and takes it back to a remote Russian base, where she and a comrade set in motion a complex plan for world domination or at least a scheme to make a lot of cash on the international weapons market. Unfortunately for them, Bond teams up with a nicer but still very resourceful

Russian Computer Programmer Babe, leaving the Agent Babe hanging and leading Bond back to the start.

**THE CAST** ➤ In his first time out as Bond, Pierce Brosnan restores 007's sense of humor (which Dalton lacked) without compromising his toughness (Roger Moore's downfall). Of course he lights up when his radar locks on a babe, but you also see that he's got the safety off in case he has to return fire in a hurry. Famke Janssen plays Onatopp, who has all the qualities of a classic Bond villain babe: She's dark, dangerous, and as devoted to action as Bond himself. Joe Don Baker is the CIA operative who's supposed to help Bond, though of course he's of little help. You'll be pleasantly surprised by the casting of Judi Dench as M, Bond's superior—she proves that Maggie Thatcher isn't the only Englishwoman who can bust balls with the boys.

### DON'T MISS
- Bond's entrance in the opening scene.
- Bond's chasing a Peugeot through the streets of St. Petersburg . . . in a tank.

### MEMORABLE LINES
While Bond and the Russian Agent Babe are in a sauna, she tries to crush him to death with her thighs. When he finally breaks free, he points his pistol at her and says, "Enough foreplay."

You see a preview or you read a box at the video rental store and you think you've found a real guy's movie. But then you see the movie and you're disappointed, because the hero is a weepy wimp or the promise of lusty babes all over the screen is just a tease. Here are six movies that women (and some men) will tell you are real guy's movies, but don't you be fooled—they've got the packaging without the goods inside. Watch them at your peril!

# BULL DURHAM (1988)

**WHAT HAPPENS** ● Baseball, even minor league baseball, is a guy's national pastime. Relationships, especially older women with younger men, is a woman's natural pastime. So when somebody takes a perfectly good story about a veteran minor league catcher brought in to help a pitcher with major league heat learn control and lets a sassy broad mess with both their heads, well, I have to call it a foul ball. And a foul ball looks like it might be a hit, but it's still scored a strike. While catcher Crash Davis and lanky righthander Ebbie "Nuke" LaRoosh should be working together on the split finger fastball, they're bickering over Annie Savoy, a certainly sexy devout fan of the Durham Bulls who tells them *she'll* decide which of *them* she will put first in her lineup for the season.

*S.S./SHOOTING STAR*

*Bull Durham:* Crash and burn.

**THE CAST** ☛ Annie, of course, is not to blame for the problems here—if you saw Susan Sarandon washing up after work in *Atlantic City,* you know that she's capable of being a distraction to the boys in the field. No, the full measure of responsibility for this baseball movie whiffing big must be divided between Nuke and Crash (Tim Robbins and Kevin Costner). They fall into Annie's game plan, let her dictate the strategy, and even listen to her advice about how to play. And when Crash finally takes control of the situation, does he restore her to her rightful place? No, he discusses their relationship. Unforgivable.

**WHY GUYS SHOULD AVOID IT** ☛ It's shown once a week on the chick channel, Lifetime. Is that proof enough?

## DON'T WATCH

- Annie reading poetry to Nuke while he's tied spread-eagle to her bed.
- Crash taking pointers from Annie at the local batting cage—she can't even hit a hanging curve.
- Nuke wearing a pair of Annie's garters while he plays.

## WOULD YOU GET AWAY WITH THIS LINE?

"Would you rather I was making love with him and using your name," Annie asks Nuke, "or making love to you and using his name?"

# CANNIBAL WOMEN IN THE AVOCADO JUNGLE OF DEATH (1989)

**WHAT HAPPENS** ◼ The Piranha Women, a renegade band of feminists living in California's Avocado Jungle, threaten the nation's supply of guacamole. How? By having sex with male avocado hunters and then eating or enslaving them. Two government men approach Margo Hunt, a serious but still babeful professor of folklore at a California university, and ask her to present their offer to relocate the Piranha Women to a condo complex in Malibu. And so she sets off on a journey to the heart of darkness—accompanied by a Valley Girl from one of her classes and a male chauvinist guide. On the way, they discover the truth behind gender stereotypes and other meaningful junk like that.

**THE CAST** ◼ Tall, blond Shannon Tweed is all buttoned up as Dr. Hunt—even when she changes into native wear; if you want to see more of her, pick up the *Night Eyes* series or the many video editions of *Playboy* she's appeared in. Her nemesis is the brunette Dr. Kurtz, a former colleague of Hunt's, who's played by the generously endowed Adrienne Barbeau, also wearing far too much clothing. *Politically Incorrect* Bill Maher wears just the right amount of clothes as the guide—plenty, that is—but he barely gets to be as incorrect as he ought to be.

### WHY GUYS SHOULD AVOID IT ⬛ After a brief tease of unclothed breast in the movie's opening sequence, you'll see nothing more than navels and cleavage throughout the rest of the movie. And with a title like this, we ought to see a bare pair in every scene.

### DON'T WATCH
- The weenie guys held hostage are liberated with nothing more than a few cans of Milwaukee's Best—talk about yer deprivation, at least they could have been given imports.
- The humiliating initiation rite to which new recruits to the Piranha Women must subject themselves.

### OH MY, IT'S A MEMORABLE LINE
The cynical general who believes that Dr. Hunt is sympathetic to the Piranha Women says to her, "I bet you want to eat me right now, don't you!"

# HARLEY-DAVIDSON AND THE MARLBORO MAN (1991)

### WHAT HAPPENS ⬛ Two buddies, a biker and a cowboy, rob an armored car to get cash to save their favorite bar. Instead of cash in that armored car, they find drugs that belong to the mob, and the Boys in the Dark Suits would like it back.

So our two heroes have to fight off a squad of goons with a bulk-rate discount on ammunition. The boys also have to keep up a few odd sexual relationships with hot babes. Nothin' wrong with that plot, right?

### THE CAST ▰ What's wrong with this movie is the cast.

Mickey Rourke and Don Johnson are, respectively, the title characters. Rourke lets his guy be sincere and dopey—he hugs everybody he meets and he pines for his dead wife. Johnson's Marlboro Man carries around saddlebags—though he has no horse—and repeatedly tells us what his daddy used to say. But his worst offense is that he, Marlboro Man, keeps his cigarettes behind his ear and never smokes a one of them. Daniel Baldwin does his best to be the lead tough guy, but he's too busy comparing his slicked back 'do to Rourke's shaggy unwashed coif or Johnson's blown-dry cut to menace anybody but Mr. Bruce, the hairdresser on location.

### WHY GUYS SHOULD AVOID IT

If the stupid nicknames these guys call each other don't send you running to rent *Drive-In Massacre* instead, consider this dialogue before you decide whether to rent it:
"You're the only family I got, Marlboro," says Rourke.
"If there is a God," Johnson says, "I'd like to meet the dude, hang out with him."

### TRIVIA

Not convinced to pass this one up? Okay, then you better be willing to sit through several scenes set to "Steel Cowboy," sung by that dreamy Jon Bon Jovi.

# POINT BREAK (1991)

**WHAT HAPPENS** ◄ A hotshot ex-football player and rookie FBI agent, Johnny Utah, from Ohio (go figure), goes undercover with a bunch of surfers to solve a string of bank robberies by guys wearing masks of ex-presidents. Utah learns to catch waves, he hooks up with a cute little surfer babe, parties with the gang, and starts to believe their leader's pseudophilosophical rap. When the surfers figure out who Utah really is, they force him to join in their games: like robbing a bank and freefalling over the California desert. But he's hobbled by a bad knee and lets them call all the shots. Most unforgivable: He lets the leader go on his own terms.

**THE CAST** ◄ Okay, I'll accept Keanu Reeves as a novice FBI agent if I must, but as a football star? Maybe flag football. And Patrick Swayze as the manic mystic named Bodhi—as in Bodhisattva? I am so sure. He's as menacing as a dance instructor at a Catskills resort. Poor Gary Busey, His Holy Sloppiness, trapped in this movie and left to die by his partner Johnny Utah, who wants so much to be liked by the other kids. Even raunchy rockers the Red Hot Chili Peppers as dope-dealin' surf Nazis cannot rescue this movie.

## WHY GUYS SHOULD AVOID IT

- On a raid into the house of a band of suspicious surf Nazis, Johnny gets his ass kicked by a naked woman.
- Ex-football player Johnny lets the slacker/surfer dude outrun him and then mock him when his trick knee collapses.
- Johnny worries more about his little honey being harmed than avenging his dead partner.

# QUIGLEY DOWN UNDER (1990)

**WHAT HAPPENS** ▬ The story seems sound on the surface. Quigley, an American sharpshooter from the Old West, answers an advertisement for a job in Australia. He arrives with his state-of-the-art rifle and demonstrates his aim by hitting a target 1,200 yards away. Then Marston, the pretentious prig who hired him, tells Quigley the job involves gunning down innocent Aborigines. Quigley declines the offer by tossing Marston out the window of his house—Marston repays Quigley by having him and a grimy, mad whore dumped together out in the desert. Now, here's where the movie breaks down. He not only saves his own carcass, but he helps her, too. Which isn't entirely bad, since she looks pretty fine after she gets cleaned up. But she miraculously recovers her sanity enough (maybe the desert sun makes crazy people lucid) to convince him to rescue a native baby. Worse, when he rides off for desperately needed supplies, she asks him to bring back a dress for her—which he does in just the shade she was hoping for.

**THE CAST** ▬ Tom Selleck is a perfectly good guy (even though his most ardent fans are surely pathetic lonely women), but let's face it, he's no Clint Eastwood. And thus, Quigley is no *High Plains Drifter* (see page 78). Quigley has deadly aim, but he has a crippling conscience and he takes orders from a woman when he's got the gun and the aim to make good on it. Sure, she's dark, sweet Laura San Giacomo, but even after her bath she's still just a clean prostitute. Alan Rickman (villain most cruel in *Die Hard*) does his best to redeem this movie, but he's reduced in the end to pleading with Quigley, and we can't cotton that.

**WHY GUYS SHOULD AVOID IT** ◆ The opening credits include Wayne Finkelman, costume designer. No mention of the guy who handles the horses or the guy who taught Selleck how to handle a gun. Just Wayne Finkelman, costume designer.

## DON'T WATCH

- Crazy Cora, the dirty (I mean unwashed) whore, tell Quigley her two-hankie tale of woe.
- The few topless Aborigines this movie teases you with. It will only make you wonder even more why Quigley doesn't just jump Cora out there in the desert—Clint can't stop thinking about jumping a nun in *Two Mules for Sister Sara* (page 80), but Quigley treats this whore like a blind date with your boss's daughter.

# TOP GUN (1986)

**WHAT HAPPENS** ◆ Hotshot pilots compete at the Navy's training school for the number one ranking. The call names of the two central characters—Maverick and Iceman—tell the whole obvious story. Maverick flaunts regulations and flies on nothing but nerve, Iceman is flawless and by-the-book. As their rivalry develops, Maverick and Iceman spend so much time staring into each other's eyes that you worry they're going to start making out at any moment. Of course, Maverick uses his smile and strut to woo a babe, who just happens to be a civilian astrophysicist and instructor at the school. You won't be surprised to see Maverick risk himself and copilot into trouble during training—so he has an opportunity to share his emotions with us—and then redeem himself in actual combat.

**THE CAST** ◆ **T**om Cruise (and his dimples) make Maverick as combat-ready as the captain of your high school pep club before the big game. Val Kilmer (and his bleached hair) plays Iceman as cool as the lifeguard at the YMCA pool. Kelly McGillis is the astrophysicist with the celestial body. Anthony Edwards (now of TV's *ER*) gets to be the passenger on Maverick's joyrides as Goose, his copilot. (He's later replaced in that job by Tim Robbins.) Regular guy Tom Skerritt (of *Picket Fences*) tries his damndest to be the firm but fair head instructor at the school.

## WHY GUYS SHOULD AVOID IT

- There are entirely too many scenes (no less than four) of these guys standing around in the locker room with just towels on. And forget about the volleyball pec-a-thon.
- The gooey sound track filled with disco songs by Giorgio Moroder.

### ENOUGH'S ENOUGH

 Yes, I realize that calling this movie a poser is heresy to some guys, but I'd rather go down in flames than have to sit through it again.

# The Guys' Guide to Guys' Videos Awards

Welcome ladies and gentlemen to the very first Guys' Guide to Guys' Videos awards, presented to honor achievement in the cinematic arts we admire most. The winners have been selected by careful consideration of the thousands of worthy nominees by a panel of no less than one guy.

## ◼ GUNS AND GORE

MOST ROUNDS FIRED TO KILL JUST ONE GUY
*Scarface,* final scene

MOST ROUNDS FIRED TO KILL TWO GUYS
*Butch Cassidy and the Sundance Kid,* final scene

MOST ROUNDS FIRED TO KILL NO GUYS
*Pulp Fiction,* Brett's apartment

MOST ROUNDS FIRED TO KILL ONE APPETITE
*Year of the Dragon,* Chinese restaurant

GRISLIEST SHOWDOWN
*High Plains Drifter*

**LONGEST SHOWDOWN**
*High Noon*

**MOST MISMATCHED SHOWDOWN (WESTERN)**
*Two Mules for Sister Sara:* Clint Eastwood versus only a
   French Army garrison

**MOST MISMATCHED SHOWDOWN (WAR)**
Patton and his .45 versus just a Messerschmitt

**HIGHEST BODY COUNT (WAR)**
*Hamburger Hill*

**HIGHEST BODY COUNT (WESTERN)**
*The Wild Bunch*

**HIGHEST BODY COUNT (URBAN)**
*Menace II Society*

**BEST BAREHANDED BRUTALITY (CLASSIC)**
*Spartacus*

**BEST BAREHANDED BRUTALITY (MARTIAL ARTS)**
*Street Fighter*

**BEST BAREHANDED BRUTALITY (OTHER)**
*Jungle Warriors,* Paul Smith

**BEST TEETH-BARED BRUTALITY**
*Midnight Express*

**MOST BLOOD SPILLED, VOLUME**
*Taxi Driver*

**MOST BLOOD SPILLED, DURATION**
*Reservoir Dogs*

MOST BLOOD SPURTED, HUMOR
*Monty Python and the Holy Grail*

MOST FLUIDS OTHER THAN BLOOD SPILLED
*The Evil Dead*

LEAST BLOODY MOVIE ADVERTISING ITSELF OTHERWISE
*Bloodsport*

AND A BRONZE MR. POTATOHEAD IS AWARDED TO
*Frankenhooker,* FOR DISTINGUISHED USE OF INDIVIDUAL BODY
PARTS

## ■ VEHICULAR SENSATIONS

BEST CAR CHASES IN PURSUIT OF CRIMINALS
*The French Connection*
*Bullitt*

BEST CAR CHASE TO ELUDE THE LAW
*Thunder Road*

BEST CAR CHASE IN PURSUIT OF NOTHING BUT SPEED
*Le Mans*

BEST CAR CHASES INVOLVING ONE CAR AND ONE PERSON ON
FOOT
*Marathon Man*
*Lethal Weapon 2*

BEST CHASE INVOLVING ONE CAR AND ONE AIRPLANE
*Iron Eagle*

BEST CHASE INVOLVING JUST ONE BUS
*Speed*

**BEST BOAT CHASE**
*Live and Let Die*

**BEST CHEVY CHASE**
*Fletch*

**BEST MOTORCYCLE CHASE**
*Great Escape*

**BEST MOTORCYCLE AND CAR CHASE**
*Billy Badd*

**BEST HARLEY, SEMICAB, AND MINIBIKE CHASE**
*Terminator 2*

**AND THE SPECIAL W. C. FIELDS BRASS BUMPER FOR EXTRAORDINARY DESTRUCTION IN PURSUIT OF A LAUGH GOES TO**
*The Blues Brothers*

# ▰ SKIN DEEP

**STRANGEST SEX SCENE**
*Angel Heart*

**FUNNIEST SEX SCENE**
*Cheerleader Camp*

**MOST GHOULISH SEX SCENE**
*To the Devil, a Daughter*

**MOST UNCOMFORTABLE SEX SCENE**
*Last Tango in Paris*

**MOST UNLIKELY SEX SCENE**
Divine raping her(him)self in *Female Trouble*

**SURPRISE SIGHTINGS OF BARE BREASTS (WESTERNS)**
The Mexican girls in *The Wild Bunch*

**SURPRISE SIGHTINGS OF BARE BREASTS (SCIENCE FICTION)**
Sigourney Weaver, *Alien*

**SURPRISE SIGHTINGS OF BARE BREASTS (LEGEND)**
Julie Andrews, *S.O.B.*

**BEST BREASTS YOU BELIEVE YOU'VE SEEN BARE, EVEN THOUGH YOU HAVEN'T**
Adrienne Barbeau's

**AS CLOSE TO NUDITY AS YOU'LL GET IN A NONPORNO MOVIE BEFORE 1960**
Jean Harlow, *Hell's Angels*

**MOST UNNERVING NUDITY**
Isabella Rossellini, *Blue Velvet*

**CREEPIEST NUDITY**
The bathtub scene in *The Shining*

**MOST DISGUSTING NUDITY IN AN OTHERWISE PERFECTLY GOOD MOVIE**
*The Krays*

**BEST USE OF SILICON IN A SUPPORTING ROLE**
Pamela Anderson, *Barb Wire*

**BEST USE OF WEIGHTLESSNESS IN A NONSUPPORTING ROLE**
Jane Fonda, *Barbarella*

**BEST USE OF LEFTOVERS IN A SEXY ROLE**
Mickey Rourke and Kim Basinger, *9½ Weeks*

AND THE JANE RUSSELL VELVET CONE GOES TO MELANIE
GRIFFITH, FOR OUTSTANDING USE OF UNDERWEAR IN A
NONSUPPORTING ROLE (CAREER)

## ■ A DOZEN DIRECTORS WHO HIT THEIR MARKS

John Ford (*The Searchers, Stagecoach, Rio Grande, How the West Was Won*)

Sam Peckinpah (*The Wild Bunch, The Osterman Weekend, Straw Dogs*)

Sergio Leone (*A Fistful of Dollars, The Good, the Bad, and the Ugly, Once Upon a Time in America*)

Stanley Kubrick (*Spartacus, A Clockwork Orange, Full Metal Jacket, The Shining*)

Martin Scorsese (*Mean Streets, Taxi Driver, Raging Bull, GoodFellas*)

Don Siegel (*Dirty Harry, Two Mules for Sister Sara, Charley Varrick, Hell Is for Heroes*)

Michael Cimino (*Year of the Dragon, The Deerhunter, Desperate Hours* [remake], *The Sicilian*)

Joel Coen (*Blood Simple, Raising Arizona, Barton Fink, Miller's Crossing*)

James Cameron (*The Terminator, Terminator 2, Aliens, The Spawning*)

John McTiernan (*Die Hard, Die Hard 3, Predator, The Hunt for Red October*)

Andrew Davis (*Under Siege, The Fugitive, Code of Silence*)

Chuck Vincent (*Hollywood Hot Tubs, Hot T-Shirts, Young Nurses in Love*)

THE WALTER JACK PALANCE LIFETIME ACHIEVEMENT AWARD IS
PRESENTED TO THE FOLLOWING ACTORS FOR VALOROUS CAREERS
IN THE SERVICE OF CREEPS, CRUDS, AND OTHER UNDESIRABLES:

**Christopher Lee:** Though he made his reputation as an impeccably mannered horror movie madman—in *Count Dracula, The House That Dripped Blood*, and *Dracula's*

*Risen from the Grave*—Lee has proved his villainy is versatile with his performances in James Bond *The Man with the Golden Gun,* Chuck Norris's *Eye for an Eye,* and *Police Academy VII: Mission to Moscow.* If you need a bad guy who uses all his well-learned politesse to lay your soul to waste, Christopher Lee is your man.

**M. Emmet Walsh:** Nobody guffaws with greater glee at the foolishness of decent people than this balding, jiggly-jowled actor. As chief of the blade runners, Walsh lays out the situation for the reluctant Harrison Ford without sugar-coating a morsel. In *The Mighty Quinn,* Walsh practically dares Denzel Washington's Chief Quinn to dig deeper into the snare of intrigue that the murder mystery becomes. Most memorably, Walsh was the P.I. without principles in *Blood Simple.*

**John Vernon:** Ah, Dean Wormer. Vernon has been the deep voice of onerous authority in *Dirty Harry, I'm Gonna Git You Sucka,* and *Savage Streets,* and he's been the two-faced manipulator in *Point Blank* (his first movie) and *The Outlaw Josey Wales.* But he will forever be Dean Wormer, the university administrator who put the Delta House on "Double Secret Probation."

**Gary Busey:** Sure, Busey has played good guys—even geeky Buddy Holly—but Busey earned his place among the guys' movie giants with his portrayals of dangerously demented henchmen: Mr. Joshua in *Lethal Weapon,* and Commander Krill in *Under Siege.* Now good action movie directors make certain they cast good wackos in the Gary Busey role: His successors in *Lethal Weapon 2* (Derrick O'Connor) and *Under Siege 2* (Everett McGill) try valiantly to meet the standard Busey set for them.

**Richard Kiel:** You probably know Kiel best for his teeth—he was the steel-dentured Jaws in two James

Bond movies. But his oversized forehead and seven-foot-two-inch frame showed up in *The Longest Yard* and *Pale Rider,* too. He even played the part of circus strongman with the King himself, Elvis, in *Roustabout.*

**Professor Toru Tanaka:** Just about every martial arts star has tried out his best stuff on this burly, limping hulk, but the professor just shakes off the hardest punches and most powerful kicks and keeps on coming. If the professor gets his mitts on a guy, the professor is likely to crush him to death—the only chance any guy has is to outsmart him, if the script allows it.

**Sybil Danning:** This former Playmate of the Year is queen of the tough chicks in the movies. No matter which side of the law she's on (as the warden in *Reform School Girls* or the kinky drug dealer in *Jungle Warriors*), Sybil is so good at being bad.

# INDEX